Knight's 24-Hour Trainer
Microsoft® SQL Server® 2008 Integration Services

Section I: Installation and Getting Started

Section II: Tasks

Section III: Data Flow

Continues

Knight's 24-Hour Trainer

Microsoft® SQL Server® 2008 Integration Services

Brian Knight
Devin Knight
Mike Davis

WILEY

Wiley Publishing, Inc.

Knight's 24-Hour Trainer: Microsoft® SQL Server® 2008 Integration Services

Published by

Wiley Publishing, Inc.

10475 Crosspoint Boulevard

Indianapolis, IN 46256

www.wiley.com

Copyright © 2009 by Wiley Publishing, Inc., Indianapolis, Indiana

Published simultaneously in Canada

ISBN: 978-0-470-49692-3

Manufactured in the United States of America

10 9 8 7 6 5 4 3 2 1

For general information on our other products and services please contact our Customer Care Department within the United States at (877) 762-2974, outside the United States at (317) 572-3993 or fax (317) 572-4002.

Wiley also publishes its books in a variety of electronic formats. Some content that appears in print may not be available in electronic books.

Library of Congress Control Number: 2009928170

To my always supporting wife and children. Thank you for making me who I am today.
—Brian Knight

James 1:17
—Devin Knight

I dedicate this book to my wife Jessica; without her support and love I would never have accomplished so much. To my son, daughter, and wife for being understanding when I work late writing instead of playing Rock Band with them. To my mother who raised me to be the man I am today.
—Mike Davis

Credits

Executive Editor
Robert Elliott

Senior Project Editor
Kevin Kent

Technical Editors
Bob Bojanic
Dustin Ryan
Carla Sabotta
Stefan Steiner

Production Editor
Kathleen Wisor

Copy Editor
Kim Cofer

Editorial Director
Robyn B. Siesky

Editorial Manager
Mary Beth Wakefield

Production Manager
Tim Tate

Vice President and Executive Group Publisher
Richard Swadley

Vice President and Executive Publisher
Barry Pruett

Associate Publisher
Jim Minatel

Project Coordinator, Cover
Lynsey Stanford

Proofreader
Dr. Nate Pritts, Word One

Indexer
Robert Swanson

About the Authors

Brian Knight, SQL Server MVP, MCITP, MCSE, MCDBA, is the owner and founder of Pragmatic Works. He is also the co-founder of SQLServerCentral.com and JumpstartTV.com. He runs the local SQL Server users group in Jacksonville (JSSUG). Brian is a contributing columnist at several technical magazines and does regular webcasts at Jumpstart TV. He is the author of ten SQL Server books. Brian has spoken at conferences like PASS, SQL Connections, and TechEd and many Code Camps. His blog can be found at http://www.pragmaticworks.com. Brian watches his 401k wither away in Jacksonville, Florida.

Devin Knight is a BI consultant at Pragmatic Works. Previously, he has tech edited the book *Professional Microsoft SQL Server 2008 Integration Services* (John Wiley & Sons, Inc.). Devin has spoken at past conferences like PASS and at several SQL Saturday events. He is a contributing member to the Business Intelligence Special Interest Group (SIG) for PASS as a leader in the SSIS Focus Group. Making his home in Jacksonville, Florida, Devin is a participating member of the local users' group (JSSUG). Visit his blog at http://pragmaticworks.com/community/blogs/.

Mike Davis (Jacksonville, Florida) is an author, developer, consultant, and trainer with Pragmatic Works. He has expertise in many areas of Business Intelligence including Integration Services, Reporting Services, Analysis Services, Database Administration, and .NET Software Development. Mike has created enterprise level BI and software solutions for numerous corporations. As a trainer he travels the world teaching classes on SQL Server and BI. He also participates as a speaker at events like SQL Saturdays, SQL Server launches, SQL server user groups, and SQL PASS. In his spare time Mike plays guitar and darts. He is a member of the North Florida Dart League.

Acknowledgments

Thanks to everyone who made this book possible. Devin and Mike were an excellent team to push this rewarding project forward. Thanks also to the voices in my head who talk to me at night when the caffeine is kicking into overdrive. Twinkles, that means you. Thank you to the wonderful team at Wrox, especially Bob Elliott, who gave this book concept a chance when it was still a drunken idea on a napkin, and Kevin Kent, who made our ramblings much more concise. As always, I owe a huge debt to my wife Jenn for putting up with my late nights and my children, Colton, Liam, and Camille for being so patient with their tired dad.

— *Brian Knight*

I must give thanks to God; without Him in my life I would not have such blessings. To my wife Erin who has only helped in strengthening my relationship with God. She's had the patience during the late nights of writing, editing, and video recording. She will be a great mother to our future child. Thanks to my brother Brian Knight. If it weren't for him an opportunity like this would have never entered my life. He's truly an inspiration in his work and personal life and I hope I can become as good a husband and dad as he is. Lastly, I would like to thank personal eating trainer, Takeru Kobayashi. With your help my hope is to join the International Federation of Competitive Eating and break the world record for hot dog eating.

— *Devin Knight*

Thanks to Brian Knight for giving me the opportunity to author a book with him and teaching me many things about SQL Server. Thanks to Devin and Brian Knight for being co-authors on this book and all of their help and advice. Thanks to technical editors Dustin Ryan, Bob Bojanic, Carla Sabotta, and Stefan Steiner who were a huge help in making sure I was accurate in my writing. Thanks to the entire Wiley staff for helping me with all parts of the book, especially Kevin Kent for putting up with all my last minute writings. And finally, thanks to the Flying Spaghetti Monster; with him all things are possible.

— *Mike Davis*

Contents

Section I: Installation and Getting Started

Contents

Contents

Contents

Contents

Section VI: Configuration

Section VII: Troubleshooting and Logging

Section VIII: Deployment and Administration

Contents

Preface

If you've picked up this book, *Knight's 24-Hour Trainer: Microsoft SQL Server 2008 Integration Services*, you've decided to learn one of SQL Server's most exciting applications, SQL Server Integration Services (SSIS). SSIS is a platform to move data from nearly any data source to nearly any destination and helps you by orchestrating a workflow to organize and control the execution of all these events. Most who dive into SSIS use it weekly, if not daily, to move data between partners, departments, or customers. It's also a highly in-demand skill — even in the worst of economic environments, jobs are still posted for SSIS developers. This is because no matter what happens in an economy, people still must move and transform data.

This book, then, is your chance to start delving into this powerful and marketable application. And what's more, this is not just a book you're holding right now. It's a video learning tool, as well. We became passionate about video training a number of years ago when we realized that in our own learning we required exposure to multiple teaching techniques to truly understand a topic — a fact that is especially true with tutorial books like this one. So, you'll find hours of videos on the DVD in this book to help you learn SSIS even better than reading about the topic alone could and to help demonstrate to you the various tutorials in the book.

Who This Book Is For

This is a beginner book and assumes only that you know SQL Server 2005 or 2008 to run queries against the database engine. Because this book is structured for a beginner, providing many tutorials and teaching you only what you'll likely use at work, it is not a reference book filled with a description of every property in a given task. It instead focuses on only the essential components for you to complete your project at work or school.

What This Book Covers

This book covers SQL Server 2008 and assumes no knowledge of SQL Server 2005. The differences in SQL Server 2005 and SQL Server 2008 are minimal, so if you are using this book as a 2005 learning tool, you will find only a few small user interface differences.

By the time you've completed this book, you'll know how to load and synchronize database systems using SSIS by using some of the new SQL Server 2008 features. You'll also know how to load data warehouses, which is a very hot and specialized skill. Even in warehousing, you'll find features in the new SQL Server 2008 release that you'll wonder how you lived without!

How This Book Is Structured

Our main principle in this book is to teach you only what we think you need to perform your job task. Because of that, it's not a comprehensive reference book. You won't find a description of every feature of SSIS in here. Instead the book blends small amounts of description, a tutorial, and videos to enhance your experience. Each lesson walks you through how to use components of SSIS and contains a tutorial. In this tutorial, called "Try It," you can choose to read the requirements to complete the lesson, the hints of how to go about it, and begin coding, or you can read the step-by-step instructions if you learn better that way. Either way if you get stuck or want to see how one of us does the solution, watch the video on the DVD to receive further instruction.

What This Book Covers

This book contains 49 lessons, which are broken into 10 sections. The lessons are usually only a few pages long and focus on the smallest unit of work in SSIS that we could work on. Each section has a large theme around a given section in SSIS:

❑   **Section 1: Installation and Getting Started** — This section covers the basic installation of SSIS and the sample databases that you'll use throughout this book. If you already have SSIS and the sample databases installed, you can review this section quickly.

❑   **Section 2: Tasks** — This section explains how to use tasks in the Control Flow of SSIS.

❑   **Section 3: Data Flow** — Seventy-five percent of your time as an SSIS developer is spent in the Data Flow tab. This section focuses on the configuration of the core sources, transforms, and destinations.

❑   **Section 4: Variables and Expressions** — Now that you've created your first package, you must make it dynamic. This section covers how you can use variables and expressions to make your package change at run time.

❑   **Section 5: Containers** — This section covers one of the key Control Flow items, containers, which control how SSIS does looping and grouping.

❑   **Section 6: Configuration** — Here you learn how to configure your packages externally through configuration files, tables, and other ways.

❑   **Section 7: Troubleshooting and Logging** — No sooner do you have an SSIS package developed than you start experiencing problems. This section shows you how to troubleshoot these problems.

❑   **Section 8: Deployment and Administration** — Now that your package is developed, here you learn how to deploy and configure the service.

❑   **Section 9: Data Warehousing** — A little more on the advanced side, this section teaches you how to load a data warehouse using SSIS.

❑   **Section 10: Wrap Up and Review** — This section was one of our favorites to write. It contains a lesson to bring everything together and also Appendixes A and B, which contain crib notes for quick reference. As trainers and consultants, we are constantly asked to leave behind a quick page of crib notes of common code. In these appendixes, you find guides on when to use which SSIS components and useful solutions and code snippets that address common situations you might face.

Instructional Videos on DVD

As mentioned earlier in this preface, because we believe strongly in the value of video training, this book has an accompanying DVD containing hours of instructional video. At the end of each lesson in the book, you will find a reference to an instructional video on the DVD that accompanies that lesson. In that video, one of us will walk you through the content and examples contained in that lesson. So, if seeing something done and hearing it explained helps you understand a subject better than just reading about it does, this book and DVD combination is just the thing for you to get started with SSIS.

Conventions

To help you get the most from the text and keep track of what's happening, we've used a number of conventions throughout the book.

> **Boxes like this one hold important, not-to-be forgotten information that is directly relevant to the surrounding text.**

Notes, tips, hints, tricks, and asides to the current discussion are offset and placed in italics like this.

 References like this one point you to the DVD to watch the instructional video that accompanies a given lesson.

As for styles in the text:

❑   We *highlight* new terms and important words when we introduce them

❑   We show URLs and code within the text like so: `persistence.properties`

❑   We present code in the following way:

```
We use a monofont type for code examples.
```

Supporting Packages and Code

As you work through the lessons in this book, you may choose either to type in all the code and create all the packages manually or to use the supporting packages and code files that accompany the book. All the packages, code, and other support files used in this book are available for download at `http://www.wrox.com`. Once at the site, simply locate the book's title (either by using the Search box or by using one of the title lists) and click the Download Code link on the book's detail page to obtain all the source code for the book.

Because many books have similar titles, you may find it easiest to search by ISBN; this book's ISBN is 978-0-470-49692-3.

Once you download the code, just decompress it with your favorite compression tool. Alternatively, you can go to the main Wrox code download page at `http://www.wrox.com/dynamic/books/download.aspx` to see the code available for this book and all other Wrox books.

Errata

We make every effort to ensure that there are no errors in the text or in the code. However, no one is perfect, and mistakes do occur. If you find an error in one of our books, like a spelling mistake or faulty piece of code, we would be very grateful for your feedback. By sending in errata you may save another reader hours of frustration and at the same time you will be helping us provide even higher quality information.

To find the errata page for this book, go to `http://www.wrox.com` and locate the title using the Search box or one of the title lists. Then, on the Book Search Results page, click the Errata link. On this page you can view all errata that has been submitted for this book and posted by Wrox editors.

A complete book list including links to errata is also available at `www.wrox.com/misc-pages/booklist.shtml`.

If you don't spot "your" error on the Errata page, click the Errata Form link and complete the form to send us the error you have found. We'll check the information and, if appropriate, post a message to the book's errata page and fix the problem in subsequent editions of the book.

p2p.wrox.com

For author and peer discussion, join the P2P forums at `p2p.wrox.com`. The forums are a Web-based system for you to post messages relating to Wrox books and related technologies and interact with other readers and technology users. The forums offer a subscription feature to e-mail you topics of interest of your choosing when new posts are made to the forums. Wrox authors, editors, other industry experts, and your fellow readers are present on these forums.

At `http://p2p.wrox.com` you will find a number of different forums that will help you not only as you read this book, but also as you develop your own applications. To join the forums, just follow these steps:

1. Go to `p2p.wrox.com` and click the Register link.
2. Read the terms of use and click Agree.
3. Complete the required information to join as well as any optional information you wish to provide and click Submit.
4. You will receive an e-mail with information describing how to verify your account and complete the joining process.

You can read messages in the forums without joining P2P but in order to post your own messages, you must join.

Once you join, you can post new messages and respond to messages other users post. You can read messages at any time on the Web. If you would like to have new messages from a particular forum e-mailed to you, click the Subscribe to this Forum icon by the forum name in the forum listing.

For more information about how to use the Wrox P2P, be sure to read the P2P FAQs for answers to questions about how the forum software works as well as many common questions specific to P2P and Wrox books. To read the FAQs, click the FAQ link on any P2P page.

Welcome to SSIS

SQL Server Integration Services (SSIS) is one of the most powerful applications in your arsenal for moving data in and out of various databases and files. Like the rest of the business intelligence (BI) suite that comes with SQL Server, it's not part of SQL Server other than being included on the DVD and in the license that you've already purchased. Because of that, even if your environment is not using a lot of SQL Server, SSIS can still be used as a platform for data movement.

Though ultimately this book is more interactive in nature, this introductory chapter first walks you through a high-level tour of SSIS so you have a life preserver on prior to jumping in the pool. Each topic touched on in this introduction is covered much deeper throughout the book in lesson form and in the supporting videos on the DVD.

Import and Export Wizard

If you need to move data quickly from almost any OLE DB–compliant data source to a destination, you can use the SSIS Import and Export Wizard (shown in Figure 1). The wizard is a quick way to move the data and perform very light transformations of data, such as casting of the data into new data types. You can quickly check any table you want to transfer as well as write a query against the data to retrieve only a selective amount of data.

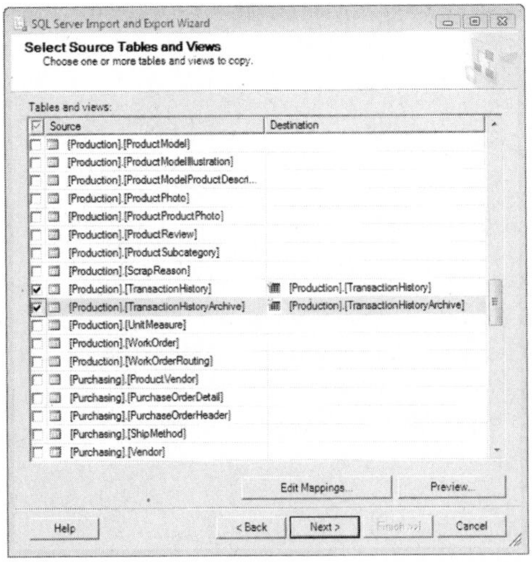

Figure 1

The Business Intelligence Development Studio

The Business Intelligence Development Studio (BIDS) is the central tool that you'll spend most of your time in as an SSIS developer. Like the rest of SQL Server, the tool's foundation is the Visual Studio 2008 interface (shown in Figure 2). The nicest thing about the tool is it's not bound to any particular SQL Server. In other words, you won't have to connect to a SQL Server to design an SSIS package. You can design the package disconnected from your SQL Server environment and then deploy it to your target SQL Server or the file system you'd like it to run on.

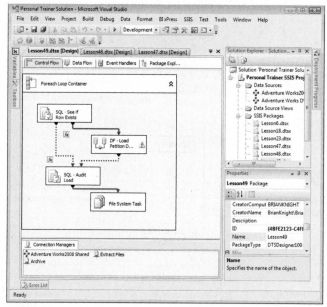

Figure 2

Architecture

SQL Server 2008 has truly evolved SSIS into a major player in the extraction, transformation, and loading (ETL) market. What's especially nice about SSIS is its price tag, which is free with the purchase of SQL Server. Other ETL tools can cost hundreds of thousands of dollars based on how you scale the software. The SSIS architecture has also expanded dramatically since the SQL Server 2000 days, as you can see in Figure 3. The SSIS architecture consists of four main components:

❏   The SSIS service

❏   The SSIS runtime engine and the runtime executables

❏   The SSIS Data Flow engine and the Data Flow components

❏   The SSIS clients

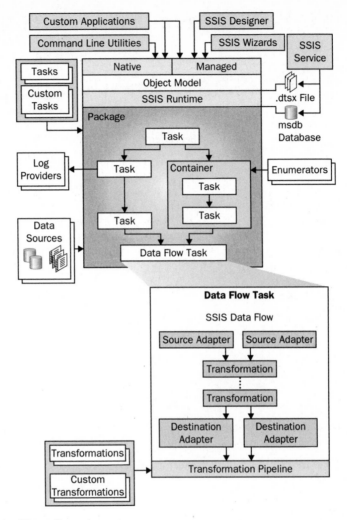

Figure 3

Let's boil this down to the essentials that you need to know to do your job. The SSIS service handles the operational aspects of SSIS. It is a Windows service that is installed when you install the SSIS component of SQL Server 2008, and it tracks the execution of packages (a collection of work items) and helps with the storage of the packages. You don't need the SSIS service to run SSIS packages, but if the service is stopped, all the SSIS packages that are currently running will in turn stop by default.

The SSIS runtime engine and its complimentary programs actually run your SSIS packages. The engine saves the layout of your packages and manages the logging, debugging, configuration, connections, and transactions. Additionally, it manages handling your events to send you emails or log into a database when an event is raised in your package. The runtime executables provide the following functionality to a package that we discuss in more detail throughout this book:

❑ **Containers** — Provide structure and scope to your package

❑ **Tasks** — Provide the functionality to your package

❑ **Event handlers** — Respond to raised events in your package

❑ **Precedence constraints** — Provider ordinal relationship between various items in your package

Packages

A core component of SSIS is the notion of a *package*. A package best parallels an executable program in Windows. Essentially, a package is a collection of tasks that execute in an orderly fashion. Precedence constraints help manage which order the tasks will execute in. A package can be saved onto a SQL Server, which in actuality is saved in the msdb database. It can also be saved as a .DTSX file, which is an XML structured file much like .RDL files are to Reporting Services. The end result of the package looks like Figure 2 that was shown earlier.

Tasks

A *task* can best be described as an individual unit of work. Tasks provide functionality to your package, much like a method does in a programming language. A task can move a file, load a file into a database, send an email, or write a set of VB.NET code for you, to name just a few of the things it can do. A small subset of the common tasks available to you comprises the following:

❑ **Bulk Insert Task** — Loads data into a table by using the BULK INSERT SQL command

❑ **Data Flow Task** — This very specialized task loads and transforms data into an OLE DB destination

❑ **Execute Package Task** — Allows you to execute a package from within a package, making your SSIS packages modular

❑ **Execute Process Task** — Executes a program external to your package, like one to split your extract file into many files before processing the individual files

❑ **Execute SQL Task** — Executes a SQL statement or stored procedure

❑ **File System Task** — This task can handle directory operations like creating, renaming, or deleting a directory. It can also manage file operations like moving, copying, or deleting files

❑ **FTP Task** — Sends or receives files from an FTP site

❑ **Script Task** — Runs a set of VB.NET or C# coding inside a Visual Studio environment

❑ **Send Mail Task** — Sends a mail message through SMTP

- ❑ **Analysis Services Processing Task** — This task processes a SQL Server Analysis Services cube, dimension, or mining model
- ❑ **Web Service Task** — Executes a method on a web service
- ❑ **WMI Data Reader Task** — This task can run WQL queries against the Windows Management Instrumentation (WMI). This allows you to read the event log, get a list of applications that are installed, or determine hardware that is installed to name a few examples
- ❑ **WMI Event Watcher Task** — This task empowers SSIS to wait for and respond to certain WMI events that occur in the operating system
- ❑ **XML Task** — Parses or processes an XML file. It can merge, split, or reformat an XML file

These are only a few of the many tasks you have available to you. You can also write your own task or download a task from the web that does something else. Writing such a task only requires that you learn the SSIS object model and know VB.NET or C#.

Data Flow Elements

Once you create a Data Flow Task, the Data Flow tab in BIDS is then available to you for design. Just as the Control Flow tab handles the main workflow of the package, the Data Flow tab handles the transformation of data. Almost anything that manipulates data falls into the Data Flow category. You can see an example of a Data Flow in Figure 4, where data is pulled from an OLE DB Source and transformed before being written to a Flat File Destination. As data moves through each step of the Data Flow, the data changes based on what the transform does. For example, in Figure 4 a new column is derived using the Derived Column Transform and that new column is then available to subsequent transformations or to the destination.

You can add multiple Data Flow Tasks onto the Control Flow tab. You'll notice that after you click on each one, it jumps to the Data Flow tab with the Data Flow Task name you selected in the drop-down box right under the tab. You can toggle between Data Flow Tasks easily by selecting the next Data Flow Task from that drop-down box.

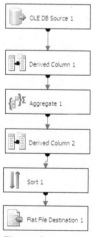

Figure 4

Sources

A *source* is where you specify the location of your source data to pull from in the data pump. Sources will generally point to a connection manager in SSIS. By pointing them to the connection manager, you can reuse connections throughout your package, because you need only change the connection in one place. Here are some of the common sources you'll be using in SSIS:

❑ **OLE DB Source** — Connects to nearly any OLE DB data source like SQL Server, Access, Oracle, or DB2 to name just a few

❑ **Excel Source** — Source that specializes in receiving data from Excel spreadsheets. This source also makes it easy to run SQL queries against your Excel spreadsheet to narrow the scope of the data that you want to pass through the flow

❑ **Flat File Source** — Connects to a delimited or fixed-width file

❑ **XML Source** — Can retrieve data from an XML document

❑ **ADO.NET Source** — The ADO.NET source is an ADO.NET connection much like you see in the .NET Framework when you use the DataReader interface in your application code to connect to a database for communication to ODBC

Destinations

Inside the Data Flow, *destinations* accept the data from the data sources and from the transformations. The flexible architecture can send the data to nearly any OLE DB–compliant data source or to a flat file. Like sources, destinations are managed through the connection manager. Some of the more common destinations in SSIS and available to you are as follows:

❑ **Excel Destination** — Outputs data from the Data Flow to an Excel spreadsheet that must already exist

❑ **Flat File Destination** — Enables you to write data to a comma delimited or fixed-width file

❑ **OLE DB Destination** — Outputs data to an OLE DB data connection like SQL Server, Oracle, or Access

❑ **SQL Server Destination** — The destination that you use to write data to SQL Server most efficiently. To use this, you must run the package from the destination

Transformations

Transformations (or transforms) are a key component to the Data Flow that change the data to a format that you'd like. For example, you may want your data to be sorted and aggregated. Two transformations can accomplish this task for you. The nicest thing about transformations in SSIS is they are all done in-memory, and because of this they are extremely efficient. Memory handles data manipulation much faster than disk IO does, and you'll find if disk paging occurs, your package that ran in 20 minutes will suddenly take hours. Here are some of the more common transforms you'll use on a regular basis:

❑ **Aggregate** — Aggregates data from a transform or source similar to a GROUP BY statement in T-SQL

❑ **Conditional Split** — Splits the data based on certain conditions being met. For example, if the State column is equal to Florida, send the data down a different path. This transform is similar to a CASE statement in T-SQL

❏ **Data Conversion** — Converts a column's data type to another data type. This transform is similar to a CAST statement in T-SQL

❏ **Derived Column** — Performs an in-line update to the data or creates a new column from a formula. For example, you can use this to calculate a Profit column based on a Cost and SellPrice set of columns

❏ **Fuzzy Grouping** — Performs data cleansing by finding rows that are likely duplicates

❏ **Fuzzy Lookup** — Matches and standardizes data based on fuzzy logic. For example, this can transform the name Jon to John

❏ **Lookup** — Performs a lookup on data to be used later in a transformation. For example, you can use this transformation to look up a city based on the zip code

❏ **Multicast** — Sends a copy of the data to an additional path in the workflow and can be used to parallelize data. For example, you may want to send the same set of records to two tables

❏ **OLE DB Command** — Executes an OLE DB command for each row in the Data Flow. Can be used to run an UPDATE or DELETE statement inside the Data Flow

❏ **Row Count** — Stores the row count from the Data Flow into a variable for later use by perhaps an auditing solution

❏ **Script Component** — Uses a script to transform the data. For example, you can use this to apply specialized business logic to your Data Flow

❏ **Slowly Changing Dimension** — Coordinates the conditional insert or update of data in a slowly changing dimension during a data warehouse load

❏ **Sort** — Sorts the data in the Data Flow by a given column and removes exact duplicates

❏ **Union All** — Merges multiple data sets into a single data set

❏ **Unpivot** — Unpivots the data from a non-normalized format to a relational format

Editions of SQL Server 2008

The features in SSIS and SQL Server that are available to you vary widely based on what edition of SQL Server you're using. As you can imagine, the higher end edition of SQL Server you purchase, the more features are available. As for SSIS, you'll have to use at least Standard Edition to receive the bulk of the SSIS features. In the Express and Workgroup editions, only the Import and Export Wizard is available to you. There are some features in SSIS that you'll have to upgrade to Enterprise or Developer Editions to see. The advanced transformations available only with Enterprise edition are as follows:

❏ Data Mining Query Transformation

❏ Fuzzy Lookup and Fuzzy Grouping Transformations

❏ Term Extraction and Term Lookup Transformations

❏ Data Mining Model Training Destination

❏ Dimension Processing Destination

❏ Partition Processing Destination

Summary

This chapter introduced you to the SQL Server Integration Services (SSIS) architecture and some of the different elements you'll be dealing with in SSIS. Tasks are individual units of work that are chained together with precedence constraints. Packages are executable programs in SSIS that are a collection of tasks. Finally, transformations are the Data Flow items that change the data to the form you request, such as sorting the data the way you want. Now that that the overview is out of the way, it's time to start the first section and your first set of lessons, and time for you to get your hands on SSIS.

> As mentioned earlier, this book comes with an accompanying DVD containing hours of instructional supporting video. At the end of each lesson in the book, you will find a box like this one pointing you to a video on the DVD that accompanies that lesson. In that video, one of us will walk you through the content and examples contained in that lesson. So, if seeing something done and hearing it explained helps you understand a subject better than just reading about it does, this book and DVD combination provides exactly what you need. There's even an Introduction to SSIS video that you can watch to get started. Simply select the Intro to SSIS lesson on the DVD.

Section I
Installation and Getting Started

Moving Data with the Import and Export Wizard

The Import and Export Wizard is the easiest method to move data from sources like Excel, Oracle, DB2, SQL Server, and text files to nearly any destination. This wizard uses SSIS as a framework and can optionally save a package as its output prior to executing. The package it produces may not be the most elegant, but it can take a lot of the grunt work out of package development and provide the building blocks that are necessary for you to build the remainder of the package. Oftentimes as an SSIS developer, you'll want to relegate the grunt work and heavy lifting to the wizard and do the more complex coding yourself.

As with most SQL Server wizards, you have numerous ways to open the tool:

❑ To open the Import and Export Wizard, right-click the database you want to import data from or export data to SQL Server Management Studio and select Tasks ➪ Import Data (or Export Data based on what task you're performing)

❑ You can also open the wizard by right-clicking SSIS Packages in Business Intelligence Development Studio (BIDS) and selecting SSIS Import and Export Wizard

❑ Another common way to open it is from the Start Menu under SQL Server 2008 by choosing Import and Export Data

❑ The last way to open the wizard is by typing **dtswizard.exe** at the command line or Run prompt

Regardless of whether you need to import or export the data, the first few screens in the wizard look very similar.

Once the wizard comes up, you see the typical Microsoft wizard welcome screen. Click Next to begin specifying the source connection. If you opened the wizard from Management Studio by selecting Export Data, this screen is prepopulated. In this screen you specify where your data is coming from in the Source drop-down box. Once you select the source, the rest of the options on the dialog box may vary based on the type of connection. The default source is SQL Native Client, and it looks like Figure 1-1. You have OLE DB sources like SQL Server, Oracle, and Access available out of the box. You can also use text files and Excel files. After selecting the source, you have to fill in the provider-specific information.

For SQL Server, you must enter the server name (localhost means go to your local machine's SQL Server instance if applicable) and the user name and password you want to use. If you're going to connect with your Windows account, simply select "Use Windows Authentication." Windows Authentication will pass your Windows local or domain credentials into the data source. Lastly, choose a database that you'd like to connect to. For most of the examples in this book, you use the AdventureWorks2008 database. You can download this database as an optional installation on CodePlex.com, or you can see Lesson 3 of this book for more information on installing this sample database.

> *You can also find the sample databases at the Wrox website at*
> `http://www.wrox.com/go/SQLServer2008RTMDataSets`.

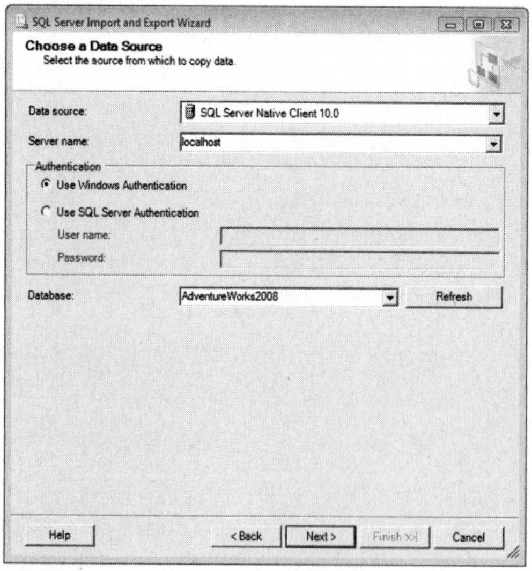

Figure 1-1

> *Additional sources such as Sybase and DB2 can also become available if you install the vendors' OLE DB providers. You can download the OLE DB Provider for DB2 for free if you're using Enterprise Edition by going to the SQL Server 2008 Feature Pack on the Microsoft website. You also have ADO.NET providers available to you in SQL Server 2008.*

After you click Next, you are taken to the next screen in the wizard, where you specify the destination for your data. The properties for this screen are exactly identical to those for the previous screen with the exception of the database. On the next screen, if you select "Copy data from one or more tables or views," you can simply check the tables you want. If you select "Write a query to specify the data to transfer," you can write an ad hoc query (after clicking Next) addressing where to select the data from or what stored procedure to use to retrieve your data.

The next screen allows you to select the table or tables you want to copy over and which table names you want them to be transferred to. If you want, you can click the Edit button to go to the Column Mappings dialog box (shown in Figure 1-2) for each table. Here you can change the mapping between each source and destination column. For example, if you want the DepartmentID column to go to the DepartmentID2 column on the destination, simply select the Destination drop-down box for the DepartmentID column and point it to the new column, or choose <ignore > to ignore the column altogether. By checking "Enabled identity insert," you allow the wizard to insert into a column that has an identity (or autonumber) value assigned. If the data types don't match between the source and destination columns, the wizard will add the necessary components to convert the data to a proper data type if possible.

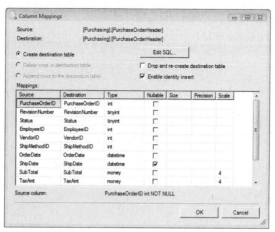

Figure 1-2

The next screen allows you to save the package or just choose to run it immediately. You can uncheck "Execute Immediately" to just save the package for later modification and execution. You can open the package that executed in the Business Intelligence Development Studio (BIDS) if you'd like. You do this by creating a project in BIDS and adding the package to the project. You cannot edit the package without a BIDS project to contain the package. We discuss how to create a project in Lesson 4 later in this book. The final screen executes the process and shows you the output log.

Try It

In this lesson, you learn how to quickly load a flat file into a database using the Import and Export Wizard. After this lesson, you'll have a clear understanding of how the Import and Export Wizard is the easiest way to load data into almost any destination and how it is accessed from Management Studio or BIDS.

Lesson Requirements

Load the file BelgiumExtract.txt (which you can download at this book's website at www.wrox.com) into any database of your choosing. We are using AdventureWorks2008 database as our target, but that's not a dependency. Note: The file's first row holds the column names.

Hints

❑ One of the fastest ways to access the Import and Export Wizard to load the data is through Management Studio. Right-click on the target database and select Tasks ➪ Import Data.

Step-by-Step

1. Open SQL Server Management Studio in the SQL Server 2008 program group.

2. Right-click the target database of your choosing (like AdventureWorks2008) and select Tasks ➪ Import Data.

3. For the Data Source, select Flat File Source, as shown in Figure 1-3. For the "File Name" property, select the BelgiumExtract.txt file that you can download from this book's website on www.wrox.com. Check the "Column names in the first data row" option to read the column names from the first row of data from the flat file. Click the Columns page in the left pane to confirm that the file is delimited by commas.

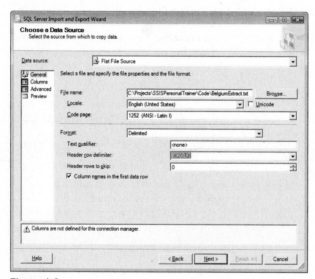

Figure 1-3

4. Click Next to configure the destination. Point to any server and database you want.

5. On the Select Source Tables and Views screen, click Edit Mappings to go to the Column Mappings page. Change the PurchaseOrderID column to an int data type. Change the OrderDate, ShipDate, and ModifiedDate columns to a datetime data type. Finally, change the SubTotal, TaxAmt, Freight, TotalDue columns all to a decimal(12,4) data type where 12 is the precision and 4 is the scale, as shown in Figure 1-4.

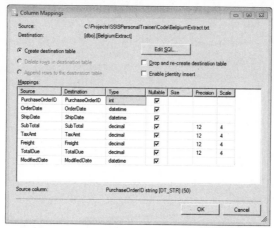

Figure 1-4

6. Click OK to leave the Column Mappings page and then click Next to review any Data Type Mapping warnings. The data mapping warnings screen shows you where you have any columns where the data types don't match. You can ignore those warnings for the time being and click Next a few times to execute the package. If you are successful, you should see a total of 4000 rows.

 Please select Lesson 1 on the DVD to view the video that accompanies this lesson.

Installing SQL Server Integration Services

This book requires that you have Business Intelligence Development Studio (BIDS) and the SQL Server Integration Services (SSIS) service installed. To develop SSIS, you cannot use Workgroup Edition or SQL Express. The SSIS runtime to run packages does ship with all editions, but that runtime on some of the lower editions may not work with all SSIS components.

On the subject of editions of SQL Server, you have a decision to make as to which edition you want to install: Standard Edition or Enterprise Edition. Developer Edition is also available. It contains all the components of Enterprise Edition at a tiny fraction of the cost but is licensed for development only. Enterprise Edition gives you a few additional SSIS components that you may be interested in for SQL Server 2008:

❑   Data Mining components

❑   Fuzzy Lookup and Group transforms

❑   Dimension and Partition Processing Destination

❑   Term Extraction and Lookup transforms

Additionally, the Enterprise Edition of SQL Server gives you database engine features that complement or may affect SSIS. One such feature is the Change Data Capture (CDC) feature, which allows you to easily synchronize two systems by querying SQL Server 2008 for only the changes that have occurred after a given date or time. Data compression is another key feature that may speed up your database reads and reduce your disk cost by 60–75 percent.

Oftentimes if you care about the Enterprise Edition features enough but don't need Enterprise Edition for the database engine, you might decide to license an SSIS server with just the minimum number of client access licenses (CALs) instead of doing a per-processor license. This approach reduces your SQL Server licensing cost sizably, but you now have new hardware cost to add.

When you're installing SQL Server, you need to ensure that the Business Intelligence Development Studio, Integration Services, and Management Tools - Basic checkboxes are selected in the Feature Selection screen (shown in Figure 2-1). The Integration Services option installs the runtime and service necessary to run the packages. The Business Intelligence Development Studio option installs the designer components, and the Management Tools option installs the DBA tools necessary to manage the packages later.

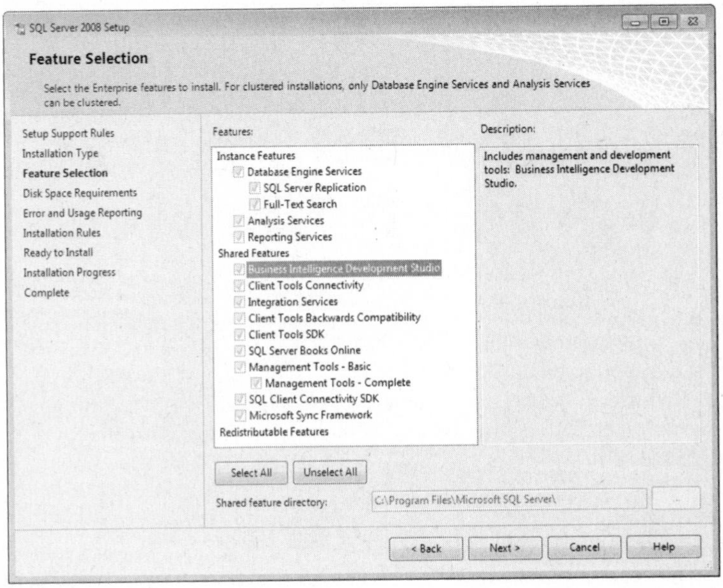

Figure 2-1

After you complete the Feature Selection screen, SQL Server installs all the necessary components without any wizard configuration required for SSIS. Once the installation is complete, open the configuration file located at C:\Program Files\Microsoft SQL Server\100\DTS\Binn\MsDtsSrvr.ini.xml. This file configures the SSIS service. Change the <ServerName> node where it currently says "." to your SQL Server's instance name where you want to store your packages. You can also change the directory from ..\Packages to the directory of your choice.

```xml
<?xml version="1.0" encoding="utf-8"?>
<DtsServiceConfiguration xmlns:xsd="http://www.w3.org/2001/XMLSchema"
xmlns:xsi="http://www.w3.org/2001/XMLSchema-instance">
  <StopExecutingPackagesOnShutdown>true</StopExecutingPackagesOnShutdown>

  <TopLevelFolders>
    <Folder xsi:type="SqlServerFolder">
      <Name>MSDB</Name>
      <ServerName>.</ServerName>
    </Folder>

    <Folder xsi:type="FileSystemFolder">
      <Name>File System</Name>
```

```
    <StorePath>..\Packages</StorePath>
    </Folder>

  </TopLevelFolders>
</DtsServiceConfiguration>
```

Once you modify this file, you need to restart the SSIS service from the SQL Server Configuration Manager or Services applet.

 Please select Lesson 2 on the DVD to view the video that accompanies this lesson.

Installing the Sample Databases

You will need two sample databases for the tutorials in this book and throughout the Microsoft Books Online tool built into SQL Server 2008. The AdventureWorks2008 database is an example database that simulates a bike retailer. It contains HR, accounting, and sales data for online transactions and store sales. The AdventureWorksDW2008 database is an example data warehouse for the same bike reseller.

The two sample databases are not installed by default with SQL Server 2008. You can download these and other sample databases from CodePlex.com (`http://www.codeplex.com/ MSFTDBProdSamples/`). CodePlex is Microsoft's community website where you can find projects and source code to extend SQL Server. The site is constantly updated and the sample databases are updated often as well.

> You can also find the sample databases at the Wrox website at
> `http://www.wrox.com/go/SQLServer2008RTMDataSets`.

The AdventureWorks2008 database requires that the Full Text Search feature be installed and that the new FileStream feature be enabled in SQL Server 2008. In addition the SQL Server Full Text service must be running. Without these, you can still install the AdventureWorksDW2008 database but not the AdventureWorks database.

To install the Full Text Search feature, you must go back to the SQL Server Installation Center under SQL Server 2008 ⇨ Configuration Tools ⇨ SQL Server Installation Center. Walk through the installation wizard again as if you were doing a new installation but when you get to the Select Components screen, ensure Full Text Search is selected.

The new FileStream feature allows you to store files quickly and easily on the file system of the server but they are treated like columns in a table. When you back up the database, it also backs up all files to which the table may refer. The feature is initially enabled in the installation wizard but can also be enabled after the installation in the SQL Server Configuration Manager under SQL

Server 2008 ⇨ Configuration Tools. Once the Configuration Manager is open, double-click the SQL Server database instance on which you want to enable the feature. This opens up the properties of the service, where you can go to the FILESTREAM tab to enable the feature, as shown in Figure 3-1.

Figure 3-1

Enabling FileStream requires that you restart the SQL Server instance. The sample database wizard can also do this automatically for you. After the installation is complete, the data files are copied to the same directory as the SQL Server system databases.

The wizard supports installation only on a local instance of SQL Server. If you need to install on a remote server, you can go to the sample directory after the installation, which is by default in the \Program Files\Microsoft SQL Server\100\Tools\Samples folder, and run the CreateAdventureWorks.cmd batch file, passing in the instance name and source path as shown in the following:

```
createadventureworks.cmd "ServerName\InstanceName" "C:\Program Files\Microsoft SQL
Server\100\" "C:\Program Files\Microsoft SQL Server\MSSQL10.MSSQLSERVER\"
```

You can also find the scripts for the databases in the C:\Program Files\Microsoft SQL Server\100\ Tools\Samples directory, where you can run them in a controlled fashion in Management Studio.

Try It

In this lesson you download and install the necessary example databases to work through the rest of the lessons in this book.

Lesson Requirements

To do this example, you need

❑ At least 300MB of hard drive space

❑ The SQL Server 2008 database engine installed

Hints

❑ Navigate to the CodePlex site to download the sample databases and make sure the Full Text service is installed and running prior to the installation

Step-by-Step

1. Browse to `http://www.codeplex.com/MSFTDBProdSamples/` in the browser of your choice and click Releases. (Or browse to `http://www.wrox.com/go/SQLServer2008RTMDataSets`.)

2. Download the appropriate version of AdventureWorks based on your server's chipset (x86, x64, or ia64). For example, if you are on a 32-bit machine, download the SQL2008.AdventureWorks_All_Databases.x86.msi setup file.

> **Prior to installation, open the SQL Server Configuration Manager to start the "SQL Full-text Filter Daemon Launcher" for your instance. Failure to do this will cause the installation to fail.**

Run the setup file to start the installation.

3. After viewing the intro and licensing screen you'll be asked to select the components that you want to be installed. The default components are fine for this screen, as shown in Figure 3-2. If you do not want to restore the databases, unselect Create AdventureWorks DBs.

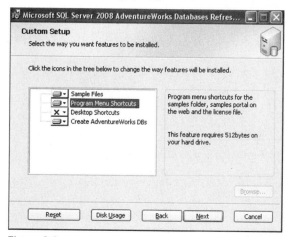

Figure 3-2

4.   Select the local instance of SQL Server that you want to install the databases to from the drop-down box.

5.   The samples are now installed and ready to use in Management Studio or in this case, SQL Server Business Intelligence Development Studio.

 Please select Lesson 3 on the DVD to view the video that accompanies this lesson.

Creating a Solution and Project

You cannot create an SSIS package in Business Intelligence Development Studio (BIDS) without first having a solution and project. Additionally, for execution of the package in debug mode, your package must be in a project and solution. Projects and solutions are containers for your packages that help you keep every component together and make you a more efficient SSIS developer.

BIDS is the program where you're going to develop your SSIS packages. In SQL Server 2008, BIDS is a Visual Studio 2008 shell. You can either open BIDS by itself under the SQL Server 2008 program group or open it by opening the full Visual Studio 2008 program.

An SSIS *project* is a container of one or more packages and other SSIS components. All the Visual Studio suite of products use the project construct to hold their files. For example, Reporting Services uses projects to hold its reports, and VB.NET uses projects to hold its VB.NET class files. In general, you want to align an SSIS project with a business project you're working on. For example, you may have an SSIS project called "Data warehouse ETL."

A *solution* is a container of one or more projects. Solutions enable many disparate types of projects to live under one container. For example, you may have a solution called "Enterprise Data Warehouse" with a SQL Server Reporting Services (SSRS) project called "Data warehouse reports," another project for SSIS called "Data warehouse ETL," and a final one for C# called "SharePoint code." All of those projects could live under one roof, so if a report developer makes a change in his SSRS project, the SSIS developer is aware of that change.

When you create a project in BIDS, a solution is automatically created at the same time. To create a project, you can open BIDS and select File ⇨ New ⇨ Project. As you can see in Figure 4-1, the solution name is "Enterprise Data Warehouse" and its project is called "Data warehouse ETL."

At first, the solution will not appear in your Solution Explorer since you only have a single project. Once you add a second project, it will appear. Subsequent projects can be added into the same

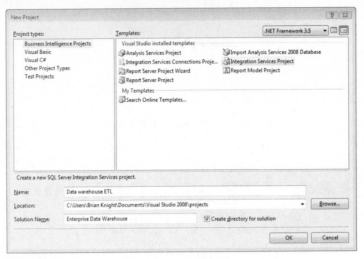

Figure 4-1

solution by going back to File ⇨ New ⇨ Project and selecting "Add to Solution" from the Solution drop-down box (which is shown in Figure 4-3 in the "Step-by-Step" later in this chapter). When you create your first project, you'll notice in the Solution Explorer, which shows you all the projects and files, that there appears to be no solution. This is because solutions are hidden from you when you have only a single project in the solution. You can choose to always see the solution file in the Solution Explorer by going to Tools ⇨ Options and checking "Always show solution" in the Projects and Solutions page. After that, your Solution Explorer will look like Figure 4-2.

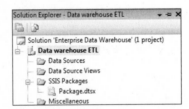

Figure 4-2

Try It

In this lesson, you learn how to create your first solution and project that you'll be using throughout the rest of the book. Examples of completed package, project, and solution files for this lesson can be downloaded from the book's website at www.wrox.com.

Lesson Requirements

To successfully complete this lesson, you need to create a solution called "Personal Trainer Solution" and a project called "Personal Trainer SSIS Project" that will be used throughout this book.

Hints

❑ To create the project, you'll want to open Business Intelligence Development Studio and select File ⇨ New ⇨ Project

Step-by-Step

1. Open BIDS from the SQL Server 2008 program group.

2. Click File ⇨ New ⇨ Project.

3. Select Business Intelligence Projects for the project type.

4. Select Integration Services Project for the template.

5. Type "Personal Trainer SSIS Project" for the Name property, as shown in Figure 4-3.

6. Type "C:\Projects\SSISPersonalTrainer" for the Location property.

7. Type "Personal Trainer Solution" for the Solution Name property.

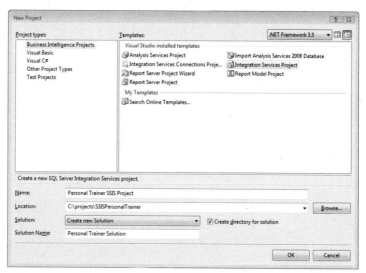

Figure 4-3

 Please select Lesson 4 on the DVD to view the video that accompanies this lesson.

Exploring Business Intelligence Development Studio

Business Intelligence Development Studio (BIDS) is a Visual Studio 2008 tool that helps you create, debug, and execute SSIS packages. When you're a business intelligence developer, it can also help you create reports in SQL Server Reporting Services (SSRS) or design cubes in SQL Server Analysis Services (SSAS). You'll be using BIDS extensively throughout this book, so it's important that in this lesson, you learn everything you need to know to make your life easier in this critical environment.

Because this is a more exploratory, introductory lesson, it doesn't have a task-based tutorial as the other lessons have.

You can open BIDS through the SQL Server 2008 program group. Depending on your PC, BIDS may take some time to open.

One hint that you can use to reduce your load time is to eliminate the splash screen. To eliminate the BIDS splash screen and reduce your load time by a few seconds each time, right-click the BIDS shortcut and select Properties. Next, add the switch -NOSPLASH *at the end of the shortcut as shown here:*

```
"C:\Program Files\Microsoft Visual Studio 9.0\Common7\IDE\devenv
.exe" -NOSPLASH
```

The Solution Explorer

Once you create your project from Lesson 4, you're ready to begin exploration of the environment. The most important pane, the Solution Explorer, is on the right. The Solution Explorer is where you can find all of your created SQL Server Integration Services (SSIS) packages, data sources, data source views, and any other miscellaneous files such as installation documents needed for the project. As discussed in Lesson 4, a solution is a container that holds a series of projects. Each project holds a myriad of objects for whatever type of project you're working in. For SSIS, it holds your packages, data source views, and shared connections. Once you create a solution, you can store many projects inside of it. For example, you might have a solution that has your VB.NET application and all the SSIS packages that support that application. In this case, you would probably have two projects: one for VB and another for SSIS.

After creating a new project, your Solution Explorer window contains a series of empty folders and a single package in the Packages folder. Figure 5-1 shows you a partially filled Solution Explorer. In this screenshot, you see a solution named PerformanceMetrics with two projects: a Reporting Services project called PerformanceMetricsReports and an Integration Services project called PerformanceMetrics. Inside the PerformanceMetrics project are two SSIS packages.

Figure 5-1

If you look into the directory that contains your solution and project files, you can see all the files that are represented in the Solution Explorer window. Some of the base files you might see will have the following extensions:

- ❑ .dtsx — An SSIS package, which uses its legacy extension from the early beta cycles of SQL Server 2008 when SSIS was still called DTS
- ❑ .ds — A shared data source file
- ❑ .dsv — A data source view
- ❑ .sln — A solution file that contains one or more projects
- ❑ .dtproj — An SSIS project file

If you copy any file that does not match the .ds, .dtsx, or .dsv extension, it is placed in the Miscellaneous folder. This folder is used to hold any files such as Word documents that describe the installation of the package or requirements documents. Anything you'd like can go into that folder, and it can all potentially be checked into a source control system like SourceSafe with the code.

The Properties Window

The Properties window (shown in Figure 5-2) is where you can customize almost any item that you have selected. For example, if you select a task in the design pane, you receive a list of properties to configure, such as the task's name and what query it's going to use. The view varies widely based on what item you have selected. Figure 5-2 shows the properties of the Execute SQL Task. You can also click the white background of the Control Flow tab to see the package properties in the Properties window. Sometimes, you can see some more advanced properties in the Properties pane than what the task's editor user interface provides you.

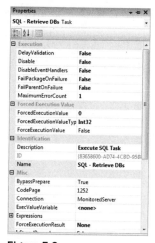

Figure 5-2

The Toolbox

The Toolbox contains all the items that you can use in the particular tab's design pane at any given point in time. For example, the Control Flow tab has a list of tasks and containers (a partial list is shown in Figure 5-3). This list may grow based on what custom tasks are installed. The list is completely different when you're in a different tab, such as the Data Flow tab. Many of the core tasks you see in Figure 5-3 are covered in Section II of this book in much more detail.

Figure 5-3

The Toolbox is organized into sections such as Maintenance Plan Tasks and Control Flow Items. These tabs can be collapsed and expanded for usability. As you use the Toolbox, you may want to customize your view by removing tasks or tabs from the default view. You can create or remove tabs by right-clicking in the Toolbox and clicking Add or Delete Tab. You can remove or customize the list of items in your Toolbox by right-clicking an item and selecting Choose Items, which takes you to the Choose Toolbox Items dialog box shown in Figure 5-4. It may take a few seconds to open. To customize the list that you see when you're in the Control Flow, select the SSIS Control Flow Items tab, and check the tasks you'd like to see. Also, after you install a custom component, you need to come back to this screen again to check the component that you installed to add it to your Toolbox.

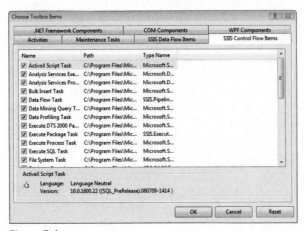

Figure 5-4

At some point, you may accidentally close a window like the Properties window. If this happens to you, you can bring that window back through the View menu. You can also click the pushpin on any particular window to hide the window because real estate is at a premium when you begin development of SSIS.

The BIDS Design Environment

The BIDS environment contains two key tabs for designing packages: Control Flow and Data Flow tabs. Each of these handles different parts of your packages. The *Control Flow* tab controls the execution of the package while the *Data Flow* tab handles the movement of data.

The Control Flow tab orchestrates the execution of your package, dictating that one task, such as an FTP Task, should execute ahead of another, for example, an Execute SQL Task. Inside the tab, you have tasks and containers you can drag over from the Toolbox onto the design pane. Each of those tasks has its own user interface to configure the task and can be accessed by double-clicking the interface.

Each package has only a single Control Flow, but can have many Data Flows. The user interface for the Data Flow task is quite different. Its user interface is the Data Flow tab. In the Data Flow tab, you can configure one or more Data Flow tasks by dragging over sources, transforms, and destinations onto the design pane. Each Control Flow can have any number of Data Flow tasks, which result in a new item in the Data Flow tab. The Data Flow is essentially where you're going to configure the movement of your data from nearly any source to nearly any destination.

When you execute a package by right-clicking it in the Solution Explorer and selecting Execute Package, you enter debug mode. Notice a new tab called Progress immediately opens. The Progress tab is where you go to debug when a package has a problem. You can also go to the Output window below to see a textual view of the same Progress tab. Once you stop debug mode by clicking the Stop button or by going to Debug ⇨ Stop Debugging, the Progress tab changes to an Execution Results tab, which shows you the last run of a package. Each of those tabs shows you more than the Output tab, which shows you only critical issues.

One other handy thing you can do from within BIDS is open Server Explorer. Server Explorer allows you to create a connection to a SQL Server database to manage just as you would in Management Studio. You can do this by selecting Tools ⇨ Connect to Database. Type in the credentials for the database, and then you're ready to run queries against the database, create stored procedures, or redesign tables, to name just a few things you can do. Now that you've taken a look at the BIDS environment, Lesson 6 covers using the environment to create your first package.

 Please select Lesson 5 on the DVD to view the video that accompanies this lesson.

Creating Your First Package

Creating packages in SQL Server Integration Services (SSIS) is a bit like Lego-block programming. You drag various tasks over, configure the tasks, chain them together, and then *voila*, execute. Well, it's not quite that easy, but you'll find it much easier than writing any program. In this lesson, you learn how to create your first SSIS package. Granted, the package does very little here, but it shows you many of the concepts that will be critical throughout the rest of the book. Many of the concepts may not make complete sense yet when it comes to configuring various components, but no worries—the concepts are deeply covered throughout the rest of the book.

To create your first package, you need an SSIS project. Creating a project is covered extensively in Lesson 4. After you create your first project, a package called Package.dtsx is automatically created. If you want to rename this package, simply right-click the package in Solution Explorer and select Rename. Once the file is renamed to something with a .dtsx extension, you will be asked, "Do you wish to rename the package object as well?" You should always say yes to this question because failure to do so results in your package name and your file name becoming out of synch, meaning that your error logs will report that a package name is failing and you won't be able to find it.

To create a new package, you can also right-click SSIS Packages in the Solution Explorer and select New Package. This action creates a new package that you will want to rename as soon as it's created because it, too, will be called Package.dtsx or some variation of it. The final result will resemble Figure 6-1, which shows a partially complete SSIS project.

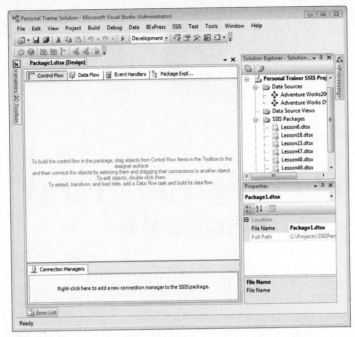

Figure 6-1

Creating and Using Connection Managers

To design a package, you want to first create connections, which are called connection managers in SSIS. A *connection manager* is a connection that can be leveraged and consumed once or many times in a package. To create a connection manager, right-click in the Connection Managers pane at the bottom of the screen in BIDS and select New <type of connection>. Any connection that you would use in SSIS, whether to a file or a database, will be stored as a connection manager here. Some of those common items would include the connections in the following table.

TYPE OF CONNECTION	CONNECTION MANAGER
Database	OLE DB Connection Manager for Oracle, SQL Server, DB ADO.NET Connection Manager for ODBC types of connections
File	Flat File Connection Manager when you want to load the file using a Data Flow Task. There is also an additional connection manager called the File Connection Manager that can be used if all you want to do is rename, delete, or perform some other type of file operation.
Excel	Excel Connection Manager
Internet Connection	SMTP Connection Manager for mail servers FTP Connection Manager for FTP servers HTTP Connection Manager for websites or web services

You can access some of the connections by right-clicking in the Connection Manager pane and selecting New Connection. This will bring up a list of all the available connection managers (shown in Figure 6-2), including third-party ones that you have installed. The handy thing about connection managers is that they're externally available to a DBA at runtime. In other words, when a DBA goes to schedule this package, he or she can point the connection to a new database or file on-the-fly for that one job.

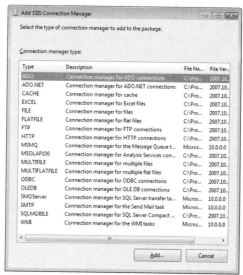

Figure 6-2

Once you create an OLE DB connection it is available to you anywhere in the package from any component that can use the connection. If you'd like, you can create a connection that can be leveraged from multiple packages by right-clicking Data Sources in the Solution Explorer and selecting New Data Source. These data sources can be leveraged from multiple packages in the project and are a design-time feature only. By creating a connection here, you type the password one time for your connection, and if you ever change any type of connection information, it changes across any package using that connection the next time you open the package. There are not any negative consequences of doing this, so generally speaking it's a great design-time practice to use shared data sources.

Because this is a design-time feature only, the connection information is folded into the package by creating a connection manager that points to the shared data source. To do this, right-click in the Connection Manager window and select New Connection From Data Source. Then, a dialog box opens asking you which shared connection you want to point to. Select that connection, and you're all done. All the metadata from the connection is now a part of the connection, and the .ds file for the shared connection is never deployed. If you delete the shared connection, the connection manager reverts to a regular OLE DB Connection Manager.

Using and Configuring Tasks

Your package would be nothing without tasks. *Tasks* in the Control Flow tab orchestrate the work that you want to do in the package. For example, one task may copy a file over from a different server while another task may load the file into a database. To use a task, simply drag it onto the design pane in the

Control Flow tab from the Toolbox. A common task that you'll use in this book is the Script Task because it requires no configuration, which makes it a great training tool.

Until most tasks are configured by double-clicking the task, you may see a yellow warning or red error indicator on the task. After you configure the task, you can link it to other tasks by using precedence constraints. Once you click the task, you'll notice a green arrow (the precedence constraint) pointing down from the task, as shown in Figure 6-3. This precedence constraint controls the execution order of the various tasks in your package and can be used by dragging the green arrow to the next task that you want to chain together. You read more about most of the core important tasks and the topic of precedence constraints in Section II of this book.

Figure 6-3

You should never keep the default name of your tasks. Instead, you should rename them to something that you can recognize in the log later. We prefer to name all of our tasks with some two- or three-digit qualifier, such as SCR for a Script Task, and then the purpose of the task such as "SCR - Encrypt File." This name then shows up in your logs when a problem occurs and can also help you self-document your package.

Exploring Package Encryption

A package is essentially an XML file behind the scenes. To prove this, you can right-click any package and select View Code to see the package's XML. As you can imagine though, storing secure information inside of an XML file could create some security problems. Luckily Microsoft already thought of that problem and has a solution—encrypting your packages.

Microsoft encrypts your package by default with your Windows user key, which is a key that protects your Windows user credentials on your PC. You can look at the property that encrypts your package by going to the Properties pane and looking at the ProtectionLevel package-level property. This property is set to EncryptSensitiveWithUserKey by default, which means that all the user names, passwords, or any other sensitive data will be locked down with your credentials. If you were to pass the package to another user, the package's encrypted data would not be visible, and the user would have to retype the secure information, such as the login information.

Another option is to change the property to EncryptSenstiveWithPassword, which locks down the package with a password instead. You can also EncryptAllWithPassword (or UserKey). This property value locks down the entire package to where no one can open it without a proper password.

> This property is usually one of the top reasons why packages fail in production. For example, if your package has sensitive information inside of it to connect to a database, the package would potentially fail when you ran the job because it was running under the SQL Server Agent's (SQL Server's scheduler) service account. You can also avoid this problem by setting the property to EncryptAllWithPassword and simply pass in the password when running the package or scheduling it.

Executing Packages

Once your package is ready to execute, you can run it in debug mode by right-clicking it in Solution Explorer and selecting Execute Package. By running the package in debug mode, you have enhanced logging views and breakpoints available to you to determine why your package is not working. While in debug mode, however, you will not be able to sizably change the package. To stop debug mode, click the Stop button or click Debug ⇨ Stop Debugging.

Try It

In this lesson, you learn how to create your first basic package that will do very little other than demonstrate some of the SSIS functionality.

Lesson Requirements

To create your first package, you can reuse the project from Lesson 4 or create a brand new project. Once created, you'll notice that one such package in your project is Package.dtsx. Rename or create a new package called Lesson6.dtsx that has two Script Tasks in it that are connected. One Script Task should be named Step 1 and the other Step 2. These two tasks will do nothing at all. Create a connection manager that points to AdventureWorks2008 and create a password on the package of your choosing that will always pop up when you open the package and execute it.

You can also find the complete package (Lesson6.dtsx) on the companion website for this book at www.wrox.com.

Hints

❑   Create a new package by right-clicking on the word Packages in Solution Explorer in BIDS

❑   Drag over the two Script Tasks and connect them together using the green precedence constraint coming out of the task

Step-by-Step

1.   Create a new package in a new solution or the existing solution you created in Lesson 4 by right-clicking Packages in Solution Explorer and selecting New Package. Rename the package to Lesson6.dtsx.

2.   Drag over two Script Tasks from the Toolbox into the Control Flow design pane.

3.   Right-click in each Script Task and select Rename. Rename one task "Step 1" and the other "Step 2."

4.   Select Step 1 and drag the green line (called a precedence constraint) onto Step 2.

5.   Right-click in the Connection Manager pane at the bottom of the screen in BIDS and select New OLE DB Connection. In the Configure OLE DB Connection Manager dialog box, you may have to click New to create a new connection or it may already be cached from a previous package. If you had to click New, type the credentials to the AdventureWorks2008 database and click OK twice.

6. Rename the newly created connection manager AdventureWorks (removing the instance name from the connection manager name).

7. Select the blank white area of the design pane in the Control Flow tab and then go to the Properties pane. Change the ProtectionLevel property to EncryptAllWithPassword and type the password of whatever you want above it by selecting the ellipsis button in the Password property right above ProtectionLevel.

8. Execute the package by right-clicking it in Solution Explorer and selecting Execute Package. The final package should look like Figure 6-4.

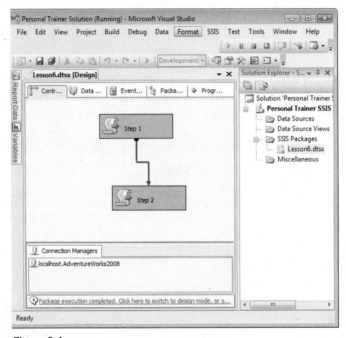

Figure 6-4

 Please select Lesson 6 on the DVD to view the video that accompanies this lesson.

Section II
Tasks

7

Connecting Control Flow Tasks with Precedence Constraints

When you create tasks in SQL Server Integration Services (SSIS), you need a way to connect these tasks. Precedence constraints are the connections between the tasks that control the execution order of each task. After you create more than one task in the Control Flow in SSIS, you can then link them together by using these precedence constraints. Click once on a task, and you see a green arrow pointing down from the task. For example, in Figure 7-1 you can see a Script Task with a green arrow below the task. This is the precedence constraint arrow. These arrows control the order of tasks in a package, and they also control which tasks will run.

Figure 7-1

To create an On Success Precedence Constraint, click the green arrow coming out of the task and drag it to the task you want to link to the first task. In Figure 7-2, you can see the On Success Precedence Constraint between the two Script Tasks. Only if the first Script Task completes successfully will the second Script Task run. To delete the constraint click once on the constraint line and press Delete on the keyboard, or right-click the constraint line and left-click Delete.

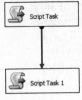

Figure 7-2

The precedence constraint arrows can be different colors to represent different commands. They can also have an FX logo to represent an expression, as shown in Figure 7-3. Placing expressions on precedence constraints gives you more advanced ways to control the execution of each package. For example, you could state that you want Script Task 1 to execute only if you're processing a month-end cycle. Each color represents a status of when a task will execute:

❑   **Green** = On Success

❑   **Red** = On Failure

❑   **Blue** = On Completion

❑   **Any color with FX Logo** = Expression, or Expression with a Constraint

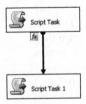

Figure 7-3

The arrows that connect tasks in a Data Flow tab look similar to the precedence constraints in the Control Flow. These Data Flow connections do not have the same properties as the Control Flow. Click a source or a transformation in the Data Flow tab, and you see a green and red arrow pointing down, as in Figure 7-4 (though in this figure you won't be able to see the colors). The green arrow is the flow of good data, and the red arrow is the flow of data with errors. This allows data with errors to be sent to another destination separate from the good data.

Figure 7-4

In the Control Flow you need to use a different approach. If you'd like the next task to execute only if the first task has failed, create a precedence constraint as explained previously for the On Success Constraint. After the constraint is created, double-click the constraint arrow and the Precedence Constraint Editor opens, as shown in Figure 7-5. This is where you set the conditions that decide if the next task will execute at runtime. The first option you want to change here is the Value to Failure, which changes the precedence constraint to an On Failure event.

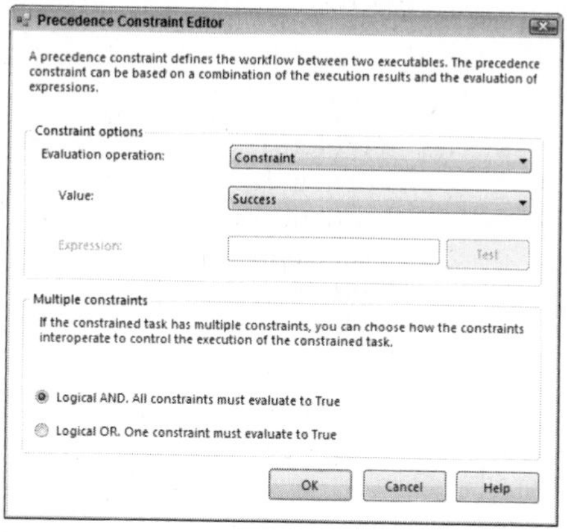

Precedence Constraint Editor

A precedence constraint defines the workflow between two executables. The precedence constraint can be based on a combination of the execution results and the evaluation of expressions.

Constraint options

Evaluation operation: Constraint

Value: Success

Expression: _____   Test

Multiple constraints

If the constrained task has multiple constraints, you can choose how the constraints interoperate to control the execution of the constrained task.

○ Logical AND. All constraints must evaluate to True

○ Logical OR. One constraint must evaluate to True

OK   Cancel   Help

Figure 7-5

In the Precedence Constraint Editor, you can also set the logical AND/OR for the preceding task. SSIS gives you the option of adding a logical AND or a logical OR when a task has multiple constraints. In the Precedence Constraint Editor you can configure the task to execute only if the group of predecessor tasks has completed (AND), or if any one of the predecessor tasks has completed (OR). A predecessor task is any task with a precedence constraint that is connected to another task. If a precedence constraint is a logical AND, the connecting lines are solid (Figure 7-6). If a precedence constraint is a logical OR, the lines are dotted (Figure 7-7), which allows the task to perform even if one or more predecessor tasks have failed.

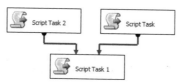

Figure 7-6

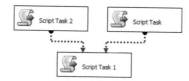

Figure 7-7

In the Evaluation Operation drop-down box of the Precedence Constraint Editor, you can edit how the task will be evaluated. The drop-down menu has four options:

❑ **Constraint** — Evaluates the success, failure, or completion of the predecessor task or tasks

❑ **Expression** — Evaluates the success of a customized condition that is programmed using an expression

❑ **Expression and Constraint** — Evaluates both the expression and the constraint before moving to the next task

❑ **Expression or Constraint** — Determines if either the expression or the constraint has been successfully met before moving to the next task

If you select any constraint with an expression, the expression box requires a valid expression. An expression is usually used to evaluate a variable before proceeding to the next task. For example, if you want to ensure that the two variables are equal to each other, use the following syntax:

```
@Variable1 == @Variable2
```

Try It

In this lesson you create four Script Tasks in a package and control when they execute with precedence constraints. After this lesson you will understand how to use precedence constraints to decide which tasks will execute in a package.

Lesson Requirements

Drag four Script Tasks into a blank package. The names of the Script Tasks will automatically be Script Task, Script Task 1, Script Task 2, and Script Task 3. Connect the Script Task so that Script Task 1 runs if Script Task is successful. Connect Script Task 1 to Script Task 2 with a success constraint. Connect Script Task 3 before Script Task 2 with a success constraint and run the package once with the logical constraints on Script Task 2 set to AND. Then change the logical constraint on Script Task 2 to OR and change the properties of Script Task 3 to Force Failure and run the package again. You should see Script Task 2 turn green each time, indicating success.

You can download the completed Lesson7.dtsx from www.wrox.com.

Hints

❑ Script Task 2 should have two incoming precedence constraint lines

❑ Look in the Properties window in the bottom right of Visual Studio to find the Force Execution Results property for the Script Task

Step-by-Step

1. Drag over four Script Tasks into the Control Flow.

2. Drag the precedence constraint from Script Task to Script Task 1.

3.   Drag the precedence constraint from Script Task 1 to Script Task 2.

4.   Drag the precedence constraint from Script Task 3 to Script Task 2. What you have should match Figure 7-8.

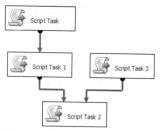

Figure 7-8

5.   Run the package; all tasks should turn green.

6.   Stop the debugging using the square stop button on the toolbar.

7.   Double-click one of the constraint arrows going into Script Task 2.

8.   Change the Logical constraint to OR; the two lines in Script Task 2 change to dotted lines.

9.   Click Script Task 3.

10.   In the Properties window change the forced execution results to Failure (Figure 7-9).

11.   Run the package. Script Task 3 should turn red, and all other tasks should turn green. Notice Script Task 2 ran even though Script Task 3 failed.

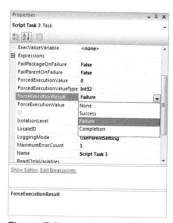

Figure 7-9

 Please select Lesson 7 on the DVD to view the video that accompanies this lesson.

Manipulating Files with the File System Task

When you need to move, delete, or rename a file, or make just about any other changes to it, the File System Task is the task to use. The File System Task allows you to make changes to files or directories and move them around without having to write custom scripts. The File System Task is a commonly used and powerful task in SSIS. A File System Task can:

- ❑ Copy a directory
- ❑ Copy a file
- ❑ Create a directory
- ❑ Delete a directory
- ❑ Delete the contents of a directory
- ❑ Delete a file
- ❑ Move a directory
- ❑ Move a file
- ❑ Rename a file
- ❑ Change the attributes of a file

You can bring up the File System Task Editor by double-clicking the File System Task or by right-clicking and selecting Edit. In the editor you see several fields to set to perform the needed operation. The Operation property is the action the task is going to perform when executing. In Figure 8-1 you can see the drop-down menu for the Operation property. What you select in this menu determines which properties will be available to you. For example, when you select Delete File, you do not need a destination, just a source file to delete, so a destination will not be available.

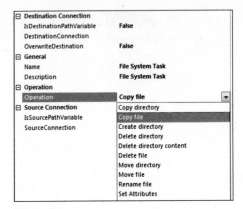

Figure 8-1

The property IsSourcePathVariable allows you to use a variable for the source. This variable will be a string variable that holds the location of the file, for example, C:\SSIS\FlatFile.csv. Instead of placing this path directly in the task, you have the location entered into a variable. The same holds true for the IsDestinationPathVariable property. The destination will not be a file name but a folder location. Figure 8-2 shows the File System Task with both the source and destination set to a variable.

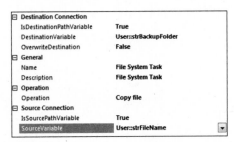

Figure 8-2

If you prefer to enter a connection instead of a variable, the connection must exist in the connection manager. You can also click <New Connection> in the Source Connection or the Destination Connection drop-down menu to create the connection in the connection manager. When you click <New Connection>, you see the screen in Figure 8-3. Here you can browse to the file or folder location and save it as the source or destination; once saved, it appears in the connection manager of the package. (If you are unfamiliar with the concept of connections and connection managers in SSIS, please refer to Lesson 6 for more explanation.)

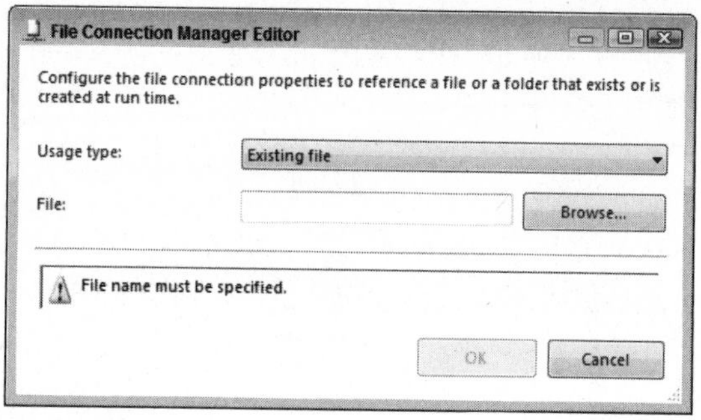

Figure 8-3

To copy a directory's contents with the File System Task you need to set up a source and destination either in the connection manager or in variables. The DestinationConnection will be the location the directory is copied into for this operation. If you have set IsDestinationPathVariable to True, the option will be DestinationVariable. Clicking the field shows a drop-down box with a list of variables. If the variable is not listed, you can click New Variable to create a variable to hold the destination name in the variable creation screen shown in Figure 8-4.

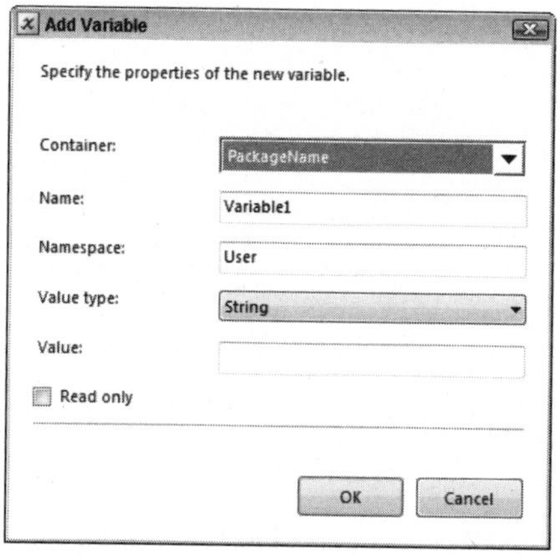

Figure 8-4

OverwriteDestination is the next option in the File System Task Editor. When you are setting this field, consider the package failures that can occur due to this setting. With this field set to True, the File System Task overwrites a directory if it already exists. This prevents errors but may overwrite a needed file. With OverwriteDestination set to False, you do not risk overwriting a file inadvertently, but if a destination file already exists, the task will fail with an error that states the file already exists.

The SourceConnection is the directory that is going to be copied. In the drop-down menu, you see the sources that are in the connection manager. If you do not see the directory, click New Connection, and this allows you to create the source connection in the connection manager just as in the DestinationConnection.

With a source folder and a destination folder set, the File System Task transfers all of the contents of the source folder and the contents of all subfolders to the destination folder. Figure 8-5 shows a completed File System Task set to back up a drive. Notice the name and description make it easy to see what the task is supposed to perform.

Figure 8-5

The next two properties are the Name and Description. The name shows in the Control Flow on the task, as in Figure 8-6, and should describe what the task is designed to do. The description should be a longer explanation.

Figure 8-6

Several of the other options in File System Task, such as Copy File, Move File, Move Directory, and Rename File, have the same options as Copy Directory. You set up these tasks using the same fields. Copy File copies a file from the source to the destination. Move File moves a file from the source to the destination.

The Rename File option is a little different. It actually performs two actions at once. It not only renames a file, but it also moves a file if the destination is different from the source. If you need to move a file and rename it, there is no need to create a Rename Task and a separate Move File Task. Both steps can be done in one File System Task. Set the source to the location of the file and set the destination to the new location the file should be moved to with this task. If you do not want to move the file and just need to rename it, set the source and destination to the same directory.

When Create Directory is selected, the first property in the File System Task is UseDirectoryIfExists, shown in Figure 8-7. If this is set to True, the task checks for the existence of the directory. If the directory exists, the File System Task takes no action. If the directory does not exist, it creates it. If UseDirectoryIfExists is set to False, and the directory already exists, the task fails with an error stating the directory already exists.

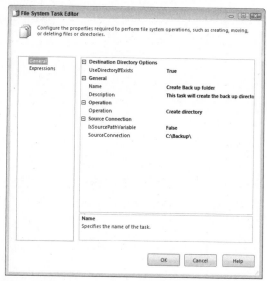

Figure 8-7

When you are setting up a File System Task to delete a directory or a file, only a source is needed. You can set the source to an existing connection manager source or to a variable. This task will delete a directory and all of its contents including all subfolders and files in the subfolders. The delete directory content operation needs only a source as well. This task leaves the directory and just deletes the contents in the directory.

When you are using a File System Task to set attributes of a file or folder, you can set four attributes on a source file. These attributes are:

- ❑ Hidden
- ❑ ReadOnly
- ❑ Archive
- ❑ System

Each file attribute can be set to either True or False. The source is changed to match the settings in the File System Task. If the source file properties match the settings in the File System Task, no changes are made to the source file.

Try It

In this lesson you create a package with a File System Task that moves a file and renames it at the same time. After this lesson you will understand how to use the File System Task to manipulate files.

Lesson Requirements

Create a file on the C: drive named CreatedFile.txt. The file will have nothing in it and can be created by using Notepad or any other tool. Create a directory named Backup on the C: drive. Then use SSIS to move and rename the CreatedFile.txt to MovedFile.txt and move it into the Backup folder on the C: drive.

Hints

❑   Only one File System Task is needed

❑   The rename operation can also move the file

Step-by-Step

1. Create a new SSIS package called Lesson8.dtsx (or download Lesson8.dtsx from www.wrox.com).

2. Navigate to the C: drive on the local machine and create a file named CreatedFile.txt (right-click in Windows Explorer and select New ⇨ Text Document).

3. Create a folder in the C: drive named Backup (right-click in Windows Explorer and select New ⇨ Folder).

4. Create a new file connection in the connection manager for C:\CreatedFile.txt (Figure 8-8) by right-clicking in the connection manager and selecting New File Connection.

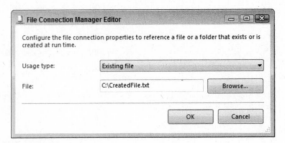

Figure 8-8

5. Create a new file connection in the connection manager to C:\Backup\MovedFile.txt (Figure 8-9) by right-clicking in the connection manager and selecting New File Connection.

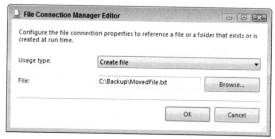

Figure 8-9

6.   Drag over a File System Task into the Control Flow.

7.   Change the Name to "Backup CreatedFile."

8.   Enter a description that describes this operation.

9.   Select Rename in the operation menu.

10. Select CreatedFile.txt as the source.

11. Select MovedFile.txt as the destination.

12. Set OverwriteDestination to True. The screen should now look like Figure 8-10.

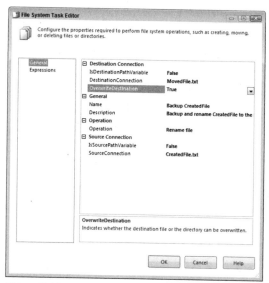

Figure 8-10

13. Click OK and run the package; the task should turn green indicating success.

 Please select Lesson 8 on the DVD to view the video that accompanies this lesson.

Coding Custom Script Tasks

When you create a new SQL Server Integration Services (SSIS) package you may find yourself wanting some functionality that the built-in tasks cannot accomplish. This situation is where the Script Task comes into play. This task can accomplish anything that can be done with any .NET programming. Interestingly, the Script Task is not a scripting language at all. In SSIS 2008 you can use VB.NET or C# to write complete coding solutions to perform just about any task your imagination can come up with.

When you drag over a Script Task and double-click it to open the Script Task Editor, you first see three nodes listed on the left: Script, General, and Expressions. Expressions are discussed in later lessons of this book (see Lessons 17, 29, and 30). In this lesson, we want to focus on the General and Script nodes.

Under the General node you see the name and description of the Script Task. This does not affect the code in the script; it is used for ease of reference when viewing the tasks in the Control Flow. The name shows on the tasks in the Control Flow. The description is usually a longer line of text describing the purpose of the Script Task. It is a best practice to always change the values of these fields to values that will make it easy for anyone to see and understand the function of the task.

In the Script node you have four properties to set.

- ❏ The first is the **ScriptLanguage**. VB.NET is used for all of the examples in this lesson
- ❏ **EntryPoint** is the next property. This is the location in the code where the task looks to execute the code first. Generally this is left at Main because Main is automatically set up in the built-in starting script

The next two properties allow you to list the variables from the package that you can use in the Script Task code.

❑ **ReadOnlyVariables** are variables that you want to use in the Script Task code, but you do not want the values of the variables edited

❑ The **ReadWriteVariables** are variables used in the Script Task that can have their values changed, meaning you can change the values of the variables to be used in the package after the Script Task completes

At the bottom of this node you can see a button labeled Edit Script. The default Script Language is C#. To change the default Script Language, click Tools ➪ Options and place a check next to Show All Settings. Click the plus next to Business Intelligence Designers and then click Integrated Services Designers. Change the default language on the right to VB in the Language drop-down menu. When you click the Edit Script button it opens the Visual Studio Script Editor. If this is your first time opening the script editor you see the first-time configuration window, as shown in Figure 9-1. After the environment is configured you see a screen similar to the one shown in Figure 9-2, which is very similar to the Visual Studio coding environment. Developers should feel right at home with this interface.

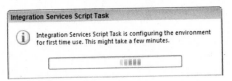

Figure 9-1

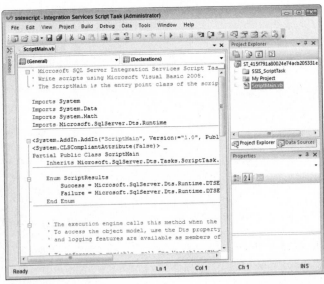

Figure 9-2

On the left you can see the Script Editor tab. On the right you see the Project Explorer with the Data Source table below and the Properties window below that. The Script Editor window is where you spend most of your time creating the script you need.

Most Script Tasks use ReadOnlyVariables, ReadWriteVariables, or a combination of both. As mentioned earlier in the lesson, to get a variable to be available in the Script Task you need to add it to the ReadWriteVariables or ReadOnlyVariables in the Script node on the Properties screen of the task. One of the most common tasks is changing a file name based on the conditions in a Script Task. You can accomplish this act by passing in a ReadWriteVariable with the file name and use the VB.NET code to change the variable.

First you have to add the variable name to the ReadWriteVariables variable property. When you click the ReadWriteVariables line an ellipsis appears on the right. Click this ellipsis button to see the list of all variables in the package, as shown in Figure 9-3. Place a check next to the variable name and click OK. Now the variable shows in the variable property as User::"*Variable name.*" This variable can now be used in the Script Task code.

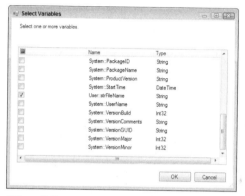

Figure 9-3

Now you can click the Edit Script button and write some code to change the value of the variable. Change the variable to "newvalue" and then make a popup box appear showing the value of the variable. Write this code below the `public sub main` starting code. Remember the entry point was left at Main in the properties of the Script Task. The following code shows how to accomplish this function.

```
Dts.Variables("strFileName").Value = "newvalue"
MsgBox(Dts.Variables("strFileName").Value)
```

Notice that the variable is called using the string literal name of the file and it is case sensitive. You use the value property of the variable to set it to a "newvalue." The next line is the typical message box in VB.NET. This causes a popup box to appear showing the value of the variable. If the value is set correctly, you see a popup box as shown in Figure 9-4.

Figure 9-4

You can use two types of variables in Script Tasks. The one just shown is the variable from the package. However, you can also create variables in the Script Task just as you would in a regular .NET application. This variable is different than the package variable and is not used outside of the Script Task. You create this variable with a `Dim` statement. The value of the variable is changed directly and does not require the use of the `DTS.Variables()` method. The following code shows how to create a variable, give it a value, and then pop up a message box with the value of the variable.

```
Dim strInternal As String
strInternal = "test"
MsgBox(strInternal)
```

This code causes a popup box to appear, as shown in Figure 9-5. Notice the value of `test` was saved in the variable value and then shown in the popup box. Again, you did this directly without using the `Dts.Variables()` method. The variable cannot be called by the package directly.

Figure 9-5

Keep in mind that you can have variables in your package with the same name as the variables in your Script Task. These variables do not pass values between the Script Task and the package. To pass values from the script variables to the package variables you need to set the package variable value to the value of the script variable. The following code shows how to do this.

```
Dts.Variables("strFileName").Value = strInternal
```

Another common function of Script Tasks is the creation of "if then" statements. These statements can be used to make decisions based on certain values. A common use for this functionality is to have an Execute SQL Task to count values from a table and pass that value into a variable. For example, say you want to see if a file name exists in an auditing table to determine if the file should be used. The Execute SQL Task saves the count value to a variable called `intAuditCount`. This value is compared with the "if then" statement and then used in further code. The following code shows an example of the "if then" statement.

```
If Dts.Variables("intAuditCount").Value > 0 Then
    'code for the file found in the audit table
Else
    'code for the file not found in the audit table
End If
```

Altering connections is another common task Script Tasks can perform. First the connection must exist in the connection manager of the package. Connections managers are explained in Lesson 6. Assume the connection is named "AdventureWorks." To alter this connection you use the `Dts.Connections()` method. The following code shows an example of changing a connection string. Notice the literal name is in parentheses and double quotes and is case sensitive. Then the `ConnectionString` property of the connection follows. You can then set the connection string equal to the needed string. This allows you to change the connection during the package runtime.

```
Dts.Connections("AdventureWorks").ConnectionString = _
"Data Source=localhost;Initial Catalog=AdventureWorks2008;" + _
"Provider=SQLNCLI10.1;Integrated Security=SSPI;"
```

Checking for the existence of a file is a common need in SSIS packages. To perform this function you must import the System.IO into the Script Task. Simply add the line `Imports System.IO` after the last Import line at the top of the Script Task code. You must create two variables on the package: a String variable to hold the file name and a Boolean variable to set to true if the file exists and false if it does not exist. Name them `strFileName` and `bolFileExist`. The code would then be:

```
If File.Exists(Dts.Variables("strFileName").Value) Then
    Dts.Variables("bolFileExist").Value = True
Else
    Dts.Variables("bolFileExist").Value = False
End If
```

Checking to see if a file is in use is another common task that can be performed with a Script Task in SSIS. Use the variables `strFileName` as the file name and `bolFileInUse` as the Boolean variable and set this to true if the file is in use. The code would be:

```
Try
    File.SetLastAccessTime(Dts.Variables("strFileName").Value, Today)
Catch e As Exception
    Dts.Variables("bolFileInUse").Value = True
End Try
```

Notice the code is catching an exception. The Script Task attempts to set the last access date of the file to today's date. If this process fails, the exception will set the Boolean variable to true to indicate the file is in use. Before running this code you may want to use the previous code that checks if a file exists to determine the file does exist. That ensures you don't catch an exception because the file does not exist when you really want to catch it because the file is being used.

After these Boolean variables are set with the Script Task you can use the expression on the precedence constraints coming from the Script Task to determine which direction the Control Flow should go. You may have two precedence constraints leaving the Script Task, both with expressions on them. One precedence constraint expression checks for a value of true and the other checks for false. The value of the Boolean variable will be evaluated, and the Control Flow will continue down the proper precedence constraint line.

Now you can use the Script Task to perform complicated decision making based on the values of the variables in the package and the values of the variables in the script. You can write these values into the ReadWriteVariables and use them later in the package. The Script Task is a very powerful component that allows developers to write complex code components to perform functions that might not exist in the built-in tasks in SSIS.

Try It

In this lesson you create a Script Task that changes the value of a variable based on the value of another variable. After completing this lesson you will understand how to use the Script Task to make changes to a package.

Lesson Requirements

You need to create two variables called `intVar` and `strVar`. You want to check the value of the `intVar`, and if it is above 10, you want to display the word "Big." If the value is 10 or less, you want to display "Small." The message box should display the value of the variable `strVar` and not the literal string of the words.

Hints

❑ You need only one message box code line in the Script Task

❑ Set the value of the `strVar` to "Big" or "Small"

Step-by-Step

1. Right-click the blank area of a blank package and left-click Variables.

2. Create a variable named `strVar` and set the type to string.

3. Create a variable named `intVar` and set the type to int.

4. Set the value of `intVar` to 5.

5. Drag over a Script Task and double-click it to open the Script Task Editor.

6. Ensure the script language is set to Microsoft Visual Basic 2008.

7. Click the ReadWriteVariables property and click the ellipsis button.

8. Place a check next the User::intVar and User::strVar and click OK; the variables should show in the property window, as shown in Figure 9-6.

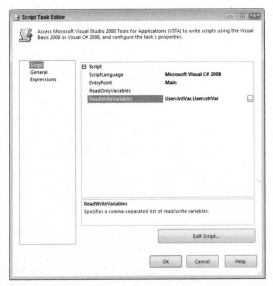

Figure 9-6

9. Click the Edit Script button in the task window.

10. Below the `public sub main()` section, type in the following code:

```
If Dts.Variables("intVar").Value > 10 Then
    Dts.Variables("strVar").Value = "Big"
Else
    Dts.Variables("strVar").Value = "Small"
End If

MsgBox(Dts.Variables("strVar").Value)
```

11. Close the script editor.

12. Click OK in the Script Task Editor window.

13. Right-click the Script Task and left-click Execute Task.

14. You should see a popup message showing the word "Small," as shown in Figure 9-7.

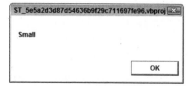

Figure 9-7

15. Click OK in the message box and click the Stop Debug button on the toolbar.

16. Change the value of the `intVar` variable to 11.

17. Execute the Script Task again; you should see a message box appear showing the word "Big," as shown in Figure 9-8.

Figure 9-8

18. Click the OK button and stop debugging.

 Please select Lesson 9 on the DVD to view the video that accompanies this lesson.

10

Using the Execute SQL Task

When you are creating a SQL Server Integration Services (SSIS) package, you will find one of the most commonly used tasks is the Execute SQL Task. This task is used to insert, update, select, and truncate data from SQL tables. Any normal SQL commands you would use can be used in this task. You can use parameters just like a stored procedure and can even call stored procedures from the task. A connection to the database must exist in the connection manager for the Execute SQL Task to reference.

Double-click on an Execute SQL Task in the Control Flow to open the Execute SQL Task Editor. The first screen on the editor lists four nodes in the left pane:

- ❑ General
- ❑ Parameter Mapping
- ❑ Result Set
- ❑ Expressions

In the General node, shown in Figure 10-1, you see the main properties that need to be set for the Execute SQL Task. The first two properties are Name and Description. These properties do not affect the task. They are used for ease of reference when viewing the task in the Control Flow. The name shows on the task in the Control Flow. The description is usually a longer line of text describing the purpose of the Execute SQL Task. It is a best practice to always change the values of these fields to values that make it easy for anyone to see and understand the function of the task.

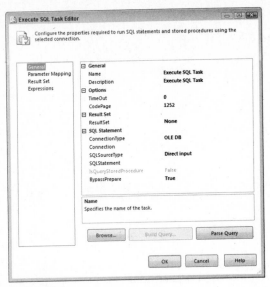

Figure 10-1

The next two options are the TimeOut and CodePage. The timeout is the number of seconds you want the Execute SQL Task to run before the task stops and reports a timeout failure. A setting of zero is infinite.

Code pages are set based on the code page used on the SQL server. In the United States the common code page is Western European (1252). If you are using a different code page, such as Korean (949), the code page would need to be changed to match the code page of the server. The code page option is available only for the following connection types:

- ❏ Excel
- ❏ OLE DB
- ❏ ADO.NET
- ❏ SQL Mobile

The ResultSet property is the type of returned data from the SQL command. This can be None when the SQL command is not returning data, as with an insert command. The result set can be a single row. This single row can be stored in a String or Integer variable. It can also be a full result set or XML, which can be stored in an object variable. These variables are set in the Result Set node.

When you click the Result Set node in the left pane of the Execute SQL Task Editor, you see the result set pane, as shown in Figure 10-2, and can create new result set variables here by clicking the Add button at the bottom. The Add button is not available here if the Result Set property on the General node is set to none. The result set name is the name of the returning data. This can be an alias you gave to a selected set of data. If you did not give the data an alias, you would enter the number 0 to indicate the first result set returned.

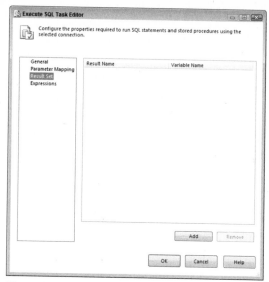

Figure 10-2

The Parameter Mapping node (also in the left pane of the Execute SQL Task Editor) is where you set up the parameters you want to pass into the SQL query. The SQL query can handle multiple parameters. In this screen, as shown in Figure 10-3, you can create the parameter mappings to connect the parameter in the SQL command to a package variable. You will see an example of parameters later this lesson.

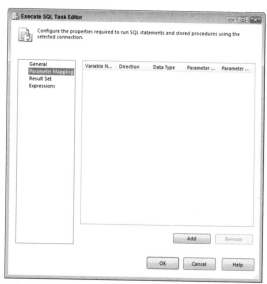

Figure 10-3

The Execute SQL Task can be used to count data in a table and return a number for the result set. If the count is returned as an alias, you can name the result set. For example, if the SQL query looks like this:

```
Select Count(*) as Counter From Products
```

The result set will be `Counter`, and you can assign it to an integer variable you create in the package using the Result Set node. If the SQL query is returning more than one row, you need to store that in an object variable. Once you have the data stored in a package variable, you can use this data throughout the rest of the package and in other tasks or expressions.

Returning to properties in the General node, you can see the next property you need to address is the ConnectionType. The Connection Type drop-down box contains six options:

- ❏ Excel
- ❏ OLE DB
- ❏ ODBC
- ❏ ADO
- ❏ ADO.NET
- ❏ SQL Mobile

These connections can be used to retrieve data from the connection types using the SQL language. This lesson covers the OLE DB connection and selecting data from a SQL Server table since this is very common.

Once you have selected the connection type you can click the Connection drop-down menu. If the connection you want to use already exists in the connection manager, you can select the connection from the drop-down menu. However, at the top you see the <New Connection ... > option. Clicking New Connection opens a corresponding connection creation window depending on the connection type you select. If you select the OLE DB connection type, you see the window shown in Figure 10-4, where you can create a new OLE DB connection.

Figure 10-4

The next property to set is the SQLSourceType. It has three options:

❑ **Direct Input** — SQL command typed into the Execute SQL Task

❑ **File Connection** — SQL command saved in an external file

❑ **Variable** — SQL command stored in a package variable

Direct Input is the easiest to use. This method allows you to type the SQL command directly into the Execute SQL Task. The advantage of this method is that the SQL is easy to enter. The disadvantage is that the SQL command cannot be altered outside of the package. So, maintenance is more difficult and requires the package to be altered and redeployed. This can be cumbersome and time consuming.

The File Connection option makes it easy to alter the SQL command from outside of the package. So, as business needs change and you need to select different data for your package, you can accomplish those changes very easily. The disadvantage here concerns maintaining and securing your files. Imagine if someone inadvertently deletes all of the SQL command files that your company's packages use daily. Any packages using these files would then fail at runtime.

The Variable option as the SQL source is similar to the direct input because the variable is stored in the package. However, because configuration files make it easy to alter variables outside of the package, you can alter the package without altering and redeploying it, giving you the best of both worlds in this situation.

Once you have selected the SQL source type, you are given an option to enter a SQL statement, select a file connection, or select a variable. The option shown changes based on the SQL source type selected.

If you have selected Direct Input, you see a SQL statement option, and clicking the property makes an ellipsis appear. Clicking this ellipsis opens a small editor window to enter the SQL command, as shown in Figure 10-5. The editor is not much more than a small notepad with fewer options. It's not an optimal place to enter SQL, and there is no color coding to help developers entering SQL code. You might find it a better option to go to SQL Server Management Studio and type the SQL command there so you receive the benefits of color coding and IntelliSense. This will make the SQL coding much easier. Then copy and paste the SQL command into the Direct Input window.

Figure 10-5

Parameters allow you to select different data with the same SQL command. The parameters are entered into the direct SQL command using question marks, as shown in the following code:

```
Select Count(*) as Counter from Products where ProductID = ?
```

This SQL command selects the number of products in a table that have the product ID in the parameter you pass into the tasks. You set this up with variables in the Parameter Mapping node. You can click the Parameter Mapping node and click the Add button to create a parameter mapping for the task. The names of the parameters start at 0 and count up. So, if you have three question marks in your SQL query, representing three parameters, your parameters mappings will be 0, 1, and 2.

Once again returning to properties in the General node, you can see the next property is IsQueryStoredProcedure. The property IsQueryStoredProcedure is available on the ADO and ADO.NET options only. This is set to true when the SQL command is calling a stored procedure from the ADO connection. This stored procedure name can be stored in direct input, a file connection, or a variable.

The BypassPrepare property indicates whether the task should prepare the query before the execution of the query. Preparing a query is similar to compiling. A prepared SQL statement does not need to be analyzed every time it is used. This property must be set to false before the Parse Query button will actually parse the SQL query.

The three buttons at the bottom of the Execute SQL Task on the General node are:

- ❑ **Browse** — Searches for .SQL files in the file system
- ❑ **Build Query** — Query builder, similar to the query builder in SQL Management Studio
- ❑ **Parse Query** — Parses the SQL query checking for syntax errors

These can be used to help build the SQL query for the task. The browse features allow users to find SQL queries stored in files in the structured file system. The query builder helps build an error-free SQL query with a visual representation of the tables and their joins. And as already mentioned, the Parse Query button will not parse the query unless the BypassQuery option is set to false.

Try It

In this lesson you build an Execute SQL Task to return data from a table in the AdventureWorks2008 database. After this lesson, you will have a grasp of how to use the Execute SQL Task to query data from a data source and store the results in a variable.

Lesson Requirements

First, you want to count the number of products with a certain product ID. Then, you are going to have a Script Task pop up the value of the variable.

You can download the completed Lesson10.dtsx from www.wrox.com.

Hints

- ❑ A Script Task and an Execute SQL Task is needed
- ❑ Create a variable to hold the return value
- ❑ Create a variable to hold the product ID
- ❑ Create a Script Task with a popup message showing the variable value

Step-by-Step

1. Drag in an Execute SQL Task and double-click on the task to open the editor.

2. Click the connection and select New Connection.

3. Create a connection to the AdventureWorks2008 database.

4. Select single row as the result set.

5. Select Direct Input as the SQL type.

6. Click the SQL command and enter the following query:

```
Select Count(*) as Counter from Products Where Product ID = ?
```

7. In the Parameter Mapping node, click Add and create a parameter with the name of 0.

8. While in the Parameter Mappings node click the Variable Name drop-down and select new variable.

9. Create an integer variable named "intProductID" and set the value to 316.

10. Click the Result Set node and click Add to create a result set with the name of 0.

11. In the Result Set node click the Variable Name drop-down and select New Variable.

12. Create an Int32 variable named "intProductCount."

13. Drag in a Script Task

14. Connect the Execute SQL Task to the Script Task with an On Success Precedence Constraint.

15. Select intProductCount in the ReadOnlyVariables of the Script Task.

16. Click the Edit Script button.

17. Type the following VB code in the script editor (refer to Lesson 9 for a Script Task explanation):

```
Msgbox(DTS.Variables("intProductCount").Value)
```

18. Close the script editor.

19. Click OK in the Script Task.

20. The package should look like Figure 10-6. Click Debug on the toolbar to run the package.

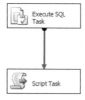

Figure 10-6

21. A popup should appear showing the intProductCount variable, which should have a value of one, as in Figure 10-7.

Figure 10-7

 Please select Lesson 10 on the DVD to view the video example that accompanies this lesson.

Using the Send Mail Task

The Send Mail Task sends email via Simple Mail Transfer Protocol (SMTP) from a SQL Server Integration Services (SSIS) package. This task allows you to receive information about the package that can be passed into the mail task through variables — system variables or user-defined variables. The Send Mail Task is most commonly used as a notification tool. The system variables in an SSIS package hold information such as package start time, errors, and warnings.

The Send Mail Task can be placed at the end of a Control Flow to send email on the successful completion of a package. The Event Handler of a package can also be a great place to place the Send Mail Task (event handlers are covered in Lesson 38). The task can be placed in the OnPreExecute Event Handler to notify you via email that a package has begun. The OnPostExecute Event Handler can send mail at the end of a package showing the start and end for a package, therefore allowing you to track the runtime of a package. When a Send Mail Task is placed in the OnError or the OnWarning Event you can be notified when an error or warning occurs anytime during the running of a package.

The Send Mail Task can also be used to send files, because it has the ability to send attachments. A Data Flow can exist in a package that creates a file, and a Send Mail Task can then send that file via email. The file can be created in a Data Flow or by a File System Task. It can also be any file not created or altered by the package.

When you first open the Send Mail Task Editor by double-clicking a Send Mail Task, you see the General node, as shown in Figure 11-1. This contains the name and description of the task. These properties are used for ease of reference when viewing the task in the Control Flow; the name shows on the tasks in the Control Flow and the description is usually a longer line of text describing the purpose of the Send Mail Task. It is a best practice to always change the values of these fields to values that make it easy to for anyone to see and understand the function of the task.

Figure 11-1

Clicking the Mail node in the left-hand pane opens the Mail properties. Here you see the main properties of the Send Mail Task, as shown in Figure 11-2. The first property is the SMTP connection. This connection must exist in the connection manager.

Figure 11-2

If the SMTP connection does not exist, you can create it by clicking <New Connection...> in the SmtpConnection drop-down menu, which opens the SMTP Connection Manager Editor, as shown in Figure 11-3. This allows you to create an SMTP connection in the connection manager. Once an SMTP connection exists in the connection manager, you can use this connection in all Send Mail Tasks.

Figure 11-3

Just as in the Send Mail Task, the SMTP connection, which is created in the connection manager, has a name and description. The name will show in the connection manager area below the Control Flow. The description is usually a longer line of text describing the purpose of SMTP connection. The SMTP server is the name of your server that will handle email sent via SMTP. Below the server name you see two check boxes, Use Windows Authentication and Enable Secure Sockets Layer (SSL). When Use Windows Authentication is checked, the package will pass the user credentials of the person running the package through to the SMTP server for verification to send the mail. Enable Secure Sockets Layer (SSL) will send the email via Secure Sockets Layer. The security type you select will vary based on your environment.

Returning to the Send Mail Task Editor, you see that the next properties of the Send Mail Task are the basic fields of an email:

- **From** — The receiver of the email
- **To** — The email address that will show as the sender
- **Cc** — Send a carbon copy email
- **Bcc** — Send a blind carbon copy
- **Subject** — Shows in the subject of the email

The From, To, and Subject properties should be very familiar to anyone who has sent an email. The carbon copy sends a copy of the email to another email address along with the To email address. The recipients can see both of the email addresses receiving the email. Blind carbon copy sends the email to another recipient along with the user in the To field, but the To recipient cannot see the Bcc email address.

The next property to set is the MessageSourceType. It has three options:

- **Direct Input** — Message is typed into the Send Mail Task
- **File Connection** — Message is saved in an external file
- **Variable** — Message is stored in a package variable

Direct Input is the easiest to use. This method allows you to type the message command directly into the Execute SQL Task. The advantage of this method is that the message is easy to enter. The disadvantage is that the message cannot be altered outside of the package. So, maintenance is more difficult and requires the package to be altered and redeployed, which can be cumbersome and time consuming.

The File Connection option makes it easy to alter the message from outside of the package. So, as business needs change and you need to select different data for your package, this process can be accomplished very easily. The disadvantage here concerns maintaining and securing your files. Imagine if someone inadvertently deletes all of the message files that your company's packages use daily. Any packages using these files would then fail at runtime.

The Variable option as the message source is similar to Direct Input because the variable is stored in the package. But configuration files make it easy to alter variables outside of the package. Thus, you can alter the package without altering and redeploying it, giving you the best of both worlds in this situation.

Once you have selected the MessageSourceType, you have an option to enter a message statement, select a file connection, or select a variable. The option shown changes based on the MessageSourceType selected.

If you selected Direct Input you see a message source option, and clicking the property makes an ellipsis appear. Clicking this ellipsis opens a small editor window in which to enter the message, as shown in Figure 11-4. The editor is not much more than a small notepad with fewer options. This is not an optimal place to enter a message. When you select Variable or File Connection for the MessageSourceType the message source changes to a drop-down menu that allows you to select the file or variable. Files and variables are easier to edit than direct input and are, therefore, a better practice.

Figure 11-4

The Priority property allows you to set the priority mail flag on an email. These are the small symbols you see in Outlook. High priority shows a red exclamation point, normal priority shows no icon, and low priority shows a blue arrow pointing down. However, remember that although this is true in Outlook, other email programs may not show icons.

The last option is Attachments. Here you can select a file that you would like to send to the recipients. This will attach the file to the email just the same as if you attached it to a standard email. This can be a file that was created in the package by a File System Task, or a completely separate file not used anywhere else in the package.

Try It

In this lesson you create a Send Mail Task to send an email. This email will be in a Control Flow. When the package is successful, the email will be sent and tell you the package has finished running, giving you an understanding of how the task can be used as a notification tool.

Lesson Requirements

You need to create a Send Mail Task. The SMTP information needs to be your own SMTP connection information so that the email can be sent via your SMTP connection.

You can download the completed Lesson11.dtsx from www.wrox.com.

Hints

- ❑ You need one Send Mail Task
- ❑ You need to set up an SMTP connection

Step-by-Step

1. Drag in a Send Mail Task to a blank package.
2. Right-click in the connection manager and select New Connection.
3. Select the SMTP connection from the list and click Add, as in Figure 11-5.

Figure 11-5

4. Change the SMTP connection name to your company name and SMTP, for example, *"My Company* SMTP."

5. Set the SMTP connection description to *"My Company's* SMTP Server."

6. Set the SMTP connection server to the actual SMTP Server connection.

7. Place a check in Windows Authentication if your company uses Windows Authentication to send SMTP email.

8. Place a check in Enable Secure Sockets Layer (SSL) if your SMTP server requires a secure connection.

9. Once you have completed the previous steps, the SMTP connection should look like Figure 11-6.

Figure 11-6

10. Click OK in both open windows to return to the Control Flow.

11. Double-click the Send Mail Task to open the editor.

12. Name the Send Mail Task "Send Package Info."

13. Set the Send Mail Task description to "Send email to users containing the package information."

14. Click the Mail node on the left-hand side of the Send Mail Task Editor window.

15. Set the SMTPConnection to the SMTP connection created in Steps 2–9.

16. Set the From address to your email address.

17. Set the To address to your email address. (If you have two email addresses, you can set the From and To to the two different email addresses. This is true as long as the SMTP server allows you to send and receive email from these email addresses.)

18. Set the Subject line to "Email From Package."

19. Set the MessageSourceType to Direct Input.

20. Set the MessageSource to "The send mail package finished." The Send Mail Task should look similar to Figure 11-7.

Figure 11-7

21. Click OK.

22. Run the package by clicking the green debug arrow on the toolbar; you should receive an email from yourself.

If you do not receive an email, but the package completes, check your SMTP server logs to see why the email was stopped.

 Please select Lesson 11 on the DVD to view the video that accompanies this lesson.

Using the FTP Task

The FTP Task works very similarly to any FTP utility. It allows you to send and receive files from an FTP location along with other FTP commands. The FTP Task comes in handy when you need to move files from an FTP server to your environment for processing or when you need to send a file to an FTP server. A common example is sending an extract file created in a Data Flow or receiving a flat file to be processed by a Data Flow and inserted into a table in your server.

Double-click on the FTP Task to open the task editor. The first screen of the FTP Task Editor shows the General node with some basic properties of the task. Under the General node you see the name and description of the FTP Task. These do not affect the FTP Task; they are used for ease of reference when viewing the tasks in the Control Flow. The name shows on the tasks in the Control Flow, and the description is usually a longer line of text describing the purpose of the FTP Task. It is a best practice to always change the values of these fields to values that make it easy to for anyone to see and understand the function of the task.

The General node also has two other properties: FTP Connection and Stop on Failure. The FTP Connection is the connection to the FTP server that must exist in the connection manager. You can create this FTP connection either by clicking the drop-down menu next to the FTP Connection field and selecting <New Connection…> or by right-clicking in the connection manager and selecting New Connection. Then select FTP in the menu of connection types. Either way opens the FTP Connection Manager Editor, as shown in Figure 12-1.

The first property of the FTP Connection Manager is the FTP Server location. The examples in this chapter use FTP.Microsoft.com. It is an FTP Server that allows anonymous connections, so you should be able to connect to it with no issues. So in the Server Name box you would type in FTP. Microsoft.Com. The port is usually 21, but if your company uses a different port for FTP, which can be due to security concerns, you would type the appropriate port in the Server Port property.

Under the Credentials section are two properties, the User Name and Password. These are the credentials used to log in to the FTP server. The Microsoft FTP Server allows Anonymous connections, so a password is not required. If you are connecting to another server, you would type in the proper user name and passwords in this section.

Figure 12-1

In the Options section are three other options. The first is Time-out. The Time-out is the number of seconds the FTP connection tries to connect before failing. The default is 60 seconds. Keep in mind that when an FTP Task is trying to connect, the package is stopped at that point in the Control Flow. So if the Time-out is set to a large number and has trouble connecting, the package may run for an extended period of time without actually performing any task. This is especially true if the package is contingent on the success of the FTP Task. So keeping this at a shorter time allows the package to fail faster due to the FTP connection issues. However, if you have an FTP server that takes a long time to validate the connection, the time may need to be higher.

The next option is Use Passive Mode. If checked, this option connects the FTP server using the passive mode instead of active mode. The Retries option is the number of times the FTP Task tries to connect to the FTP Server before failing out. The last property of the FTP Connection Manager Editor is the Chunk Size. This is the size of the data that is sent out in succession until the entire file is sent or received. Some networks have restrictions that may require this to be adjusted, so check with your network admin for your restrictions. Generally the 1KB default is acceptable.

Once you have the connection information set up to connect to the FTP location, you can click Test Connection at the bottom of the FTP Connection Manager Editor window, and a test message is sent to the FTP server to ensure the connection exists and that the user name and password meet the FTP server credentials. If it is a successful connection, you receive the message "Test connection succeeded," as shown in Figure 12-2.

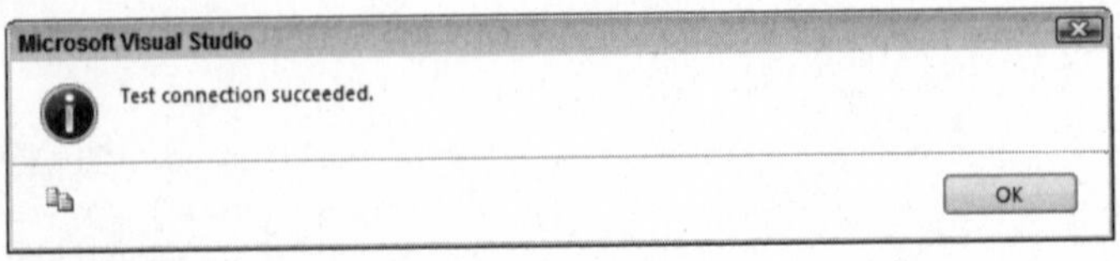

Figure 12-2

If the FTP server does not exist or the user credentials fail to pass the login process, you receive the message "Connection cannot be established. Server name, port number, or credentials may be invalid," as shown in Figure 12-3.

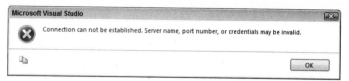

Figure 12-3

After you have created the FTP server connection in the connection manager you can then rename the connection by clicking it in the connection manager one time, and the name will highlight blue. Then you can type a more meaningful name for the FTP connection. This capability is particularly helpful when you have multiple FTP connections in the connection manager.

Once you have the FTP connection set up in the connection manager, you can select it in the FTP Connection drop-down menu in the FTP Task. The next property is Stop on Failure. This property stops the FTP from performing a transfer if there is a failure during the transfer process. Keep in mind the task will still send a failure message to the package or parent container if it has a failure regardless of this property's setting. The Stop on Failure property is available simply to allow the transfer to continue if part of the transfer fails.

When you click the File Transfer node in the FTP Task Editor, you see the operations that are available for the FTP Task to perform and the parameters for this operation. Of course, the parameters change based on the operation you select. The Operation drop-down menu has several options, as shown in Figure 12-4:

- ❑ **Send Files** — Send files to the FTP server from a local source
- ❑ **Receive Files** — Retrieve files from the FTP server to a local destination
- ❑ **Create Local Directory** — Create a folder on a local drive
- ❑ **Create Remote Directory** — Create a folder on the remote directory
- ❑ **Remove Local Directory** — Delete a local folder and all of the contents
- ❑ **Remove Remote Directory** — Delete a remote folder and all of its contents
- ❑ **Delete Local Files** — Delete files on the local directory
- ❑ **Delete Remote Files** — Delete files on the remote FTP server

If you select Receive Files you see the most common options used in an FTP Task. IsLocalPathVariable is a Boolean that tells the FTP Task whether the location on the local destination is saved in a variable. When this is set to true, the drop-down menu of the Local Path changes to a drop-down menu of variables. When the IsLocalPathVariable option is set to false, the LocalPath drop-down shows the available folder location in the connection manager.

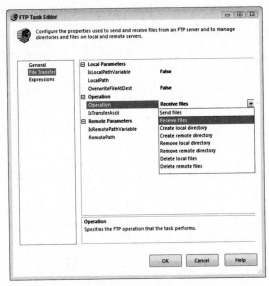

Figure 12-4

If the IsRemotePathVariable is true, the RemotePath shows a drop-down or variables to choose from. If the IsRemotePathVariable is false, the RemotePath shows an ellipsis that will connect to the FTP server and show a browse window allowing you to select the file to be retrieved with the FTP Task.

The last property to set is OverwriteFileAtDest. If set to true, this property allows the FTP Task to overwrite an existing file if the FTP Task attempts to move the file into a directory that already contains the file being moved. If it is set to false, the FTP Task fails if the file already exists.

Try It

In this lesson you retrieve a file from the FTP server from Microsoft. After this lesson, you will understand how you can use the FTP Task download a file to a local destination.

Lesson Requirements

You need to create an FTP Task with the proper credentials and server settings to connect to FTP. Microsoft.Com. You then look in a folder on the FTP server and retrieve a single file.

You can download the completed Lesson12.dtsx from www.wrox.com.

Hints

❑   You need a single FTP Task

❑   Microsoft's FTP server allows you to connect anonymously

Step-by-Step

1.   Drag an FTP Task into a blank package and double-click the task to open the FTP Task Editor.

2.   Click the FTP Connection drop-down menu and select the only option, <New Connection...>. This opens the FTP Connection Manager Editor.

3.   In the FTP Connection Manager Editor set the Server Name to FTP.Microsoft.Com and leave the other options at the defaults. The window should match Figure 12-5.

Figure 12-5

4.   Click Test Connection to ensure you have a connection to the FTP server. If your connection fails, check with your network admin to determine your FTP abilities in your environment.

5.   Click OK in the FTP Connection Manager Editor; the FTP Task Editor should still be open.

6.   Change the name of the FTP Task to "Get MS File."

7.   Change the description to "Retrieve File from Microsoft."

8.   Click the File Transfer node in the left pane of the FTP Task Editor.

9.   Select Receive Files in the Operation drop-down menu.

10. From the drop-down menu for Local Path select <New Connection...>. This selection opens the File Connection Manager Editor.

11. Set the usage type to Existing Folder.

12. Click Browse and select the C:\Projects\SSISPersonalTrainer.

13. Click the ellipsis next to Remote Path and browse to the SoftLib directory in the Microsoft FTP Server.

14. Select the file name index.txt. Click OK.

15. Click OK in the FTP Task.

16. Click the green debug arrow on the toolbar. The FTP Task should turn green to indicate success.

17. Ensure you have the index.txt file in the SSISPersonalTrainer folder on your local drive.

 Please select Lesson 12 on the DVD to view the video that accompanies this lesson.

Creating a Data Flow

This lesson covers the basics of the Data Flow Task. Section III comprises chapters covering the sources, destinations, and transformations in detail. However, this lesson gives you the tools to get started creating a Data Flow and understanding the purpose of it.

The Data Flow Task is used to transfer data from a source to a destination and can transform the data as needed. The source can be any of several different types such as a flat file or database and can contain millions of rows of data. The Data Flow Task is capable of handling large amounts of data. The destination can be of several types also.

The Data Flow Task can be used to extract data from a database and write to a flat file location or move the data from a flat file to a database. This capability allows you to receive files from outside sources and write this data to your database. You can also use the Data Flow Task to move data from one database to another database.

The transforms that exist in the Data Flow allow you to make changes to the data as you move it from a source to a destination. For example, if you are receiving flat files from a vendor and the data is not formatted correctly, say, the Social Security numbers need to have dashes, you can fix that before writing it to a database. Fixing things like that prior to writing to your database prevents you from running updates on your database later.

And these transforms are faster in SSIS. SSIS performs the transforms in memory, which is why it is much faster than reading and writing the data to a drive. This speed is especially evident in the case of running updates to a table. SQL update commands read data from a database and write data back to the same database. This reading and writing to the same location makes the process very slow compared to SSIS.

The Data Flows allow you to save data to multiple locations simultaneously, which also improves performance when you are saving data. You can receive a flat file from a vendor, open it with an SSIS package, parse through the data, make decisions on where data needs to be written, and write the data to multiple locations all in one Data Flow.

You have two ways to create a Data Flow in a package. You can drag out the Data Flow Task from the Toolbox, or you can click the Data Flow tab at the top and click the blue link in the middle of the screen. This link states, as shown in Figure 13-1, "No Data Flow tasks have been added to this package. Click here to add a new Data Flow task."

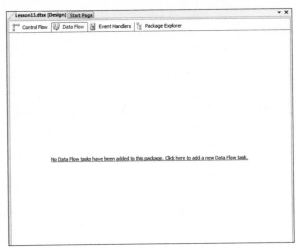

Figure 13-1

If there is already a Data Flow in the package, clicking the Data Flow tab shows that Data Flow. If multiple Data Flows are in a package, you see a drop-down menu at the top of the Data Flow screen showing the list of all the Data Flows in the package. It is a best practice to give the Data Flows a name that is descriptive. With descriptive names you can then easily select the correct Data Flow you are trying to alter. Descriptive naming is a major help when your package contains a large number of Data Flows.

After you enter the Data Flow tab by either method previously mentioned, the Toolbox will contain a new set of tools. The top section contains the sources, the middle the transforms, and the bottom the destinations. These are the tasks that can be used only in the Data Flow Task and cannot be used in the Control Flow screen.

Several sources have the same type as a destination. For example, there is an Excel Source and an Excel Destination. These tasks are not interchangeable. A source can only read data and a destination can only write data. Keep in mind that because of the connection manager (the connection manager is explained in Lesson 6) you can use the same connection repeatedly. So a source in a Data Flow can connect to an Excel file, and an Excel Destination can connect to the same Excel file. The connection exists just once in the connection manager but can be used multiple times in a package.

Once you drag a source into a Data Flow, two lines will appear from the bottom of the task. The green line is the good data. The red line is the bad data. Sources and destinations, including how to use these green and red lines, are explained in detail in the lessons following this one. Double-clicking the source opens the source editor for that source type. In the editor you can select the location of the source.

After your source is established you can connect it to a transform from the transformation section of the Toolbox. This transform can manipulate the data to be in the form you want for your destination. The transform can also make complex decisions to send data to different destinations.

Once the sources and transforms are created you can drag out a destination and connect the last step of the transforms to the destination. If the Data Flow does not contain any transforms, the source can be connected directly to the destination, which simply moves data from one location to another without changing the data. This arrangement is the simplest form of a Data Flow.

Try It

In this example you create a package with a Data Flow Task. The Data Flow is going to move data from a SQL database table to a flat file. After this lesson, you will have an understanding of how to create a Data Flow Task in the Control Flow of a package.

Lesson Requirements

You need to create a Data Flow in a package and create a source and a destination. The source is going to be an OLE DB connection to the AdventureWorks2008 database to the Products table. The destination is going to be a flat file you create.

You can download the completed Lesson13.dtsx from www.wrox.com.

Hints

❑   You need only one Data Flow Task for this example

❑   The Data Flow needs a source and a destination

❑   The package needs two connections in the connection manager

Step-by-Step

1.   Drag a Data Flow Task into a blank package.

2.   Double-click the Data Flow Task to enter the Data Flow tab.

3.   Drag in an OLE DB Source.

4.   Double-click the OLE DB Source to open the source editor.

5.   Click the New button. The Configure OLE DB Connection Manager dialog box opens (see Figure 13-2). Select the source connection to AdventureWorks2008, and click OK. Note: If the connection exists in this window, you can skip Steps 6–8.

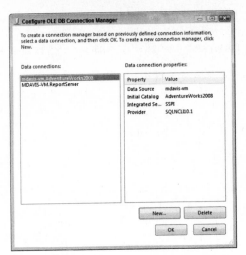

Figure 13-2

6.   If the AdventureWorks2008 connection does not show in the Configure OLE DB Connection Manager dialog box, click the New button, which takes you to the Connection Manager dialog box (see Figure 13-3).

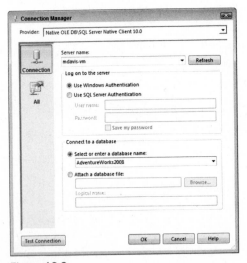

Figure 13-3

7.   Set the Server Name to the location of the server with the AdventureWorks2008 database. Usually this name is LocalHost.

8.   Select AdventureWorks2008 in the "Select or enter a database name" drop-down and click OK twice.

9.   In the OLE DB Source Editor click the drop-down menu of tables and select the Production. Product table.

10. Click the Columns node in the left-hand pane. You should see columns in the Products table.

11. Click OK.

12. Right-click the OLE DB Source and select Rename.

13. Change the Name to "AW Products."

14. Drag a Flat File Destination into the Data Flow.

15. Connect the green line from the bottom of the AW Products Source to the Flat File Destination.

16. Double-click the Flat File Destination to open the Flat File Destination Editor.

17. Click the New button.

18. Select Delimited in the Flat File format window and click OK.

19. In the Flat File Connection Manager Editor change the name to "AW Products Extract."

20. Change the Description to "All AW product data."

21. Type "c:\AWProducts.txt" in the File Name text box.

22. Click OK.

23. Click the Mappings node in the left-hand pane; the mappings should look like Figure 13-4.

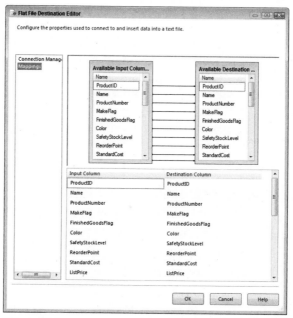

Figure 13-4

24. Click OK.

25. Right-click the Flat File Destination and click Rename. Change the name to "AW Products Extract File." The Data Flow should match Figure 13-5.

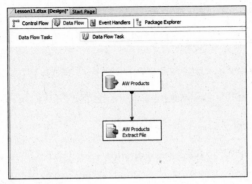

Figure 13-5

26. Click the green debug arrow on the toolbar. A new file will be created in your C: drive containing all the data from the product table. (If you do not see a file, you may not have rights to create a file and may need to start BIDS in administrative mode.)

27. Click the Stop Debug button on the toolbar and go look at the content of the file on your C: drive.

28. You can delete the text file when you are done viewing it.

 Please select Lesson 13 on the DVD to view the video that accompanies this lesson.

Section III
Data Flow

Extracting Data from Sources

Generally when you create SQL Server Integration Services (SSIS) packages, it is for the purpose of moving data from one point to another. A *source* is where you specify the location of the data you want to move or transform.

Most sources point to the connection manager in SSIS. By pointing to the connection manager, you can reuse connections throughout your package because you need only change the connection in one place. In this lesson the most frequently used sources (OLE DB, Excel, and flat file) are described thoroughly.

OLE DB Source

The most common type of source used is the OLE DB Source, which can point to any Object Linking and Embedding Database (OLE DB)–compatible data source such as SQL Server, Oracle, and DB2. To configure the OLE DB Source, double-click the source once you've added it to the design pane in the Data Flow tab. In the Connection Manager page of the OLE DB Source Editor, shown in Figure 14-1, select the connection manager of your OLE DB Source from the OLE DB Connection Manager drop-down box. You can also add a new connection manager in the editor by clicking the New button.

The Data Access Mode option sets how you can retrieve the source data. The OLE DB Source has four different data access modes available:

- ❑ A table or view
- ❑ A table or view indicated in a variable
- ❑ The results of a SQL statement
- ❑ The results of a SQL statement initiated in a variable

SSIS does allow for a stored procedure to be accessed when using the SQL command mode. Additionally, you can pass a variable into the query by substituting a question mark (?) for where the parameter should be and then clicking the Parameters button.

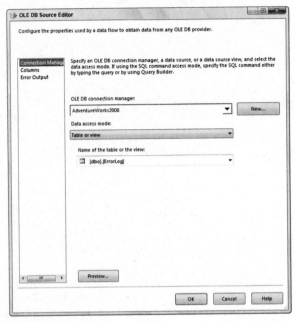

Figure 14-1

After these configurations have been completed you can go to the Columns page to check each column you need from the table. Figure 14-2 shows that once the needed columns are checked, you can assign a new name by typing the new name in the Output Column.

Here's a best practice: when you are selecting columns, check only what you will need to use. With a smaller data set you gain better performance. For the same reason it is always better to type a query with only the needed columns instead of selecting a table. Using the select table option essentially does a Select * *on the table bringing all that data across the network when you might need only 5 out of 25 columns.*

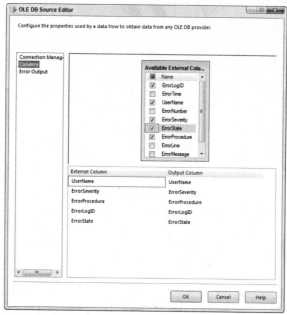

Figure 14-2

Sometimes incompatible data types can cause conversion issues, and you may want to send these errors to a different path in the Data Flow. This configuration can be accomplished within the Error Output page shown in Figure 14-3, where you specify how to handle these issues when they occur. On each column, you can specify that if an error occurs, you want the row to be ignored, be redirected, or fail. If you choose to ignore failures, the column for that row is set to NULL. If you redirect the row, the row is sent down the red path in the Data Flow coming out of the OLE DB Source.

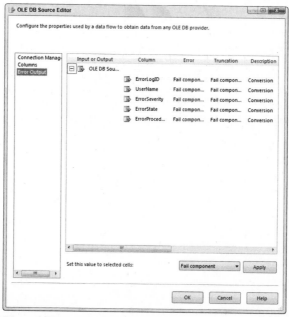

Figure 14-3

Try It

In this lesson, you set up an OLE DB Source to bring in transaction history data from the Adventure-Works2008 database. You can download the AdventureWorks2008 database at CodePlex.com (http://www.codeplex.com/MSFTDBProdSamples/). (Please see Lesson 3 if you haven't yet installed the AdventureWorks2008 database.) After this lesson, you will know how to use an OLE DB Source to extract data from a SQL Server table.

> *You can also find the sample databases at the Wrox website at*
> http://www.wrox.com/go/SQLServer2008RTMDataSets.

Lesson Requirements

Create a new package named Lesson14 and make the following change. You can find Lesson14.dtsx on the book's website at www.wrox.com:

❑ Use the following query to return needed rows from AdventureWorks2008:

```
SELECT TransactionID
      ,ProductID
      ,TransactionDate
      ,Quantity
      ,ActualCost
      ,ModifiedDate
  FROM Production.TransactionHistory
 WHERE Quantity > 2
```

Hints

❑ You need only one OLE DB Source and one OLE DB Connection Manager.

Step-by-Step

1. Create an SSIS package and name it Lesson14 or download Lesson14.dtsx from www.wrox.com. Add a Data Flow Task to the Control Flow design surface and name it "OLE DB Extract."

2. Drag an OLE DB Source in the Data Flow design surface and double-click to open the OLE DB Source Editor.

3. Click the New button for the OLE DB Connection Manager to create a new connection to a SQL Server Source, which is shown in Figure 14-4.

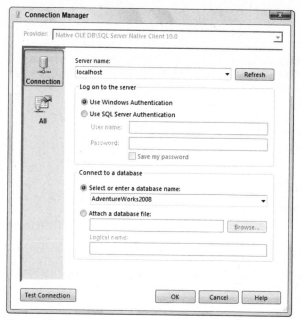

Figure 14-4

4. Back in the OLE DB Source Editor after the connection manager is created, select SQL Command as the data access mode and type the following query:

```
SELECT TransactionID
      ,ProductID
      ,TransactionDate
      ,Quantity
      ,ActualCost
      ,ModifiedDate
  FROM Production.TransactionHistory
WHERE Quantity > 2
```

Once your screen looks like Figure 14-5, click OK to continue.

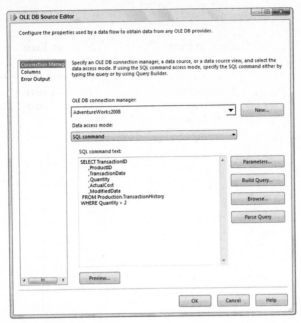

Figure 14-5

5. Drag a Union All onto the Data Flow designer. The Union All serves as a placeholder until you learn about destinations in the next lesson. Connect the Flat File Source to the Union All and execute just this Data Flow by right-clicking in the designer and selecting Execute Task. Figure 14-6 shows the results.

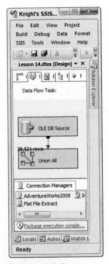

Figure 14-6

Excel Source

The Excel Source is used to extract data from an Excel spreadsheet. To use an Excel Source you must first create an Excel Connection Manager that points to the location of the spreadsheet. Figure 14-7 shows that once you point to an Excel Connection Manager, you can select the sheet from the Name of the Excel Sheet drop-down box. The Excel Source works much the same the OLE DB Source, which means you can even run a query by changing the data access mode to SQL Command. This source treats Excel just like a database, where an Excel sheet is the table and the workbook is the database.

Figure 14-7

SSIS supports Excel data types, but unfortunately it does not translate well to how most databases are constructed. If you right-click a column and select Format Cells in Excel, you can find that most of the columns in your Excel spreadsheet have probably been set to General. SSIS interprets the General format as a Unicode data type. In SQL Server, the Unicode translates into nvarchar, which is not typically what you find in databases. If you have a Unicode data type in SSIS and you try to insert into a varchar column, it can potentially fail. Lesson 16 shows you this exact problem and how to correct it.

If you are connecting to an Excel 2007 spreadsheet or later, ensure that you select the proper Excel version when creating the Excel Connection Manager. You will not be able to connect to an Excel 2007 spreadsheet otherwise.

Additionally, the Excel driver is a 32-bit driver only, and your packages will have to run in 32-bit mode when using Excel connectivity. To enable 32-bit mode, right-click and select Properties on the project file in the Solution Explorer window. Change to the Debugging tab and change Run64BitRuntime to False, shown in Figure 14-8.

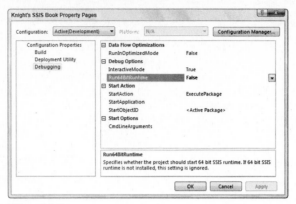

Figure 14-8

Try It

In this lesson, you set up an Excel Source to bring in inventory data. You will use an Excel spreadsheet as your source, which you can download from www.wrox.com. After this lesson, you will know how to use an Excel Source to extract data from an Excel spreadsheet.

Lesson Requirements

Make the following changes to your Lesson14 package. You can find Lesson14.dtsx at www.wrox.com:

❑ Download the file Inventory_Worksheet.xls as your source from www.wrox.com and save it to C:\Projects\SSISPersonalTrainer\

Hints

❑ You need only one Excel Source and one Excel Connection Manager

Step-by-Step

1. Open the SSIS package named Lesson14 or download Lesson14.dtsx from www.wrox.com. Add a Data Flow Task to the Control Flow design surface and name it "Excel Extract."

2. Drag an Excel Source in the Data Flow designer surface and double-click to open the Excel Source Editor.

3. Click the New button for the connection manager. This opens the Excel Connection Manager dialog.

4. For the Excel file path, click Browse to select the location C:\Projects\SSISPersonalTrainer\ that you downloaded the spreadsheet file to. Once you have selected the correct spreadsheet make sure the Microsoft Excel version is Excel 97-2004 and that the "First row has column names" option is checked. Figure 14-9 shows what your screen should look like.

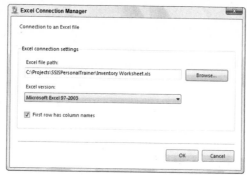

Figure 14-9

5. Back in the Excel Source Editor after the connection manager is created, select Inventory_ Worksheet in the Name of the Excel Sheet drop-down and click OK, as shown in Figure 14-10.

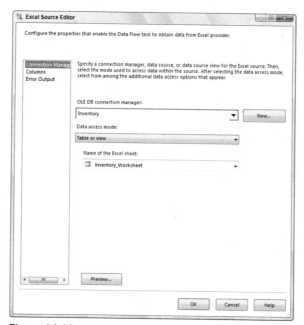

Figure 14-10

6. Drag a Union All onto the Data Flow designer. The Union All serves as a placeholder until you read about destinations in the next lesson. Connect the Excel Source to the Union All and execute just this Data Flow by right-clicking in the designer and selecting Execute Task. Figure 14-11 shows the results.

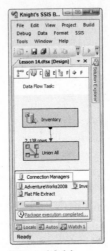

Figure 14-11

Flat File Source

The Flat File Source provides a data source for text files. Those files are typically comma- or tab-delimited files, or they could be fixed-width or ragged-right. A fixed-width file is typically received from the mainframe, and it has fixed start and stop points for each column. This method makes for a fast load but takes longer at design time for the developer to map each column.

You specify a Flat File Source the same way you specify an OLE DB Source. Once you add it to your Data Flow pane, you point it to a connection manager connection that is a flat file. After that, you go to the Columns tab of the Flat File Source Editor to specify what columns you want to be presented to the Data Flow. Figure 14-12 shows columns being selected from a Flat File Source. All the specifications for the flat file, such as delimiter type, were previously set in the Flat File Connection Manager.

Figure 14-12

Similar to the Excel Source, the data types of a Flat File Source are set up by default, and SSIS may not assign them correctly. All columns are brought in as a string data type regardless of their true content. To correct this, go to the Advanced tab in the Flat File Connection Manager and select the column and then the correct data type.

Try It

In this lesson, you set up a Flat File Source to bring in employee benefits data from a flat file. The comma-delimited file to use for this example is called EmployeeList.txt and you can find it at www.wrox .com. After this lesson, you will know how to use a Flat File Source to extract data from a text file.

Lesson Requirements

Make the following changes to your Lesson14 package. You can find Lesson14.dtsx at www.wrox.com:

❏ Download the file EmployeeList.txt as your source from www.wrox.com and save it to C:\Projects\SSISPersonalTrainer

❏ Set the Flat File Connection Manager as comma-delimited

❏ Note the first row in the file comprises column names

❏ Data types should be as follows:

    ❏ **EmpID** — int

    ❏ **Name** — string

    ❏ **SickDays** — int

    ❏ **VacationDays** — int

Hints

❏ You need only one Flat File Source and one Flat File Connection Manager

Step-by-Step

1. Open the SSIS package named Lesson14 or download Lesson14.dtsx from www.wrox.com. Add a Data Flow Task to the Control Flow design surface and name it "Flat File Extract."

2. Drag a Flat File Source in the Data Flow designer surface and double-click to open the Flat File Source Editor.

3. Click the New button for the connection manager. This opens the Flat File Connection Manager Editor.

4. In the General tab, name the connection manager "Flat File Extract" and select the file name EmployeeList.txt for the source file. You can download this file from www.wrox.com. Last, check the "Column names in the first data row" check box. Once these changes have been made, your screen should look like Figure 14-13.

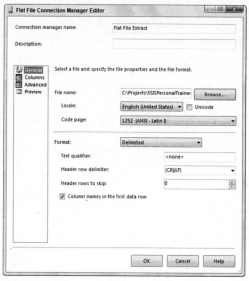

Figure 14-13

5. Select the Columns tab and ensure the Column Delimiter drop-box has Comma {,} selected, as shown in Figure 14-14.

Figure 14-14

6. By default all columns are assigned a string data type, but this can be corrected in the Advanced tab of the Flat File Connection Manager Editor. In the Advanced tab you can manually change the data type or have SSIS suggest the data type (the Suggest Types button). SSIS suggestions are fairly accurate, but don't always give the desired results. For example, on the columns EmpID, SickDays, and VacationDays change the DataType to four-byte signed integer (int). Had you done a Suggest Types for these columns, SSIS would have assigned these columns single-byte signed integer (tinyint), which is not what you want this time. Once these changes have been made, your screen should look like Figure 14-15. Click OK to complete creating the Flat File Connection Manager.

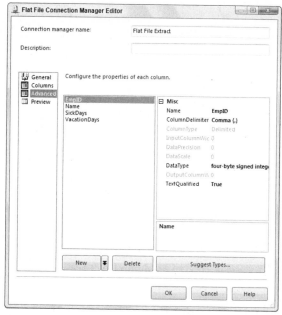

Figure 14-15

7. Click OK in the Flat File Source Editor and drag a Union All onto the Data Flow designer. The Union All serves as a placeholder until you read about destinations in the next lesson. Connect the Flat File Source to the Union All and execute just this Data Flow by right-clicking in the designer and selecting Execute Task. Figure 14-16 shows the results.

Figure 14-16

Here's another best practice: using Fast Parse can drastically improve performance of your package when you are using a Flat File Source. By default, SSIS validates any numeric or date columns but with Fast Parse set to True this step will be bypassed. To enable Fast Parse, follow these steps (shown in Figure 14-17):

❑ *Right-click the Flat File Source or Data Conversion Transformation, and click Show Advanced Editor*

❑ *In the Advanced Editor dialog box, click the Input and Output Properties tab*

❑ *In the Inputs and Outputs pane, click the column for which you want to enable Fast Parse*

❑ *In the Properties window, expand the Custom Properties node, and set the FastParse property to True*

❑ *Click OK*

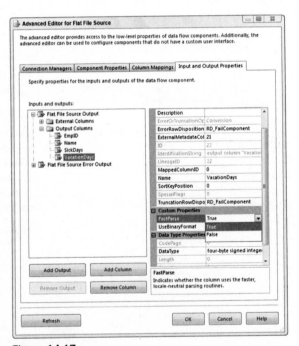

Figure 14-17

 Please select Lesson 14 on the DVD to view the video that accompanies this lesson.

Loading Data to a Destination

After you have set up a source to bring the needed data to the Data Flow you need somewhere to put it. A *destination* accepts data from data sources or transformations and sends them to the location specified in the destination's connection manager.

The difference between configuration of sources and destinations is the Mappings page shown in Figure 15-1. The Mappings page points each column from your Data Flow's pipeline to each column that is available in your destination. By default, SSIS will match columns together with the same name, but you can easily match columns by dragging one of Available Input Columns to the appropriate Available Destination Columns if your column names do not correspond. As you can see in the figure, it is not mandatory that these columns be in the same order from the source to the destination.

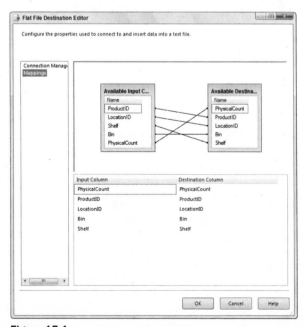

Figure 15-1

Until the destination is connected to the rest of pipeline you cannot configure it. To make the connection, select the source or a transformation and drag the green arrow to the destination. If you want to output a transformation's bad data to a destination, you would drag the red arrow to that destination. In this lesson the most frequently used destinations (OLE DB, flat file, and Excel) are demonstrated.

OLE DB Destination

The most common type of destination is the OLE DB Destination. It can write data from the source or transformation to any Object Linking and Embedding Database (OLE DB)–compatible data source such as SQL Server, Oracle, and DB2. You configure it like any other source or destination, by using an OLE DB Connection Manager. The Connection Manager page of the OLD DB Destination Editor is shown in Figure 15-2.

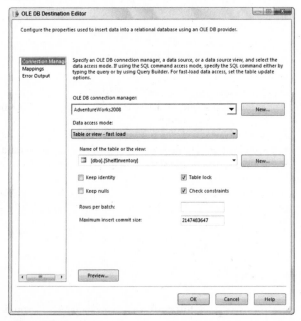

Figure 15-2

Selecting "Table or view - fast load" under Data Access Mode specifies that SSIS loads data in bulk into the OLE DB Destination's target table. The Fast Load option is available only for SQL Server database instances. When Fast Load is selected, you have options like Table Lock, Rows Per Batch, and Maximum Insert Commit Size available to configure.

❏   If you decide to employ **Table Lock**, it prevents others from accessing the table while your package is inserting to it, but speeds up the load

❏   Setting **Rows Per Batch** allows you to specify how many rows are in each batch sent to the destination

❏ The **Maximum Insert Commit Size** sets how large the batch size is going to be prior to sending a commit statement. Usually setting the Max Insert Commit Size to a number like 10,000 increases performance, but it really depends on how wide the columns are in the table

As a best practice, when possible, use a SQL Server Destination instead of an OLE DB Destination. This destination is optimized for SQL Server and achieves performance gains by using the bulk insert features that are built into SQL Server. The SQL Server Destination can be used only if the package is running on the same machine as the SQL Server database you are loading.

Try It

In this lesson, you are going to set up an OLE DB Destination to load a new EmployeeList table you are going to create in the AdventureWorks2008 database. You can download the AdventureWorks2008 database at CodePlex.com (http://www.codeplex.com/MSFTDBProdSamples/). (Please see Lesson 3 if you haven't yet installed the AdventureWorks2008 database.) After this lesson, you will know how to use an OLE DB Destination to load a SQL Server table.

You can also find the sample databases at the Wrox website at http://www.wrox.com/go/SQLServer2008RTMDataSets.

Lesson Requirements

Open the package created from the last lesson or download the completed package called Lesson15.dtsx at www.wrox.com and make the following changes:

❏ Using the following code, create a table in the AdventureWorks2008 database named EmployeeList to load the content of the flat file to:

```
CREATE TABLE [EmployeeList] (
    [EmpID] int,
    [Name] varchar(50),
    [SickDays] int,
    [VacationDays] int
)
```

Hints

❏ You already created the source for this package in Lesson 14 so all you need is an OLE DB Destination this time

Step-by-Step

1. Open the package created from the last lesson or download the completed package called Lesson15.dtsx at www.wrox.com.

2. Open the Data Flow Task named "Flat File Extract" and drag an OLE DB Destination to the designer surface. If you have a Union All that was serving as a placeholder, delete it. Rename the destination "EmployeeList."

3. Connect the green arrow from the Flat File Source to the new destination and double-click to open the destination's editor.

4. By default, the destination assumes you are using the only OLE DB Connection Manager already created in the package. Click the New button next to Name of the Table or the View option to create a new SQL Server table to load.

5. The Create Table dialog box appears with a query to create the table already prepared, just like Figure 15-3. Ensure the query is the following and click OK:

```
CREATE TABLE [EmployeeList] (
    [EmpID] int,
    [Name] varchar(50),
    [SickDays] int,
    [VacationDays] int
)
```

Figure 15-3

6. Notice now that in the bottom of the OLE DB Destination Editor a warning flag has been raised. This warning flag is shown in Figure 15-4. This warning means you're not quite done yet. Select Mappings to go to the Mappings page.

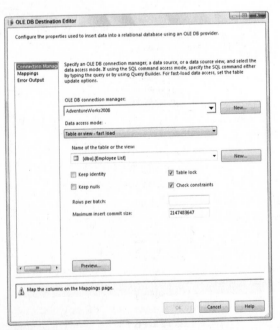

Figure 15-4

7. The Mappings page automatically matches columns with the same names; therefore, all your columns are now input columns and are now mapped to destination columns, as shown in Figure 15-5. Now, click OK to complete the configuration of this destination.

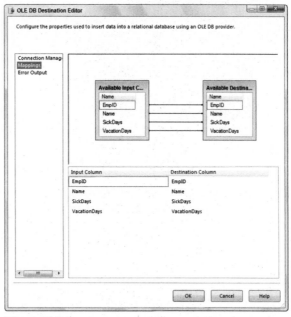

Figure 15-5

8. Execute just this Data Flow by right-clicking in the designer and selecting Execute Task. Figure 15-6 shows the results.

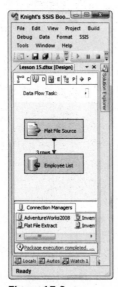

Figure 15-6

9. If you open the EmployeeList table now, you find the results shown in Figure 15-7.

	EmpID	Name	SickDays	VacationDays
1	1	Devin Knight	4	10
2	2	Brian Knight	5	14
3	3	Mike Davis	0	9

Figure 15-7

Flat File Destination

The Flat File Destination is used to load data into a flat file. The flat file can be either a fixed-width or delimited file. A file that is fixed-width uses width measurements to define columns and rows, whereas a delimited file uses special characters to define columns and rows. When you are configuring a Flat File Destination, you can choose to overwrite data in the file and add a custom header to the file by typing it into the Header window.

Try It

In this lesson, you are going to set up a Flat File Destination to bring in inventory data from an Excel Source to a flat file. You can find the Excel file as part of the Lesson 15 download at www.wrox.com. After this lesson, you will know how to use a Flat File Destination to load data into a text file.

Lesson Requirements

Open the package you created from the last lesson or download the completed package named Lesson15.dtsx at www.wrox.com and make the following changes:

❑ Create a new Flat File Connection Manager that is comma-delimited and save the file anywhere on your computer

Hints

❑ This example requires one Flat File Destination and one Flat File Connection Manager, making a total of two Flat File Connection Managers for this package

Step-by-Step

1. Open the package created from the last lesson or download the completed package named Lesson15.dtsx at www.wrox.com.

2. Open the Data Flow Task named "Excel Extract" and drag a Flat File Destination to the designer surface. If you have a Union All that was serving as a placeholder, delete it.

3. Connect the green arrow from the Excel Source to the new destination and double-click the destination to open the destination's editor.

4. By default, the destination assumes you are using the only Flat File Connection Manager already created in the package. However, in this case, you need to make a new connection manager, so click the New button next to the Flat File Connection Manager.

5. Make the file comma-delimited, find a location to save the file on your computer, and click OK.

6. Back in the Flat File Destination Editor, go to the Mappings page to ensure all columns are mapped appropriately, as shown in Figure 15-8. Then click OK.

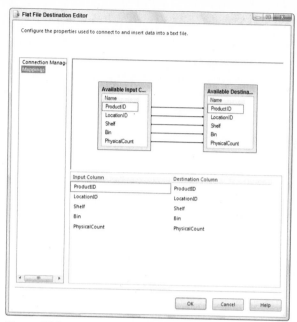

Figure 15-8

7. Execute just this Data Flow by right-clicking in the designer and selecting Execute Task. Figure 15-9 shows the results.

Figure 15-9

Excel Destination

The Excel Destination works the same basic way the Excel Source does, except the destination takes in data instead of sending that data out. As in all sources and destinations a connection manager must be specified, in this case an Excel Connection Manager. The Excel Connection Manager must point to a worksheet you want to load data into. Unlike with the Flat File Destination, however, a spreadsheet must already exist to load; otherwise, you will receive an error.

Try It

In this lesson, you set up an Excel Destination to load a worksheet named TransactionHistory with data from an AdventureWorks2008 database source. After this lesson, you will know how to use an Excel Destination to load data into an Excel spreadsheet.

Lesson Requirements

Open the package created from the last lesson or download the completed package named Lesson15.dtsx at www.wrox.com and make the following changes:

❏ Use the Excel file Inventory_Worksheet that you can download from www.wrox.com as the destination.

❏ Point the destination to the Excel sheet named TransactionHistory.

Hints

❏ You need only one Excel Destination for this example

Step-by-Step

1. Open the package created from the last lesson or download Lesson15.dtsx at www.wrox.com.

2. Open the Data Flow Task named "OLE DB Extract" and drag an Excel Destination to the designer surface. If you have a Union All that was serving as a placeholder, delete it. Rename the destination "Transaction History."

3. Connect the green arrow from the OLE DB Source to the new destination and double-click to open the destination's editor.

4. By default, the destination assumes you are using the only Excel Connection Manager already created in the package. Click the New button next to the Name of the Excel Sheet option and click OK to create the sheet using the query SSIS has generated, as shown in Figure 15-10.

Figure 15-10

5. Back in the Excel Destination Editor, select the Mappings page and ensure all columns are mapped appropriately, as in Figure 15-11. Then click OK.

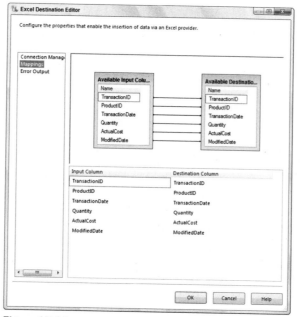

Figure 15-11

6. Execute just this Data Flow by right-clicking in the designer and selecting Execute Task. Figure 15-12 shows the results.

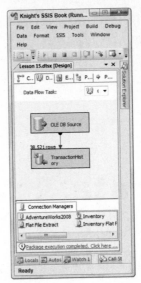

Figure 15-12

 Please select Lesson 15 on the DVD to view the video that accompanies this lesson.

Changing Data Types with the Data Conversion Transform

Often when working with data, you have various reasons why you may need to make changes to a column's data type. For example, SQL Server Integration Services (SSIS) supports Excel data as a source, but it may not support the data the way you intend by default. By default the general data type is set, which is a Unicode data type. In SQL Server, Unicode translates to an nvarchar, which is most likely not what you want because it requires twice the space and may be slower. If you have a Unicode data type in SSIS and you try to insert into a varchar column, it will potentially fail.

The Data Conversion Transform performs the T-SQL equivalent of the CONVERT or CAST functions on a selected column. To configure this transform, drag it onto the Data Flow designer and double-click it to open the Data Conversion Transformation Editor (shown in Figure 16-1). Here you check the columns you need to convert and use the Operation drop-down box select the data type you want to convert to.

Something that can be frustrating with SSIS is how it deals with SQL Server data types. For example, a varchar maps in SSIS to a string data typed column. It was made this way to translate well into the .NET development world. The following table shows how the data types translate from a SQL Server data type to an SSIS data type.

SQL Server Data Type	SSIS Data Type
Bigint	Eight-byte signed integer [DT_I8]
Binary	Byte stream [DT_BYTES]
bit	Boolean [DT_BOOL]
datetime	Database timestamp [DT_DBTIMESTAMP]

Continued

(continued)

SQL Server Data Type	SSIS Data Type
decimal	Numeric [DT_NUMERIC]
float	Float [DT_R4]
int	Four-byte signed integer [DT_I4]
image	Image [DT_IMAGE]
nvarchar or nchar	Unicode string [DT_WSTR]
ntext	Unicode text stream [DT_NTEXT]
numeric	Numeric [DT_NUMERIC]
smallint	Two-byte signed integer [DT_I2]
text	Text stream [DT_TEXT]
timestamp	Byte stream [DT_BYTES]
tinytint	Single-byte unsigned integer [DT_UI1]
uniqueidentifier	Unique identifier [DT_GUID]
varbinary	Byte stream [DT_BYTES]
varchar or char	String [DT_STR]
xml	Unicode string [DT_WSTR]

Figure 16-1

The Output Alias is the column name you want to assign to the new column generated after it is transformed. If you don't assign it a new name, it defaults to "Copy of *ColumnName*." It's always a good idea to give the Output Alias a new name so it can be identified as the converted column.

The Data Conversion Transform Editor dialog box also has length, precision, and scale columns. *Length* for a numeric data type is the total bytes required to store the number and length for a string data type is the total characters the column can store. *Precision* is the total number of digits in a number (including the values to the right of the decimal), and *scale* is the number of digits to the right of the decimal point. For instance, the integer 9876543.21 has a precision of 9 and a scale of 2.

The Data Conversion Transform is a synchronous transform, meaning rows flow into memory buffers in the transform and the same buffers come out. Essentially this means no rows are held or blocked and typically these transforms perform very quickly with minimal impact to your Data Flow.

> *Here's a best practice: the Data Conversion Transform and the Flat File Source are the only two tools that can use the performance enhancement called Fast Parse. Fast Parse can be enabled only in the tools' Advanced Editor. When you enable a column with Fast Parse, verification of that column is turned off. Use this feature only when you are certain your data is reliable.*

Try It

In this lesson, your company has an Excel file called Inventory Worksheet that needs to be imported into your AdventureWorks2008 database. Your requirements are to create a package that uses a Data Conversion Transform to convert all column data types. Your manager tells you that the results after the conversion should be populated into a new table. After this lesson, you'll know how to convert a column's data type using the Data Conversion Transform and load tables of different data types.

Lesson Requirements

Download the Inventory Worksheet.xls Excel file from the www.wrox.com. This file will be your source for populating a new table you create called ShelfInventory in the AdventureWorks2008 database. Save the Excel file to a location on your computer called C:\Projects\SSISPersonalTrainer. You can also download the creation script for this lesson from www.wrox.com. Your goal in this lesson is to select all columns and convert them to the specified data types with a new destination table:

Columns	Convert To
Shelf	varchar(255)
Product	int
LocationID	int
Bin	int
PhysicalCount	int

Hints

❏ Only one Excel Source and Excel Connection Manager are needed

❏ A Data Conversion Transform is needed to convert the columns to the required data type

❏ Only one OLE DB Destination and OLE DB Connection Manager are needed

Step-by-Step

1. Create a new SSIS package called Lesson16.dtsx (or download Lesson16.dtsx from www.wrox.com).

2. Create a new Excel Connection Manager using the Inventory Worksheet.xls file you downloaded from www.wrox.com and make sure the option "First row has column names" is checked. (You can find more information on using an Excel Source in Lesson 14.)

3. Drag over a Data Flow Task onto the design pane and name the new task "DF – Data Conversion."

4. In the Data Flow tab, drag a new Excel Source onto the Data Flow design pane and name it "Excel SRC - Inventory Worksheet."

5. Double-click the Excel Source and change the OLE DB Connection Manager option to your only connection manager. Then change the "Name of the Excel sheet" option to Inventory_Worksheet and click OK.

6. Drag a Data Conversion Transform onto the design pane and connect it to the Excel Source.

7. Open the Data Conversion Transformation Editor by double-clicking the new transform and check each column from the Available Input Columns table. Change the Output Alias of all columns to Converted*ColumnName*, as shown in Figure 16-2.

8. For the Data Type select string [DT_STR] for the Input Column Shelf and four-byte signed integer [DT_I4] for all other columns and click OK.

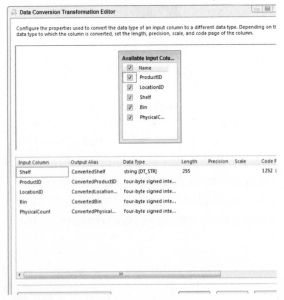

Figure 16-2

9. Back in the designer, drag an OLE DB Destination onto the design pane and connect it to the Data Conversion Transform.

10. Open the OLE DB Destination and click New to create a new OLE DB Connection Manager, where you will select AdventureWorks2008.

11. Still in the OLE DB Destination Editor click New to create a new table and ensure the following statement is used:

```
CREATE TABLE [ShelfInventory] (
    [Shelf] varchar(255),
    [ProductID] int,
    [LocationID] int,
    [Bin] int,
    [PhysicalCount] int
)
```

12. Go to the Mappings page and delete all connections between the Input Columns and Destination Columns. Now connect all Input Columns with the Converted prefix to the associated Destination Columns (Figure 16-3) and click OK.

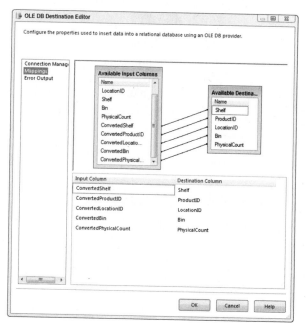

Figure 16-3

13. Execute the package. A successful run should look like Figure 16-4.

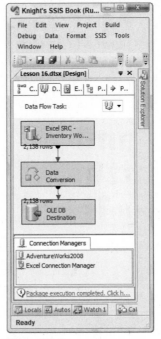

Figure 16-4

 Please select Lesson 16 on the DVD to view the video that accompanies this lesson.

Creating and Replacing Columns with the Derived Column Transform

The Derived Column Transform allows you to either create or replace a column in the data stream. This component can be used for many problems you may run into and, therefore, is one of the most useful tools you have in the Data Flow. As you are going to see in this lesson's "Try It" example, the transform can be used for things like adding row auditing and editing incoming data using the available SQL Server Integration Services (SSIS) expressions.

You open the Derived Column Transformation Editor as you open other transform editors, by dragging it into the Data Flow and then double-clicking. To configure this transform, drag the column or variable into the Expression column, as shown in Figure 17-1. Then add any functions to it. You can find a list of functions to use as a reference in the top-right corner of the Derived Column Transformation Editor; the functions can be dragged into the Expression property. You must then specify, in the Derived Column drop-down box, whether you want the output of the expression to replace an existing column or create a new column. Lastly, if you create a new column give it a name in the Derived Column Name column.

In Figure 17-1, the expression states that if the column PhysicalCount is null, then convert it to 0; otherwise, keep the existing data.

To get the most bang for your buck with this transform, explore the different functions available. The functions and the availability of variables makes the Derived Column Transform one of the top five transforms that you find yourself using to satisfy the need for T-SQL scripting in your package.

Figure 17-1

The expression language is marketed as being a heavily C#-based syntax. However, you can't just start writing C# because some quirks are mixed into the scripting language. Still, the following common operators are irrefutably from a C# ancestry:

Expression Operator	Description
||	Logical OR operation
&&	Logical AND operation
==	Comparison of two expressions to determine if equivalent
!=	Comparison of two expressions to determine inequality
?:	Conditional operator

Now look at an example of how to write an expression using one of these operators. The following statement uses the conditional operator (? :) to check the column PhysicalCount to see if it contains any nulls and, if it does, to change them to 0. Otherwise, it keeps the column the same. The shell of such a script uses code like this:

```
<<boolean_expression>> ? <<when_true>> : <<when_false>>
```

This shell translates the previously mentioned example into this code:

```
ISNULL( [PhysicalCount] ) ? 0 : [PhysicalCount]
```

Sometimes you run into functions that look like they would function like T-SQL. For example, the GETDATE() function is typically what you would use to return the current date in T-SQL. In this circumstance, GETDATE() performs exactly the same in the SSIS expression language. However, some functions look like T-SQL functions but work in ways that are not the same:

Expression Function	Description	Difference
DATEPART()	Parses the date part from a date	Requires quotes on the date part
ISNULL()	Tests an expression for NULL	Doesn't allow for default value

The statement that follows uses the DATEPART() function to return an integer representing the desired part of a date. In this example the expression is returning the year from today's date. The shell of this script uses code that looks like this:

```
DATEPART( <<datepart>>, <<date>> )
```

This shell translates the previously mentioned code example into this code:

```
DATEPART( "yy",GetDate ( ) )
```

Many times it is useful to build string data within an expression. You can use string data to populate the body of an email message or to build file paths for processing. Here are some of the most commonly used string functions:

Expression Operator	Description
REPLACE()	Replaces a character string
UPPER()	Converts lowercase characters to uppercase
SUBSTRING()	Returns a character value that starts at a specified position with a specified length

Using the REPLACE() function allows you to search through a string for a specific value and replace it with another. In the example that follows the expression searches the column named [Shelf] for the word "Development" and replaces it with "Production". The shell of this script uses code that looks like this:

```
REPLACE( <<character_expression>>, <<search_expression>>, <<replace_
expression>> )
```

This would translate the example into this code:

```
REPLACE( [Shelf] , "Development", "Production" )
```

Another common string function is UPPER(), which changes all lowercase characters to uppercase. The shell of this function is written like this.

```
UPPER( <<character_expression>> )
```

This example uses the system variable PackageName to return the name of the package in all uppercase. The result looks like this: LESSON 17.

```
UPPER(@[System::PackageName] )
```

The last example of a string function we want to show is SUBSTRING(). This function allows you to retrieve a predetermined amount of characters from a string field.

```
SUBSTRING( <<character_expression>>, <<start>>, <<length>> )
```

The following expression is bringing back just the first letter of the FirstName column with a period (.) followed by the entire contents of the LastName column. The results would look like this: D. Knight.

```
SUBSTRING( [FirstName] , 1, 1 )+". " +[LastName]
```

Many other string functions are available, so be sure to explore all the functions available in the reference guide in the top-right section of the Derived Column Transform Editor.

It is very likely that you might find it necessary to convert or cast certain values within an expression so they are compatible with the column's data type. Here are some of the most common cast functions available:

Cast Operator	Additional Parameters
DT_STR(<<length>>, <<code_page>>)	length — Final string lengthcode_page — Unicode character set
DT_WSTR(<<length>>)	length — Final string length
DT_NUMERIC(<<precision>>, <<scale>>)	precision — Max number of digits scale — Number of digits after decimal
DT_DECIMAL(<<scale>>)	scale — Number of digits after decimal

A common opportunity to use a cast operator involves converting dates to fit in inputs that accept only strings. The following example uses the DT_WSTR cast function to convert the date to a string. The code shell for this function looks like this:

```
(DT_WSTR, <<length>>)
```

This shell translates the previously mentioned code example into this code:

```
(DT_WSTR, 30) GETDATE()
```

For more on the SSIS expression language, read Lessons 29 and 30.

Try It

In this lesson, your company decides that it would be best to include a date that each row is populated in your SSIS package from Lesson 16. Your manager tells you that they really need to have this date for auditing purposes. Once these changes have been made to the package, delete the content of the table before you run the package again. After this lesson, you'll know how to add to the pipeline of an SSIS package a derived column built by assigning an expression to it.

Lesson Requirements

Make the following changes to the package you created in Lesson 16 or open the completed Lesson 17 package from www.wrox.com:

❑   Add a column to the pipeline that uses the system variable @[System::StartTime] to populate the RowStartDate column that is already in the ShelfInventory table

❑   Delete the content of ShelfInventory table and repopulate it with the new column included

Hints

❑   Use the Derived Column Transform to add the new date column to the file stream

Step-by-Step

1.   Open a Query Window in Management Studio and run this query to empty the table's data:

```
TRUNCATE TABLE ShelfInventory
```

2.   Now run this query to add a column to the ShelfInventory table with the following query:

```
ALTER TABLE ShelfInventory
ADD RowStartDate datetime
```

3.   Open the SSIS package Lesson16.dtsx that you created in the previous lesson or you can find the completed Lesson17.dtsx at www.wrox.com.

4.   Click the Data Flow tab and delete the precedence constraint between the Data Conversion Transform and the OLE DB Destination.

5.   Drag a Derived Column Transform into the Data Flow and connect it between the Data Conversion Transform and the OLE DB Destination.

6.   Open the Derived Column Transformation Editor and add a new column by typing RowStartDate in the Derived Column Name property. Then in the Expression property add the system variable @[System::StartTime] by dragging it down from the variables list in the top-left section of the editor, as shown in Figure 17-2. Then click OK. This will add the current date and time to the column when the package is run.

Figure 17-2

7. Now that this column has been added, you need to make sure the destination knows to use this column. Open the OLE DB Destination and add the column RowStartDate to the mapping as shown in Figure 17-3.

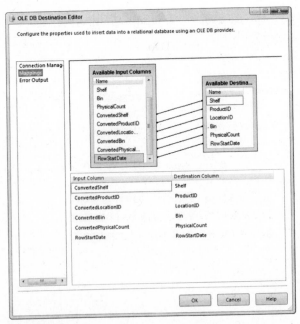

Figure 17-3

8. Now execute the package. A successful run should look like Figure 17-4. The ShelfInventory table has now been repopulated with the new column that holds the date and time the package was run.

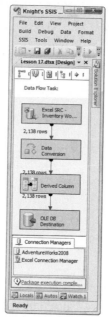

Figure 17-4

 Please select Lesson 17 on the DVD to view the video that accompanies this lesson.

Rolling Up Data with The Aggregate Transform

Do you have a large amount of data that you want to roll up to a different granularity? The Aggregate Transform allows you to essentially apply a GROUP BY statement on data entering it. Aggregate Transforms are one of the more expensive operations you can perform against data, much like a GROUP BY statement is in T-SQL, and they can be very memory intensive.

> The Aggregate Transform is an asynchronous transform and is fully blocking. This means that every row must enter the transform prior to sending the first row out. Because of this, your transform will need as much RAM as the source retrieves. For example, if your Data Flow is reading a 1GB file, your Aggregate Transform will require at least 1GB of memory.

Once you drag the transform over, simply check the columns in the Aggregations tab that you want to aggregate or sum. The Operation drop-down box allows you to select what type of aggregation function you want to apply to the data. The most important operation is a Group By operation, which allows you to roll the data up to that grain. For example, if you have a dozen sales of three products, and you grouped by the ProductID, you'd have only three rows come out of the transform. You can see a list of all the operations allowed in the following table.

Data Type	Operations Allowed
String	Group by, Count, Count distinct
Numeric	Group by, Count, Count distinct, Minimum, Maximum
Date	Group by, Count, Count distinct, Minimum, Maximum, Average, Sum

Like any GROUP BY statement, only the columns that are being grouped by or aggregated on a different way as with a SUM or MAX function are returned. Other columns are dropped and will not be available to you in the next Data Flow.

You can tune the Aggregate Transform by estimating how many distinct groups you will retrieve from the operation. In the Advanced tab (see Figure 18-1), you can type the estimated number of groups in the "Number of keys" text box. This will optimize the transform for that level of distinct values.

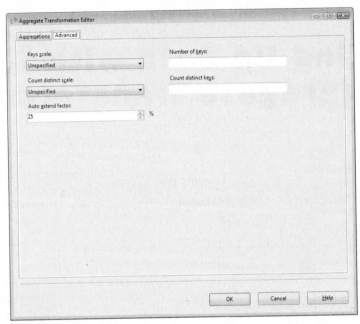

Figure 18-1

The Aggregate Transform is one of the most powerful and simple transforms to configure. However, it should be used sparingly due to its speed. If you pull data out of a flat file, it's a good application for the Aggregate Transform, but when you're pulling data out of a database, consider writing a SQL statement that pulls the data out already aggregated.

Try It

In this lesson, you create an extract file that contains a rolled-up version of the Production. TransactionHistory table. The Production.TransactionHistory table has hundreds of thousands of records in it containing very granular data of every transaction for your company's history. Your partner only needs to know how many of each product you've sold and other data such as the last sale of that product. After this lesson, you'll know how to apply grouping to your data to see your data at a higher grain.

Lesson Requirements

In this lesson, you need to read the Production.TransactionHistory table from the AdventureWorks2008 database and create a new file with the following columns without using T-SQL's GROUP BY statement:

- ❑ **ProductID** — One row for each product
- ❑ **LastTransactionDate** — The date of the last purchase
- ❑ **TotalQuantity** — The total quantity for all transactions for a given product
- ❑ **TotalCost** — The total cost for all transactions for a given product

Hints

- ❑ To perform a GROUP BY clause against data in a Data Flow you use the Aggregate Transform after pulling data out of the Production.TransactionHistory table with the OLE DB Source
- ❑ Write the data to the flat file with the OLE DB Destination

Step-by-Step

1. Create a new SSIS package called Lesson18.dtsx.

2. Create a new OLE DB Connection Manager that connects to your AdventureWorks2008 database.

3. Drag over a Data Flow Task onto the design pane and call the new task "DF - Aggregate Data."

4. In the Data Flow tab, drag a new OLE DB Source onto the Data Flow design pane and name it "OLE SRC – TransactionHistory."

5. Double-click the OLE DB Source and change the OLE DB Connection Manager option to your only connection manager. Change the Data Access Mode to SQL Command and type the following query into the SQL Command text box:

```
SELECT
TransactionID, ProductID, TransactionDate,
TransactionType, Quantity, ActualCost, ModifiedDate
FROM Production.TransactionHistory
```

6. Drag an Aggregate Transform onto the design pane and connect it to the OLE DB Source.

7. Open the Aggregate Transformation Editor by double-clicking the new transform and check the ProductID, TransactionDate, Quantity, and ActualCost columns.

8. Change the Output Alias column for each of the checked columns. Change the alias to LastTransactionDate for the TransactionDate column. Change the Quantity column to TotalQuantity and ActualCost to TotalCost.

9. In the Operation column, change ProductID to Group By, LastTransactionDate to Maximum, TotalQuantity to Sum, TotalCost to Sum, as shown in Figure 18-2.

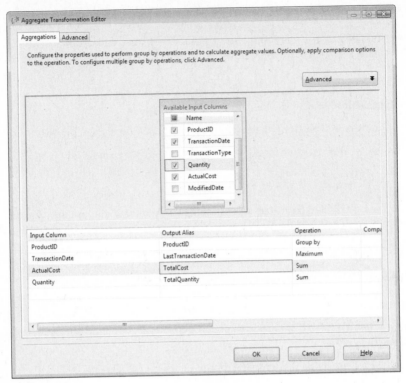

Figure 18-2

10. Back in the designer, drag a Flat File Destination onto the design pane and connect it to the Aggregate Transform.

11. Open the Flat File Destination and click New to create a new Flat File Connection Manager. When prompted, click that the file will be delimited (separated by a given symbol).

12. Name the connection manager "Extract." Place the file wherever you'd like and check "Column names in first data row."

13. Go to the Mappings page and click OK.

14. Execute the package. A successful run should look like Figure 18-3.

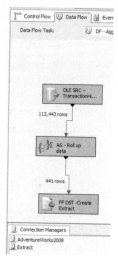

Figure 18-3

You can download the completed Lesson18.dtsx package from the book's website at www.wrox.com.

 Please select Lesson 18 on the DVD to view the video that accompanies this lesson.

Ordering Data with the Sort Transform

The Sort Transform allows you to sort data based on any column in the path. To configure the Sort Transformation Editor after it's been connected, open the transform and check the columns you need to sort by (Figure 19-1). Uncheck any columns you don't want passed through the path from the Pass Through column. By default, every column passes through the pipeline.

You can optionally check the "Remove rows with duplicate sort values" box. When this is checked, if a second value comes in that matches your same sort key, it is disregarded, and the row is dropped.

> The Sort Transform is a fully blocking asynchronous transform and will slow down your Data Flow performance. Use these only when you have to and sparingly.

The Sort Transform is one of the most frequently used transforms. This is because many other transforms that can be used require data to be presorted with either a Sort Transform or an ORDER BY statement
in the OLE DB Source. You should avoid using the Sort Transform when you can because of speed constraints.

If you place an ORDER BY statement in the OLE DB Source, SSIS is not aware of the ORDER BY statement because it can just have easily been in a stored procedure, so you must notify SSIS that the data is presorted. To do this right-click the source and select Advanced Editor; then go to the Input and Output Properties and select the OLE DB Source Output. In the Properties pane, change the IsSorted property to True (shown in Figure 19-2).

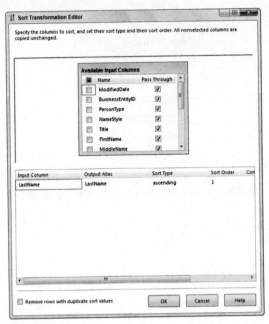

Figure 19-1

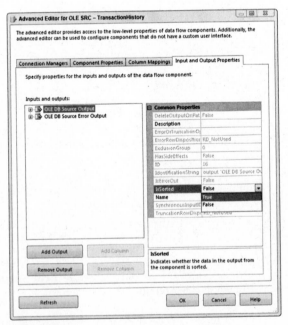

Figure 19-2

Then, under Output Columns, select the column you are ordering on in your SQL statement and change the SortKeyPosition to 1, if you're sorting only by a single column ascending, as shown in Figure 19-3. If you have multiple columns, you could change this SortKeyPosition value to the column position in the ORDER BY statement starting at 1. A value of –1 would sort the data in descending order.

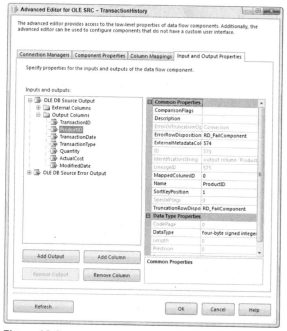

Figure 19-3

Try It

In this lesson, your company has decided it really needs the extract file you created in Lesson 18 to show the products in order by total sold. Your manager tells you to make sure that once you've made these changes to your package to delete the content of the extract file before you run the package again. After this lesson, you'll know how to sort data using SSIS.

Lesson Requirements

You can either make the following changes to the package you created in Lesson 18 or download the Lesson 18 package from www.wrox.com and make these changes:

❑   TotalQuantity — Sort in descending order

❑   Delete the contents of the flat file and repopulate it with newly ordered records

Be sure you are using the Lesson 18 package as a starting place. The Lesson 19 package that you can download at www.wrox.com is the version of the package after this Step-by-Step example has already been completed.

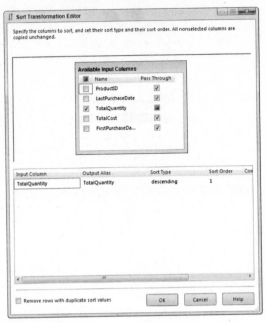

Figure 19-4

Hints

❏ You need to add only one Sort Transform to the package

Step-by-Step

1. Open the SSIS package Lesson18.dtsx that you created in the last lesson or download it from www.wrox.com.

2. Click the Data Flow tab and delete the precedence constraint between the Aggregate Transform and the Flat File Destination.

3. Drag a Sort Transform into the Data Flow and connect it between the Aggregate Transform and the Flat File Destination.

4. Open the Sort Transformation Editor, select TotalQuantity to sort by, and change the Sort Type to descending, as shown in Figure 19-4. Then click OK.

5. After making these changes, notice that the Flat File Destination has a red X on it. This occurred only because of the new transform that was added to the path. To fix this error try to open the Flat File Destination; this opens the Restore Invalid References Editor dialog box. Click Select All and Apply to Map using column name.

6. Now execute the package. A successful run should look like Figure 19-5. The flat file has now been repopulated sorted by TotalQuantity in descending order.

7. Upon completion your package will look like the completed Lesson19.dtsx available from www.wrox.com.

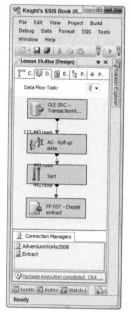

Figure 19-5

 Please select Lesson 19 on the DVD to view the video that accompanies this lesson

Joining Data with the Lookup Transform

Are you looking for a way to join data from a new source into your Data Flow pipeline? The Lookup Transform in SQL Server Integration Services (SSIS) allows you to perform the equivalent of an inner and outer hash join. The only difference is that the operations occur outside the realm of the database engine.

This transform is used in many different situations but would typically be found in an ETL process that populates a data warehouse. For example, you may want to populate a table by joining data from two separate source systems on different database platforms. The component can join only two data sets at a time, so in order to join three or more data sets you would need to string multiple Lookup Transforms together.

The Lookup Transform is a synchronous transform; therefore, it does not block the pipeline's flow of data. As new data enters the transform, rows that have been joined are leaving through one of the possible outputs. The caveat to this is that in certain caching modes the component will initially block the package's execution for a period of time while it charges its internal caches.

Sometimes rows will not join successfully. For example, you may have a product that has no purchase history and its identifier in the product table would have no matches in the sales table. SSIS supports this by having multiple outputs on the Lookup Transform; in the simplest (default/legacy) configuration you would have one output for matched rows and a separate output for non-matched and error rows.

Cache Modes

The transform provides several modes of operation that allow you to trade off performance and resource usage. Often there is a logical rationale for choosing a particular cache mode, which is discussed later in this lesson. To configure the Lookup Transform drag one from the toolbar to the Data Flow design surface and double-click it to open the editor. Figure 20-1 shows the Lookup Transformation Editor where you select the cache mode and data source.

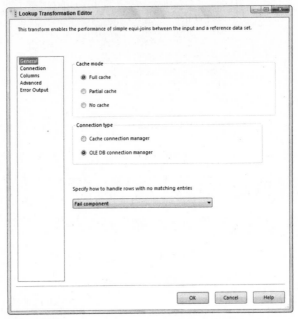

Figure 20-1

In *full-cache mode,* one of the tables you are joining is loaded entirely into memory, then the rows from the other table are flowed through the pipeline one buffer at a time, and the selected join operation is performed.

However, sometimes the reference table used in a lookup is too large to cache all at once in the system's memory. In these circumstances you have two options: either you can cache some of the data or cache nothing.

For *no-cache mode* there is no up-front caching done, and each incoming row in the pipeline is compared one at a time to a specified relational table. Depending on the size of the reference data, this mode is usually the slowest, though it scales to the largest number of reference rows.

> **Use no-cache mode carefully because this can cause a high performance overhead on the system.**

The *partial-cache mode* gives you a middle ground between the no-cache and full-cache options. In this mode the transform caches only the most recently used data within the memory boundaries specified. As soon as the cache grows too big, the least-used cache data is thrown away.

Try It

In this lesson, your company needs you to alter a package to show the product names with the sales of each product. Your manager tells you to create a new flat file to store the results. After this lesson, you'll know how to join data into the Data Flow pipeline using SSIS.

Lesson Requirements

Make the following changes to the package (Lesson20a.dtsx), which you can find at www.wrox.com:

❑ Join the data from the Production.Product table to bring in the product names with this query:

```
SELECT ProductID, Name
FROM Production.Product
```

❑ Create a new flat file and populate it with new results

Hints

❑ Use the Lookup Transform to join Product data to your package data stream

Step-by-Step

1. You can either continue the work you did from the last lesson or open the completed SSIS package Lesson20a.dtsx from www.wrox.com.

2. Click the Data Flow tab and delete the connecting lines between the Sort Transform and the Flat File Destination.

3. Drag a Lookup Component into the Data Flow and rename it "LKP - Product Name"; then connect it between the Sort Transform and the Flat File Destination.

4. Once you connect to the Flat File Destination, the Input Output Selection dialog box will open, and you should select Lookup Match Output from the Output drop-down box, shown in Figure 20-2.

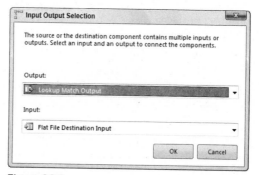

Figure 20-2

5. Open the Lookup Transformation Editor, navigate to the Connection tab, and select the option "Use results of an SQL query."

6. In the query window write the following select statement. Figure 20-3 shows how the editor should look at this point.

```
SELECT ProductID,Name
FROM Production.Product
```

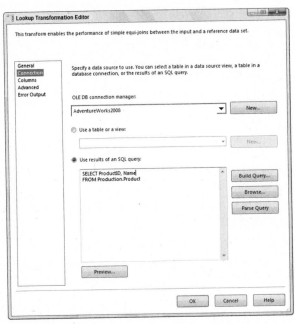

Figure 20-3

7. Navigate to the Columns tab and select the mapping, as shown in Figure 20-4. Then click OK.

8. Open the Flat File Destination and create a new Flat File Connection Manager, as you did in Lesson 18. Name it Extract 2 but make sure this time the Name column is included. Ensure that the "Column names in the first data row" option is checked in the Flat File Connection Manager Editor and click OK. Once this is completed make sure all columns are mapped in the destination and click OK again.

9. Now execute the package. A successful run should look like Figure 20-5. The new flat file has now been created with the new column included.

Figure 20-4

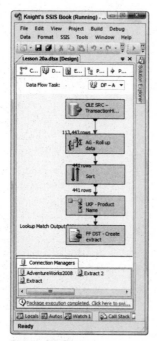

Figure 20-5

 Please select Lesson 20a on the DVD to view the video that accompanies this lesson.

The Cache Connection Manager and Transform

In previous versions of SSIS, the Lookup Transform could use source data for its cache only from specific OLE DB connections, and the cache could be populated by using only a SQL query. The current version of the Lookup Transform allows you to populate the cache using a separate pipeline in either the same or a different package. You can use source data from just about anywhere.

Previously you needed to reload the cache every time it was used. For example, if you had two pipelines in the same package that each required the same reference data set, each Lookup Transform would load its own copy of the cache separately. Now you can persist the cache to virtual memory or to permanent file storage. This means that within the same package, multiple Lookup Transforms can share the same cache, and the cache does not need to be reloaded during each iteration of a looping operation. You can load the cache to a file and share it with other packages. The cache file format is optimized for speed and can be orders of magnitude faster than reloading the reference data set from the original relational source.

The Cache Connection Manager (CCM) and Cache Transform allow you to load the Lookup cache from any source. The Cache Connection Manager is the more critical of the two — it holds a reference to the internal memory cache and can both read and write the cache to a disk-based file. In fact the Lookup Transform internally uses the CCM as its caching mechanism.

Like other connection managers in SSIS, the CCM is instantiated in the Connection Managers pane of the package design surface. You can also create new CCMs from the Cache Transform Editor and Lookup Transform Editor. At design time the CCM contains no data, so at runtime you need to populate it. Figure 20-6 shows the Cache Connection Manager Editor.

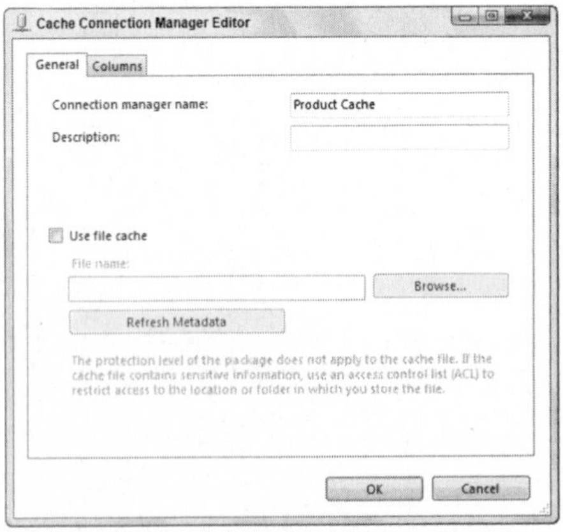

Figure 20-6

When you configure a CCM, it allows you to specify which columns of the input data set will be used as index fields and which columns will be used as reference fields. This is a necessary step — the CCM needs to know up front which columns you will be joining on so that it can create internal index structures to optimize the process. See Figure 20-7.

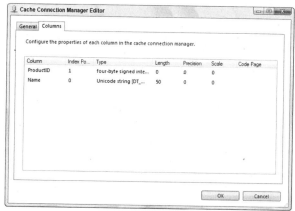

Figure 20-7

Try It

In this lesson, your company needs you to alter the package you worked on earlier in this lesson to show the product names using the new caching methods. Your manager tells you to use the same flat file to store the results. After this lesson, you'll know how to use the new caching tools provided for SSIS 2008.

Lesson Requirements

Make the following changes to the package you created earlier in this lesson:

- ❑ Send the needed columns from Production.Product into a CCM
- ❑ Change the source for the lookup to use the CCM

Hints

- ❑ Use the Cache Transform to put the product data into the Cache Connection Manager
- ❑ Use the CCM in the lookup instead of the OLE DB Connection Manager

Step-by-Step

1. Either open the completed SSIS package Lesson20b.dtsx from www.wrox.com or alter the package used earlier in this lesson.

2. Add a new Data Flow to the Control Flow and name it "Cache Product Table." Then connect it to the existing Data Flow.

3. Open the new Data Flow and drag over an OLE DB Source. Then configure it as shown in Figure 20-8. Click OK.

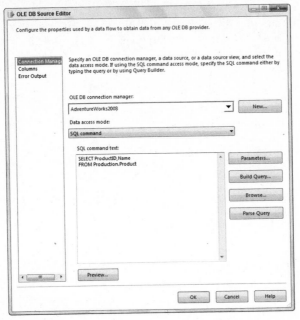

Figure 20-8

4. Bring a Cache Transform into the Data Flow and open the Cache Transformation Editor. Select New to create a Cache Connection Manager, which opens the Cache Connection Manager Editor.

5. On the Columns tab of the editor change the Index Position for ProductID to 1, as shown in Figure 20-9. Then click OK.

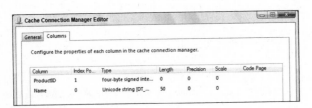

Figure 20-9

6. Ensure that all columns are mapped by clicking the Mappings tab in the Cache Transformation Editor. Then click OK.

7. Now enter the "DF – Aggregate Data" Data Flow to change the source of the lookup by opening the "LKP – Product Name" and changing the Connection Type to Cache Connection Manager. Then click OK. You will see the results in Figure 20-10.

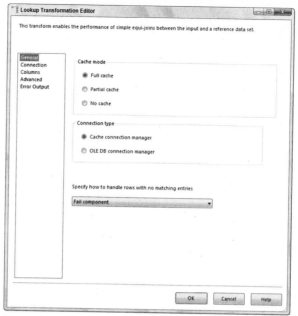

Figure 20-10

8. Empty the content of the flat file and then execute the package again. The results will be the same as the original package but now the cached data can be used several times throughout the package.

 Please select Lesson 20b on the DVD to view the video that accompanies this lesson.

Auditing Data with the Row Count Transform

Often in an ETL process you may be required to create an auditing table that records how many rows were loaded. SSIS has made this easy to accomplish with the Row Count Transform.

This transform has the ability to count rows in a Data Flow and record that count for later use in conjunction with an Execute SQL Task. The count must be placed into a variable, which can then be used in the Control Flow for inserting into an audit table.

To configure the Row Count Transform, connect it to any point in the Data Flow that you want to record the number of rows. Double-click the transform to open the Advanced Editor for Row Count. In the VariableName property you specify what variable will store the row count that the transform records.

Another valuable way to use the Row Count Transform is as a destination to send your data to. Because you don't physically have to commit stream data to a table to retrieve the count, it can act as a destination, terminating your data stream and allowing you to view the Data Flow's data with a data viewer.

Try It

In this lesson, your company needs you to create a package that runs only if there are any rows in the ErrorLog table in the AdventureWorks2008 database. After this lesson, you'll know how to insert a row count into a variable and use it dynamically in your package.

Lesson Requirements

Create a new package named Lesson21 and make the following changes. You can also find the completed Lesson21.dtsx package at www.wrox.com:

❑ Count the rows in the ErrorLog table and place that number in a variable

❑ Set the precedence constraint to run a Script Task if the table has at least one row

Hints

❑ You need only one OLE DB Source in a Data Flow and one Row Count Transform that counts how many rows are in the ErrorLog table

❑ Use a Script Task that executes only if at least one row is found in the ErrorLog table

Step-by-Step

1. Create an SSIS package named Lesson21 or download Lesson21.dtsx from www.wrox.com. Add a Data Flow Task to the Control Flow design surface.

2. In the Control Flow tab, add a variable named "MyRowCount." Ensure that the variable is package-scoped and of type Int32 (Figure 21-1). If you don't know how to add a variable, select Variable from the SSIS menu and click the Add Variable button.

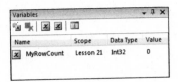

Figure 21-1

3. Create a connection manager that connects to the AdventureWorks2008 database. Add an OLE DB Data Source to the Data Flow design surface. Configure the source to point to your AdventureWorks2008 database's connection manager and the ErrorLog table.

4. Add a Row Count Transform to the Data Flow. Open the Advanced Editor and select the variable named "User::MyRowCount" as the VariableName property. Your editor should resemble Figure 21-2.

Figure 21-2

5. Return to the Control Flow tab and add a Script Task. This task is not really going to perform any action. Instead it will be used to show the conditional ability to perform steps based on the value returned by the Row Count Transform.

6. Connect the Data Flow Task to the Script Task.

7. Right-click the arrow connecting the Data Flow Task and Script Task. Select the Edit menu. In the Precedence Constraint Editor, change the Evaluation Operation to Expression. Set the Expression to "@MyRowCount>0" (Figure 21-3).

Figure 21-3

8. Now execute the package. A successful run should look like Figure 21-4. The Script Task should not change to green because there are no rows in the ErrorLog table.

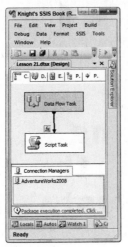

Figure 21-4

 Please select Lesson 21 on the DVD to view the video that accompanies this lesson.

22

Combining Multiple Inputs with the Union All Transform

The Union All Transform combines multiple inputs in the Data Flow into a single output rowset. It is very similar to the Merge Transform, but does not require the input data to be sorted. For example, in Figure 22-1, three different transforms are combined into a single output using the Union All Transform. The transformation inputs are added to the output one after the other; thus, no rows are reordered.

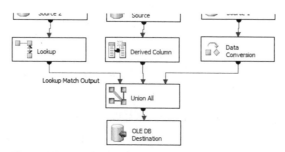

Figure 22-1

To configure this transform, bring the green precedence constraints from the sources or transformations you want to combine to the Union All Transform. SSIS automatically maps the columns if they have the same name, but if you want to verify the columns are correctly mapped, open the Union All Transformation Editor. The only time you really must open the Union All Transformation Editor is if the column names from the different inputs do not match. During development if upstream components get tweaked or something else changes to disrupt the column mappings of the Union All Transform, those mappings will have to be fixed manually.

The transform fixes minor metadata issues. For example, if you have one input that is a 20-character string and a different one that is 50 characters, the output of this from the Union All Transform will be the longer 50-character column. Occasionally though, when you make changes above the transform, you might see red on the Union All Transform indicating an error. In these cases, it's faster to delete the transform and re-add it than it is to spend time debugging the error.

The Union All Transform can be used as a temporary destination while you are developing to test your package. This practice allows you to test the rest of your package without landing data.

Try It

In this lesson, your company needs you to create a package that has three different sources but places the data into one flat file. After this lesson, you will know how to combine data from different sources and place that data in one flat file destination.

Lesson Requirements

Create a new package named Lesson22 and make the following changes, or download the completed Lesson22.dtsx from www.wrox.com:

❑ Use the following tables from the AdventureWorksDW2008 database:

   ❑ FactInternetSales

   ❑ FactResellerSales

❑ Combine these columns from each table:

   ❑ ProductKey

   ❑ SalesAmount

❑ After the data is combined, export it to a flat file

Hints

❑ You need two OLE DB Sources: one for FactInternetSales and one for FactResellerSales

❑ Use a Union All Transform to combine the previously mentioned columns

❑ Send the results of the package to a Flat File Destination

Step-by-Step

1. Create an SSIS package named Lesson22 or download the completed Lesson22.dtsx from www.wrox.com. Add a Data Flow Task to the Control Flow design surface.

2. In the Control Flow tab, add a new Data Flow Task to the design surface and name it "DF - Union All Sales."

3. Create a new OLE DB Connection Manager using the AdventureWorksDW2008 database as the source. Then drag two OLE DB Sources on the designer and rename them "Reseller Sales" and "Internet Sales."

4. In the Internet Sales Source select SQL Command as the Data Access Mode and enter the following query:

```
Select ProductKey,SalesAmount
From FactInternetSales
```

5. In the Reseller Sales Source select SQL Command as the Data Access Mode and enter the following query:

```
Select ProductKey, SalesAmount
From FactResellerSales
```

6. Drag a Union All Transform and connect both green arrows from the sources to it. Verify that the columns mapped correctly by opening the Union All Transformation Editor (Figure 22-2).

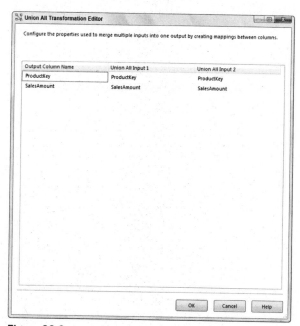

Figure 22-2

7. Now bring a Flat File Destination to the design surface and connect the Union All Transform to it. Then name the destination Sales Export.

8. Open the Flat File Destination and select New to create a delimited Flat File Connection Manager.

9. Name the Flat File Connection Manager "Flat File Sales Export." Then call the file SalesExport.txt, and select C:\Projects\SSISPersonalTrainer as the location for it. Also, check the "Column names in the first data row" option.

10. The package is now complete. When the package is executed, your results will look like Figure 22-3.

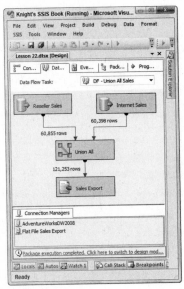

Figure 22-3

 Please select Lesson 22 on the DVD to view the video that accompanies this lesson.

23

Cleansing Data with the Script Component

Sometimes you can't accomplish your data cleansing goal in a Derived Column Transform, and you must get more advanced. Say, for example, you want to run a routine where any character data is removed from the data or if the data coming in is not a date, perhaps you replace it with today's date. In these examples, you can use a Script Component in the Data Flow Task. The Script Component can play three roles: a transform, source, or destination.

❑ Generally, the focus of your Data Flow will be on using the script as a transform. In this role, you can use it to perform advanced cleansing that can be done with the out-of-the-box components

❑ When the script is used as a source, you can apply advanced business rules to your data as it's being pulled out of the source system. This happens sometimes with Cobol files

❑ Lastly, when the script is used as a destination, you can use the script to write out to a non-OLE DB destination like XML or SharePoint

Your script can be written in VB.NET or C#, but once you select a language, you can't change it. You can select the language by double-clicking on the Script Component and going to the Script page of the Script Transformation Editor (shown in Figure 23-1). You can also select any variables you want to pass into the script in this page. Make sure to select the variable for ReadWrite only if the variable is needed to be written to. Otherwise, the variable might be locked for the duration of the script's execution.

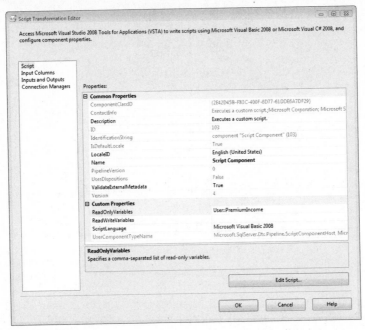

Figure 23-1

In the InputColumns page (Figure 23-2), select each column that you want to be passed into the script from the Data Flow and if you want to allow them to be accessed for writing. If you don't need the column for writing, make sure it's set to ReadOnly, because ReadWrite columns require more resources. All columns that are not checked are passed through to the next transform or destination seamlessly.

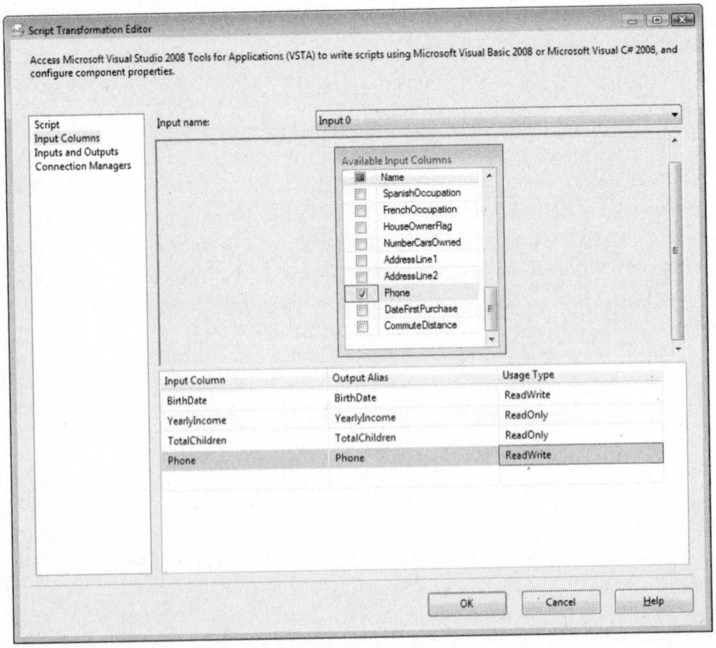

Figure 23-2

You can also add more columns that are not part of the source or a previous transform in the Input and Outputs page. This page additionally lets you add other buckets of data that you can use to direct the data down multiple paths. To do this, you must first create an additional output by clicking New Output. Then you need to set the SynchronousInputID property to the same number for each output. Then, you need to set the ExclusionGroup to the same non-zero number. In the script, you can then use the DirectRowTo<outputbuffername> method to send the data to each of the paths. Because this is in the script, the data can be sent to multiple paths at the same time.

To edit the script, go to the Script page and click Edit Script. This opens the Visual Studio environment. Three subroutines are the most important to your design: PreExecute, PostExecute, and ProcessInputRow:

❑ PreExecute executes once per transform execution and is a great place to initialize objects or connections that you hope to later use

❑ PostExecute is where you can close connections and objects or set variables

❑ ProcessInputRow is run for every row going through the transform, and from this subroutine, you cannot set variables

Accessing a row is simple from the ProcessInputRow subroutine. To do so, you must use the Row object, which contains an individual row as it is looping. For example, to read rows coming into the transform like BRIAN KNIGHT and translate that to a proper-cased value like Brian Knight, use the following code, where ColumnName holds the customer name. The StrConv is a string conversion function to convert a string to a new format.

```
Public Overrides Sub Input0_ProcessInputRow(ByVal Row As Input0Buffer)
  'This is the line that performs the magic to Proper Case.
  Row.ColumnName = StrConv(Row.ColumnName, VbStrConv.ProperCase)
    End Sub
```

Variables can be read from any subroutine, but you will only be able to write to them in the PostExecute subroutine. To read or write to a variable, you can use a Me.Variables statement as shown in the following:

```
Row.YearlyIncome = Row.YearlyIncome + Me.Variables.PremiumIncome
```

Though breakpoints were allowed in the Script Task, they are not allowed in the Data Flow. Because of this fact, you have to use more arcane debug techniques like message boxes to notify you of which step the engine is at in the code.

Try It

In this lesson, you have recently begun to receive data from an entity that has issues occasionally with date data. The source application allows users to enter whatever they'd like for the birth date so occasionally you receive invalid characters in the date or invalid dates. After completing this lesson, you'll have a better idea of how to use the Script Component to perform more complex cleansing or checking of your data.

Lesson Requirements

You can find the Lesson23Data.txt source file on the Wrox website (www.wrox.com). In this lesson, you need to check dates of the BirthDate column as each row is read into the script and send the data to one of two buckets: ValidatedData or BadData. Additionally, if the DateFirstPurchase column is anything but a date, change the row to today's date as a default. Normally, you would send the data in the BadData bucket to another business rule to cleanse it further or to an auditing table. However, the point of this lesson is not to write the data to a destination table, so if you'd like, you can just send the data to two Union All Transforms to simulate two data streams.

Hints

- ❏ The IsDate() function can determine if a column is in a date
- ❏ You will want to create two buckets in the Input and Outputs page
- ❏ Make sure the SynchronousInputID column is set to the same input and the ExclusionGroup property is set to 1 for each of the outputs

Step-by-Step

1. Create a new package called Lesson23.dtsx (or download the completed Lesson23.dtsx from www.wrox.com).

2. Create a connection to the file that you downloaded off the Wrox website called Lesson23Data.txt.

3. Create a new Flat File Connection Manager called "Extract" (creating connection managers is covered in Lesson 6) and point to the Lesson23Data.txt file. In the General page, check the "Column names in the first data row" and ensure that the EmailAddress column in the Flat File Connection Manager is set to 100 characters in the Advanced page.

4. Create a Data Flow Task and in the Data Flow tab, create a Flat File Source that points to the new connection manager called Extract you just created.

5. Drag a Script Component onto the design pane. You will immediately be prompted for what type of script you wish to use (source, transform, destination). Select Transformation for the type, and connect the transform to the Flat File Source.

6. In the Script Transform Editor, select the Input Columns page and check BirthDate and DateFirstPurchase. Ensure that DateFirstPurchase is set to ReadWrite.

7. Go to the Input and Outputs page and highlight the Output 0 Buffer and click Remove Output. Then click Add Output twice. Rename the first output you just created to BadData and the second to ValidatedData. For both of the outputs set the SynchronousInputID to the same input buffer and set the ExclusionGroup property to 1, as shown in Figure 23-3.

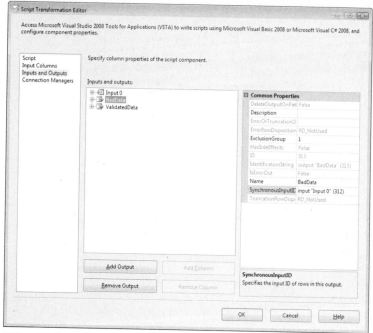

Figure 23-3

8. Go to the Script page, select VB.NET, and click Edit Script. Then add the following script in the ProcessInputRow subroutine (note that the subroutine will already exist in your code block).

```vb
Public Overrides Sub Input0_ProcessInputRow(ByVal Row As Input0Buffer)

    If IsDate(Row.DateFirstPurchase) = False Then
        Row.DateFirstPurchase = Now
    End If

    If IsDate(Row.BirthDate) = True Then
        Row.DirectRowToValidatedData()
    Else
        Row.DirectRowToBadData()

    End If
End Sub
```

9. Close the script after ensuring there is nothing underlined (showing bad code) and return to the designer.

10. Drag two Union All Transforms onto the design pane and connect the Script Transform to each of the Union All Transforms.

11. Execute the package, and you should see five bad rows go down the BadData path as shown in Figure 23-4.

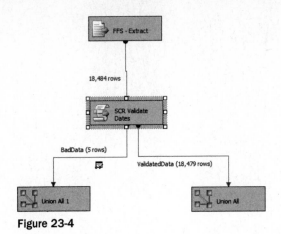

Figure 23-4

 Please select Lesson 23 on the DVD to view the video that accompanies this lesson.

Separating Data with the Conditional Split Transform

Sometimes you deal with source data that may require different treatments applied to it. For example, you want to generate a mailing list for a direct mail campaign, but you want to target only customers with children. You want to make sure to separate the customers without kids before preparing the list. You would also like anyone who has more than five kids to receive a buy-two-get-one-free coupon with the mailer.

The best way to separate data within a package to apply different types of actions is with the Conditional Split Transform. With this transform you can send data from a single data path to multiple outputs based on conditions set in the Conditional Split Transformation Editor, shown in Figure 24-1. To open the editor drag the transform in the design surface and double-click it.

The Conditional Split Transform uses the SSIS expression language to determine how the data pipeline should be split. If you need a reminder on how the SSIS expression language works, refer back to Lesson 17 where we cover it in more detail. For this example just know that the Conditional Split Transform is checking to see if customers have more than five kids so they can receive the extra coupon. This check will produce three possible outputs:

- ❏ For customers with more than five children
- ❏ For customers with between one and four children
- ❏ For customers with no children

It may look like there are only two outputs but if you look on the bottom of the Conditional Split Transformation Editor the Default Output Name provides an output for data that doesn't apply to the conditions declared. In the case of this package, you need only those customers with at least one child so you will see them in the final package (shown in Figure 24-2). You do not need to use the output for customers with no children.

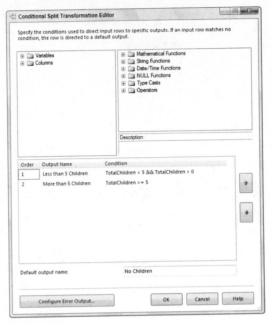

Figure 24-1

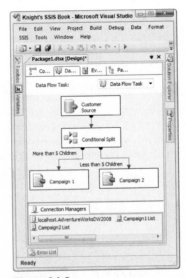

Figure 24-2

Try It

In this lesson, your company needs a list of customers for a direct mail campaign that is only going to be sent regionally. You need to create an SSIS package that generates two different mailing lists because one region is going to receive a different promotion than the other. After completing this lesson you will know how to split data within a package based on set conditions using the Conditional Split Transform.

Lesson Requirements

Create a new package named Lesson24 and make the following changes. You can also find the completed Lesson24.dtsx at www.wrox.com:

❑ Use the following tables from AdventureWorksDW2008 database:

    ❑ DimCustomer

    ❑ DimGeography

❑ Bring back the following columns from DimCustomer:

    ❑ Title

    ❑ FirstName

    ❑ MiddleName

    ❑ LastName

    ❑ EmailAddress

    ❑ AddressLine1

    ❑ AddressLine2

    ❑ Phone

❑ Using the GeographyKey use any method to join the DimCustomer and DimGeography tables together and bring back the following columns from DimGeography:

    ❑ StateProvinceCode

    ❑ PostalCode

❑ Create a Conditional Split with these conditions:

    ❑ **Campaign 1** — StateProvinceCode == "FL" || StateProvinceCode == "GA"

    ❑ **Campaign 2** — StateProvinceCode == "CA" || StateProvinceCode == "WA"

❑ Send these two outputs to two separate flat files to create the regional mailing lists

Hints

❑ In the Data Flow you need only one OLE DB Source to bring in customer data

❑ A Lookup Transform is needed to join geography data to each customer

❑ Use a Conditional Split Transform to separate the different state codes

❑ You need two separate Flat File Destinations for the results

Step-by-Step

1. Create an SSIS package named Lesson24 or download Lesson24.dtsx from `www.wrox.com`. Add a Data Flow Task named "DF - Regional Mailing List" to the Control Flow design surface.

2. Create a new OLE DB Connection Manager using the AdventureWorksDW2008 database as the source. Then drag an OLE DB Source on the designer and rename it "Customer Source."

3. In the Customer Source select AdventureWorksDW2008 as the connection manager and SQL Command as the Data Access Mode.

4. Enter the following query in the Data Access Mode window:

```
Select FirstName,
MiddleName,
LastName,
AddressLine1,
AddressLine2,
EmailAddress,
Phone,
GeographyKey
From DimCustomer
```

5. Drag a Lookup Transform on to the design pane and name it "Geography LKP." Open the Lookup Transformation Editor and select AdventureWorksDW2008 as the connection manager.

6. Next, select Use Results of a SQL Query and use the following query:

```
SELECT GeographyKey, StateProvinceCode
FROM DimGeography
```

7. Go to the Columns tab to add the StateProvinceCode to the data stream shown in Figure 24-3.

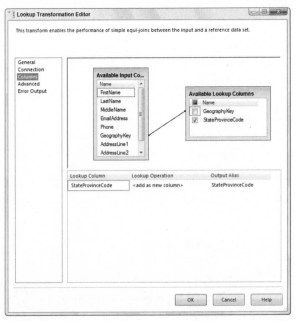

Figure 24-3

8. Now bring a Conditional Split Transform to the design surface and connect it to the Lookup Transform.

9. Open the Conditional Split Transformation Editor. Add a new output in the Conditional Split Transformation Editor called Campaign1, and then add the following condition:

```
StateProvinceCode == "FL" || StateProvinceCode == "GA"
```

10. Add a second output named Campaign2 with the following condition:

```
StateProvinceCode == "CA" || StateProvinceCode == "WA"
```

11. Make "No Ad Campaign" the Default Output Name and click OK. After making these changes the editor should look like Figure 24-4.

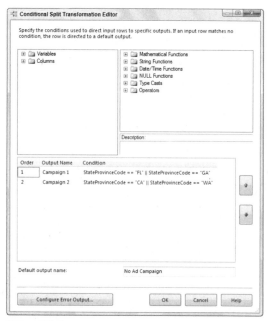

Figure 24-4

12. Bring two Flat File Destinations into the Data Flow and name them "Campaign1 Mailing List" and "Campaign2 Mailing List." Create separate connection managers for them pointing to the file location of your choice.

13. The Conditional Split will have three green output arrows. When you connect the first green arrow to one of the two destinations a dialog box opens asking which output you want. Connect each output to the destination that has the name associated with it. This action leaves one output unused: "No Ad Campaign."

14. Open each Flat File Destination to make sure the mapping is set correctly.

15. The package is now complete. When the package is executed, your results will look like Figure 24-5.

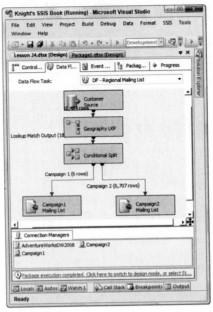

Figure 24-5

 Please select Lesson 24 on the DVD to view the video that accompanies this lesson.

Altering Rows with the OLE DB Command Transform

The OLE DB Command Transform is used to run a SQL statement for each row in the Data Flow. It sounds innocent enough, doesn't it? The reality is that the statement "for each row" should immediately make alarms go off in your head. This involves kicking off an update, insert, or delete statement for each row in an input stream.

To put this into perspective, imagine you are loading a product dimension table in your ETL process. Your predecessor decided it would be best to update and delete these rows using an OLE DB Command. The company you work for is a major department store, and the new spring clothing line is coming in. So, all the winter clothes are being marked down. This means you are going to get an update with a price reduction for all the winter clothes your company has in inventory at one time. Using the OLE DB Command Transform would mean that your package would be running several thousand update statements and your package would run for hours. A situation like that one is why we recommend you avoid using the OLE DB Command Transform.

So if we recommend not using the OLE DB Command Transform, what are your options? The best practice would be to insert all rows marked as updates into a staging table and then in the Control Flow use an Execute SQL Task to update the destination table. Why is this better than using the OLE DB Command Transform? The Execute SQL Task performs this operation in bulk versus the several thousand update statements required in the OLE DB Command Transform. This method is explained in greater detail in Lesson 47 on loading a dimension table.

This doesn't mean you should never use this transform, but it is important to understand its shortcomings when working with large amounts of data.

To use the OLE DB Command Transform drag it from the Toolbox to the Data Flow design surface and double-click it. The configuration looks more complicated than it really is. From the Connection Managers tab specify which OLE DB Connection you want to execute the SQL statement on. Figure 25-1 shows the AdventureWorks2008 database as the connection manager.

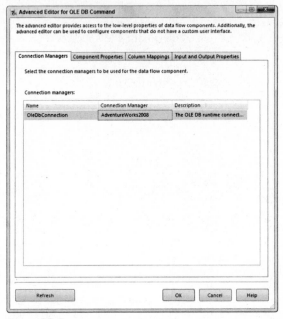

Figure 25-1

The SQL statement you plan to execute will be set on the Component Properties tab. To enter your SQL statement, click the ellipsis next to the SqlCommand property. Remember that to tell SSIS that you are going to be using parameters in a SQL statement you use a question mark (?).

You can also configure the amount of time before a timeout occurs in the CommandTimeout property, shown in Figure 25-2. This uses an interval of seconds where 0 denotes no timeout.

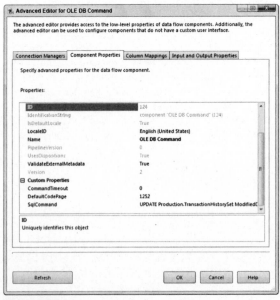

Figure 25-2

The Column Mappings tab in the Advanced Editor for OLE DB Command window is similar to the Mappings page in a destination editor. (Configuring destinations is discussed in more detail in Lesson 15.) It displays the input stream and destination columns, which are really the parameters indicated in the SqlCommand property. Any input column mapped to a parameter replaces the parameter with the value of that field. When you are mapping, remember that the order in which you place the parameters while writing the SQL statement is also the order in which they must be mapped. In Figure 25-3 you see how to map the following Update statement:

```
Update Production.TransactionHistory
Set ModifiedDate = ?
Where ProductID = ?
```

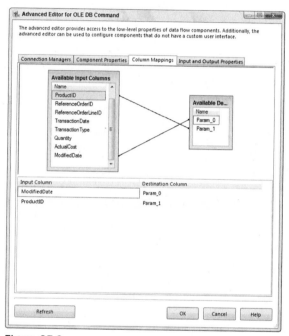

Figure 25-3

The last tab is the Input and Output Properties tab, which you will likely not have to ever change. It simply provides another place where you can add or remove columns that are used in the transform.

Try It

In this lesson, you work for a company that sells dartboard supplies. As new supplies are added to your inventory, some of the older products are being discounted. Use the flat file extract provided and update the price on all required products. After completing this lesson you will know how to use the OLE DB Command Transform to alter data with a SQL statement inside the Data Flow.

The small package created in this example is meant only to show the capabilities of the OLE DB Command Transform. Our recommendations stated earlier in the lesson for why you might want to avoid using the OLE DB Command Transform for these sorts of situations still stand.

Lesson Requirements

Create a table in the AdventureWorks2008 database named Product_OLEDBCommand. You can find the code to create this table in the download for this lesson available at www.wrox.com.

Download the flat file named OLEDBCommandExample.txt from www.wrox.com to use as your source. Save this file to the C:\Projects\SSISPersonalTrainer directory.

Update the current flag and row end date columns in the Product_OLEDBCommand table and then create new rows in the table representing the new list price.

Hints

❑   Use the OLD DB Command Transform to update only two columns

❑   After updating these fields, send the rest of the input stream to a regular OLE DB Destination to insert new records with the new list price

Step-by-Step

1.   Create a new package and name it Lesson25 or download the completed Lesson25.dtsx package from www.wrox.com.

2.   Drag a Data Flow Task onto your designer and name it "DFT - OLE DB Command."

3.   Create a new Flat File Connection Manager, name it "Product Price Change," and point it to C:\Projects\SSISPersonalTrainer\OLEDBCommandExample.txt. Also, check the "Column names in the first data row" option. The editor should look like Figure 25-4.

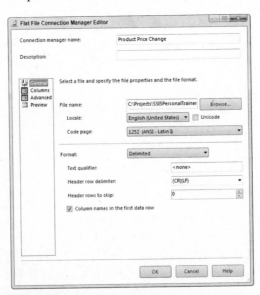

Figure 25-4

4. In the Data Flow bring a new Flat File Source over and name it "Discounted Products." Open the editor and make the connection manager the newly created Product Price Change.

5. Open Management Studio and run the following query to create a new table called Product_OLEDBCommand (you can download the query from www.wrox.com):

```
CREATE TABLE [dbo].[Product_OLEDBCommand](
    [ProductID] [smallint] IDENTITY(1,1) NOT NULL,
    [ProductBusinessKey] int,
    [ProductName] [varchar](50) NOT NULL,
    [ListPrice] [money],
    [CurrentFlag] [smallint],
    [RowStartDate] [datetime],
    [RowEndDate] [datetime]
 CONSTRAINT [PK_Product_OLEDBCommand_ProductID] PRIMARY KEY CLUSTERED
(
        [ProductID] ASC
) ON [PRIMARY]
) ON [PRIMARY]

GO
INSERT INTO [dbo].[Product_OLEDBCommand] Select 101,
    'Professional Dartboard','49.99','1','1/1/2006',Null
INSERT INTO [dbo].[Product_OLEDBCommand] Select 102,
    'Professional Darts',15.99,1,'1/1/2006',Null
INSERT INTO [dbo].[Product_OLEDBCommand] Select 103,
    'Scoreboard',26.99,1,'1/1/2006',Null
INSERT INTO [dbo].[Product_OLEDBCommand] Select 104,
    'Beginner Dartboard',45.99,1,'1/1/2006',Null
INSERT INTO [dbo].[Product_OLEDBCommand] Select 105,
    'Dart Tips',1.99,1,'1/1/2006',Null
INSERT INTO [dbo].[Product_OLEDBCommand] Select 106,
    'Dart Shafts',7.99,1,'1/1/2006',Null
```

6. Next, create another connection manager, this time an OLE DB Connection Manager using the AdventureWorks2008 database.

7. Bring an OLE DB Command Transform onto the design surface, connect it to Discounted Products, and after opening the transform's editor, select AdventureWorks2008 as the connection manager on the Connection Managers tab.

8. Enter the following SQL statement in the SqlCommand property on the Component Properties tab, shown in Figure 25-5:

```
Update Product_OLEDBCommand
Set CurrentFlag = 0,
    RowEndDate = GETDATE()
Where ProductBusinessKey = ?
and RowEndDate is null
```

This statement means that for every ProductBusinessKey you have, the CurrentFlag will be set to 0, and the RowEndDate will be given today's date.

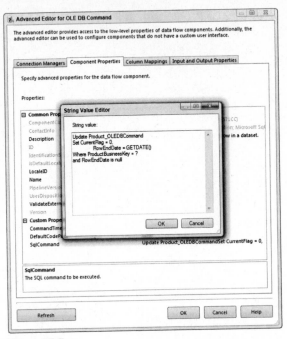

Figure 25-5

9. Next, on the Columns Mapping tab you need to connect ProductBusinessKey from the Input Columns to Param_0 in the destination. Figure 25-6 shows there is only one parameter in this statement, so there is only one destination column.

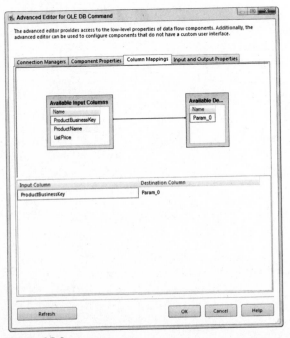

Figure 25-6

10. Now bring a Derived Column Transform to the Data Flow and connect the source to it. Open the Derived Column Transform Editor and add two new columns called RowStartDate and Current-Flag. For the RowStartDate column use the GETDATE() function in the Expression field, and CurrentFlag just needs 1 in the Expression box. The Derived Column Transform Editor should look like Figure 25-7. Click OK.

Figure 25-7

11. To finish this package you need to load the new rows' results into the Product_OLEDBCommand table. Bring an OLE DB Destination onto the design surface and from within the editor select Product_OLEDBCommand as the destination table.

12. Go to the Mappings page of the OLE DB Destination Editor, and you notice all the columns are automatically mapped except for RowEndDate, which is set in the OLE DB Command Transform. Figure 25-8 shows how the final mapped columns should look.

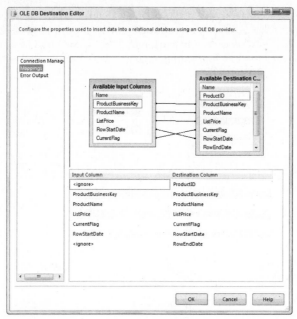

Figure 25-8

13. A successful run of this package should look like Figure 25-9.

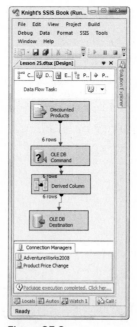

Figure 25-9

14. Take a look at the table in Figure 25-10 to see the results of a completed package. Notice the package created a new row for each product with the new price. It also closed the old row by updating the row's end date and the current flag. This is what's known as a Type 2 change in a dimension table. To learn more about data warehousing best practices read Lessons 47 and 48.

	ProductID	ProductBu...	ProductName	ListPrice	CurrentFl...	RowStartDate	RowEndDate
1	1	101	Professional Dartboard	49.99	0	2006-01-01 00:00:00.000	2009-02-21 19:45:27.910
2	2	102	Professional Darts	15.99	0	2006-01-01 00:00:00.000	2009-02-21 19:45:27.927
3	3	103	Scoreboard	26.99	0	2006-01-01 00:00:00.000	2009-02-21 19:45:27.927
4	4	104	Beginner Dartboard	45.99	0	2006-01-01 00:00:00.000	2009-02-21 19:45:27.927
5	5	105	Dart Tips	1.99	0	2006-01-01 00:00:00.000	2009-02-21 19:45:27.927
6	6	106	Dart Shafts	7.99	0	2006-01-01 00:00:00.000	2009-02-21 19:45:27.927
7	7	101	Professional Dartboard	44.99	1	2009-02-21 19:45:27.920	NULL
8	8	102	Professional Darts	11.99	1	2009-02-21 19:45:27.920	NULL
9	9	103	Scoreboard	17.99	1	2009-02-21 19:45:27.920	NULL
10	10	104	Beginner Dartboard	38.99	1	2009-02-21 19:45:27.920	NULL
11	11	105	Dart Tips	1.09	1	2009-02-21 19:45:27.920	NULL
12	12	106	Dart Shafts	4.99	1	2009-02-21 19:45:27.920	NULL

Figure 25-10

Please select Lesson 25 on the DVD to view the video that accompanies this lesson.

Handling Bad Data with the Fuzzy Lookup Transform

More often than not when you are working in the real world, data is not going to be perfect like it is in the AdventureWorks database. Real-world situations call for cleansing dirty data or data that has abnormalities like misspellings and truncation.

Imagine you are attempting to retrieve a foreign key from a dimension table, but strangely you find rows without a match. Upon investigation you find bad data is being supplied to you. One technique might be to divert these rows without matches to a table to be dealt with later, or another might be just to add the bad data regardless of misspellings and other mishaps that occur during data entry.

The Fuzzy Lookup Transform, discussed in this lesson, and Fuzzy Grouping Transform, discussed in the next lesson, give another alternative to dealing with dirty data while reducing your number of unmatched rows. The Fuzzy Lookup Transform matches input records with data that has already been cleansed in a reference table. It returns the match and can also indicate the quality of the match. This way you know the likelihood of the match being correct.

> *A best practice tip is to use the Fuzzy Lookup Transform only after trying a regular lookup on the field. The Fuzzy Lookup Transform is a very expensive operation that builds specialized indexes of the input stream and the reference data for comparison intentions. Therefore, it is recommended to first use a regular Lookup Transform and then divert only those rows not matching to the Fuzzy Lookup Transform.*

During the configuration of the transform you must specify a reference table that will be used for comparison. Figure 26-1 shows the reference table selection being made in the Fuzzy Lookup Transformation Editor. The transform uses this reference data and builds a token-based index, which despite its name is actually a table, before it begins the process of comparing entries.

Figure 26-1

Using the Fuzzy Lookup Transform requires at least one field to be a string, either a DT_WSTR or DT_STR data type. On the Columns tab in the editor you need to map at least one text field from the input to the reference table for comparison.

The Advanced tab contains the settings that control the fuzzy logic algorithms. You can set the maximum number of matches to output per incoming row. The default is set to 1, which means pull the best record out of the reference table if it meets the similarity threshold. Incrementing this setting higher than the default might generate more results that you'll have to sift through, but it might be required if there are too many closely matching strings in your data. A slider controls the similarity threshold. When you are experimenting, a good strategy is to start this setting at 0.5 and move up or down as you review the results. This setting is normally decided based on a businessperson's review of the data, not the developer's review. If a row cannot be found that's similar enough, the columns that you checked in the Columns tab will be set to NULL. The token delimiters can also be set if, for example, you don't want the comparison process to break up incoming strings by a period (.) or spaces. The default for this setting is all common delimiters. See Figure 26-2 for an example of an Advanced tab.

Figure 26-2

The transform will create several output columns that you may or may not decide are useful to store in a table. Either way they are important to understand:

❑ **Input and Pass-Through Field Names and Values** — This column contains the name and value of the text input provided to the Fuzzy Lookup Transform or passed through during the lookup

❑ **Reference Field Name and Value** — This column contains the name and value(s) of the matched results from the reference table

❑ **Similarity** — This column contains a number between 0 and 1 representing similarity. Similarity is a threshold that you set when configuring the Fuzzy Lookup Transform. The closer this number is to 1, the closer the two text fields must match

❑ **Confidence** — This column contains a number between 0 and 1 representing confidence of the match relative to the set of matched results. Confidence is different from similarity, because it is not calculated by examining just one word against another but rather by comparing the chosen word match against all the other possible matches. Confidence gets better the more accurately your reference data represents your subject domain, and it can change based on the sample of the data coming into the ETL process

You may not want to use each of these fields, but it is important to appreciate the value they could provide.

Try It

In this lesson, you are going to use the Fuzzy Lookup Transform to attempt to correct some bad data that you receive in a flat file. After this lesson, you should have an idea how useful the Fuzzy Lookup Transform can be in cleansing your data.

Lesson Requirements

Create a table in the AdventureWorks2008 database named Occupation using the following code (which you can find as part of this lesson's download on the book's website at www.wrox.com):

```
CREATE TABLE [dbo].[Occupation](
    [OccupationID] [smallint] IDENTITY(1,1) NOT NULL,
    [OccupationLabel] [varchar](50) NOT NULL,
 CONSTRAINT [PK_Occupation_OccupationID] PRIMARY KEY CLUSTERED
(
    [OccupationID] ASC
) ON [PRIMARY]
) ON [PRIMARY]

GO
INSERT INTO [dbo].[Occupation] Select 'CUSTOMER SERVICE REPRESENTATIVE'
INSERT INTO [dbo].[Occupation] Select 'SHIFT LEADER'
INSERT INTO [dbo].[Occupation] Select 'ASSISTANT MANAGER'
INSERT INTO [dbo].[Occupation] Select 'STORE MANAGER'
INSERT INTO [dbo].[Occupation] Select 'DISTRICT MANAGER'
INSERT INTO [dbo].[Occupation] Select 'REGIONAL MANAGER'
```

Download the flat file named FuzzyExample.txt from www.wrox.com to use as your source. Save this file to the C:\Projects\SSISPersonalTrainer directory. Correct the bad data from this flat file and insert it to a new table called EmployeeRoster.

Hints

❑   Remember the best practice tip mentioned earlier in this lesson and first attempt to use a regular lookup before attempting the fuzzy lookup to catch the bad data

Step-by-Step

1. Create a new package and name it Lesson26 or download the completed Lesson26.dtsx package from www.wrox.com.

2. Drag a Data Flow Task onto your designer and name it "DFT - Fuzzy Lookup."

3. Create a new Flat File Connection Manager (creating connection managers is discussed in Lesson 6), name it "New Employee," and point it to C:\Projects\SSISPersonalTrainer\ FuzzyExample.txt. Also, check the "Column names in the first data row" option. The editor should look like Figure 26-3.

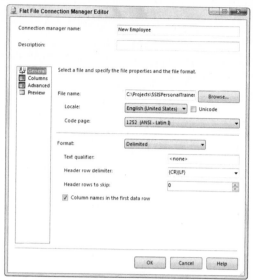

Figure 26-3

4. In the Data Flow bring a new Flat File Source over and name it "New Employee Load." Open the editor and make the connection manager the newly created New Employee.

5. On the Columns tab change the name of the output columns to LastName, FirstName, and OccupationLabel.

6. Open Management Studio and run the following query to create a new table called Occupation (you can download the query from www.wrox.com):

```
USE AdventureWorks2008
CREATE TABLE [dbo].[Occupation](
    [OccupationID] [smallint] IDENTITY(1,1) NOT NULL,
    [OccupationLabel] [varchar](50) NOT NULL,
 CONSTRAINT [PK_Occupation_OccupationID] PRIMARY KEY CLUSTERED
(
    [OccupationID] ASC
) ON [PRIMARY]
) ON [PRIMARY]

GO
INSERT INTO [dbo].[Occupation] Select 'CUSTOMER SERVICE REPRESENTATIVE'
INSERT INTO [dbo].[Occupation] Select 'SHIFT LEADER'
INSERT INTO [dbo].[Occupation] Select 'ASSISTANT MANAGER'
INSERT INTO [dbo].[Occupation] Select 'STORE MANAGER'
INSERT INTO [dbo].[Occupation] Select 'DISTRICT MANAGER'
INSERT INTO [dbo].[Occupation] Select 'REGIONAL MANAGER'
```

7. Next, create another connection manager, this time an OLE DB Connection Manager using the AdventureWorks2008 database.

8. Bring a Lookup Transform on the design surface and use the new Occupation table to bring back the OccupationID based on the OccupationLabel that exists in both the source and the reference table. (Refer back to the Lesson 20 if you need help with a regular lookup.) Figure 26-4 shows what your mapping should look like. Lastly, before closing the editor make sure to specify in the General tab that non-matching entries should redirect rows to no match output.

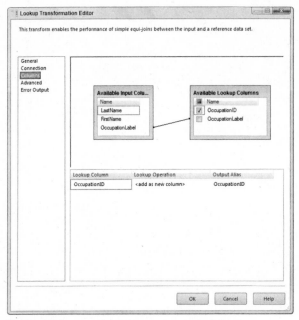

Figure 26-4

9. You already know from the lesson description that the source data is dirty, so now you're going to use a Fuzzy Lookup Transform to catch all the bad data the regular lookup doesn't recognize. Drag a new Fuzzy Lookup Transform in the Data Flow and connect the green lookup no match output arrow from the Lookup Transform to it.

10. Figure 26-5 shows the Fuzzy Lookup Transformation Editor using the Occupation table as the reference table.

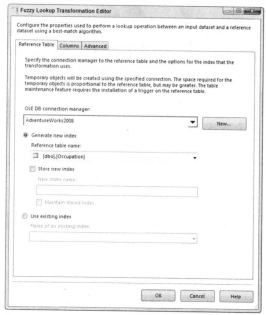

Figure 26-5

11. The Columns tab should be joined by OccupationLabel as shown in Figure 26-6. It should also return the OccupationID and OccupationLabel from the reference table, which you can ensure by checking the boxes in the Available Lookup Columns box. The OccupationLabel from the reference table should replace the same column from the input stream to correct bad data. To do this, uncheck the OccupationLabel column from the Available Input Columns.

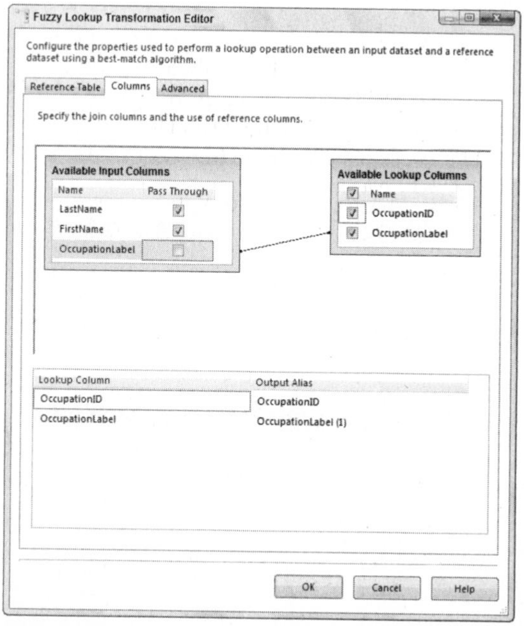

Figure 26-6

12. Next, in the Advanced tab you leave the Similarity threshold the default setting and change the token delimiters to use only a period in the Additional Delimiters box, as reflected in Figure 26-7.

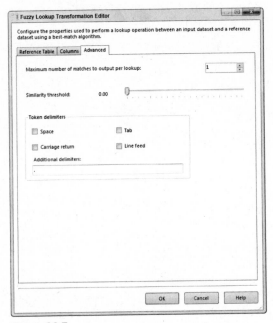

Figure 26-7

13. To bring together the data from both the lookup transforms drag a Union All over and connect the two lookups to it. First connect the green arrow from the Fuzzy Lookup Transform and then connect the green arrow from the regular Lookup Transform. Then open the Union All Transformation Editor and delete the unneeded columns by right-clicking and selecting Delete on the columns that are not pictured in Figure 26-8. You may also need to rename the output of OccupationLabel to not include (1) in the name.

Figure 26-8

14. To finish off this package you need to load the results into a new table. Bring an OLE DB Destination onto the design surface and from within the editor select New to create a new table. Use the following code to create the EmployeeRoster table or download the code from www.wrox.com:

```
CREATE TABLE [EmployeeRoster] (
    [EmployeeID] [smallint] IDENTITY(1,1) NOT NULL,
    [LastName] varchar(50),
    [FirstName] varchar(50),
    [OccupationID] smallint,
    [OccupationLabel] varchar(50)
)
```

15. Once the mapping has been set in the destination, click OK and your package is complete. A successful run of this package should look like Figure 26-9. Compare the EmployeeRoster table to the original flat file you started with, and you will see the fuzzy lookup using the reference table corrected 10 rows of dirty data.

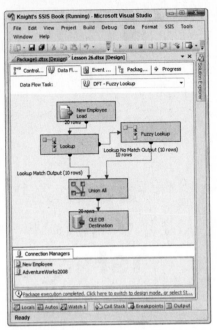

Figure 26-9

 Please select Lesson 26 on the DVD to view the video that accompanies this lesson.

Removing Duplicates with the Fuzzy Grouping Transform

In the previous lesson you saw how to prevent bad data from being loaded in your dimension tables with the Fuzzy Lookup Transform, but what if the bad data is already in your table or if you are just beginning to build your data warehouse?

In these circumstances you can use the Fuzzy Grouping Transform to examine the contents of suspect fields and provide groupings of similar words. The matching information provided by this transform can be used to clean up the table and eliminate redundancy.

The Fuzzy Grouping Transform uses the same logic as the Fuzzy Lookup Transform and therefore requires many of the same things. It must have a connection to an OLE DB Connection Manager to generate temporary tables that the transform uses in its algorithm. At development time the Connection Manager tab is where you make this setting.

Also just as was the case with the Fuzzy Lookup Transform, this transform expects an input stream with a string, either a DT_WSTR or DT_STR data type. The Columns tab of the Fuzzy Grouping Transform Editor (which you open by double-clicking the transform), shown in Figure 27-1, is where you select the string field that you want to be analyzed and grouped into logical matches. Notice in the top part of the Columns tab that each column can also be selected to Pass Through, which means the data is not analyzed, but is accessible in the output stream. If you move down to the bottom part of the Columns tab, you see a table of options for each input column. You can choose the names of any of the output columns: Group Output Alias, Output Alias, and Similarity Output Alias. Often the only column you want from this group is the Group Output Alias. If you select more than one column to be analyzed, the minimum similarity evaluation is configurable at the column level.

The Numerals option allows for configuration of the numbers in the input stream when grouping text logically. This may be necessary when comparing an address field because more than likely it will have leading numerals. For example, 834 West Elm Street has leading numerals.

Comparison flags provide the options to ignore or pay attention to case, kana type, nonspacing characters, character width, symbols, and punctuation.

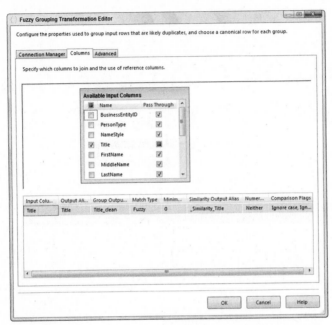

Figure 27-1

The Advanced tab is where you see some of the familiar configurations you saw in the Fuzzy Lookup Transform that control the logic algorithm used. A slider controls the similarity threshold. It is recommended you start this at 0.5 to test and move the slider up or down until you get the results you are looking for. This setting is normally decided based on a business person's review of the data, not the developer's review. The token delimiters can also be set if, for example, you don't want the comparison process to break up incoming strings by a period (.) or spaces. Figure 27-2 shows the default settings for the Advanced tab.

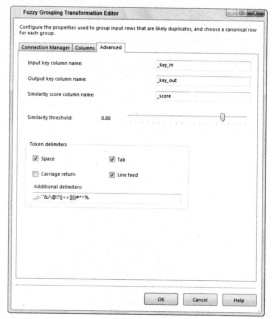

Figure 27-2

One new feature that was not in the Fuzzy Lookup Transform is that you can set the names of the three additional fields that are added automatically to the output of this transform. By default, these fields are named _key_in, _key_out, and _score. These new outputs that will be added to the data stream are important to understand:

❏ **_key_in** — This column uniquely identifies each row in the stream

❏ **_key_out** — This column identifies a group of duplicate rows. Any rows that have the same _key_out value are rows that are in the same group

❏ **_score** — This column indicates the similarity of the row with a value between 0 and 1

Try It

In this lesson, you are going to create a new dimension table to populate occupations for your company. The import file contains several different versions of the same occupation, and you need to determine which will be the best fit. After this lesson, you will have an understanding of how to use the Fuzzy Grouping transform to remove duplicates.

Lesson Requirements

Download the flat file named FuzzyExample.txt from www.wrox.com to use as your source. Save this file to the C:\Projects\SSISPersonalTrainer directory.

After determining which version of the occupation field is best, create a table named Occupation_FuzzyGrouping and load it.

Hints

❑ After using the Fuzzy Grouping Transform to determine the correctly spelled occupation, use a Conditional Split to bring back only the rows where _key_in == _key_out

❑ The only column you need to load into the table is the clean version of the OccupationLabel

Step-by-Step

1. Create a new package and name it Lesson27 or download the completed Lesson27.dtsx package from www.wrox.com.

2. Drag a Data Flow Task onto your designer and name it "DFT - Fuzzy Grouping."

3. Create a new Flat File Connection Manager (creating connection managers is discussed in Lesson 6), name it "Occupations," and point it to C:\Projects\SSISPersonalTrainer\ FuzzyExample.txt. Also, check the "Column names in the first data row" option. The editor should look like Figure 27-3.

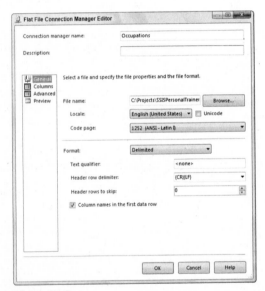

Figure 27-3

4. In the Data Flow bring a new Flat File Source over and name it "Occupation Load." Open the editor and make the connection manager the newly created Occupations.

5. On the Columns tab select only the TITLE column to return and change the name of the output column to OccupationLabel. Then click OK.

6. Next, create another connection manager, this time an OLE DB Connection Manager, using the AdventureWorks2008 database.

7. Bring a Fuzzy Grouping Transform in the Data Flow and open the editor. Set the OLE DB Connection Manager to AdventureWorks2008.

8.   On the Columns tab there is only one column to bring back, so check the OccupationLabel. Figure 27-4 shows what the Columns tab should look like now.

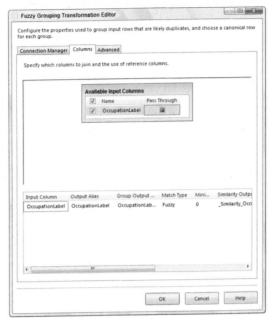

Figure 27-4

9.   Next, in the Advanced tab change the Similarity Threshold to 0.50 and change the Token Delimiters to reflect Figure 27-5. Then click OK.

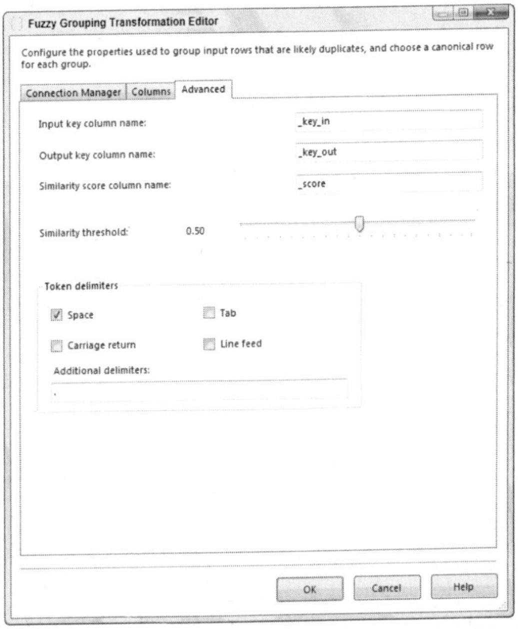

Figure 27-5

10. If you ran this now and loaded a table, you would have 22 rows of the clean data, but you would also have several duplicate records. Remember you are trying to create a dimension table, so to prevent duplicates in this package add a Conditional Split Transform with an Output Name "Best Match" and a Condition of "_key_in == _key_out." If these two values match, the grouped value is the best representative candidate for the natural key in a dimension table. All other rows are not needed, so you can name the Default Output Name "Delete." Figure 27-6 shows how your Conditional Split Transform should be configured.

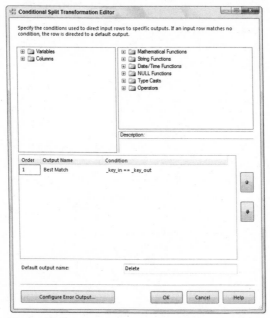

Figure 27-6

11. To finish off this package you need to load the results into a new table. Bring an OLE DB Destination onto the design surface and from within the editor select New next to Name of the table or name of the view to create a new table. Use the following code to create the Occupation_FuzzyGrouping table or download the code from www.wrox.com:

```
CREATE TABLE [dbo].[Occupation_FuzzyGrouping](
    [OccupationID] [smallint] IDENTITY(1,1) NOT NULL,
    [OccupationLabel] [varchar](50) NOT NULL
    )
```

12. Remember from the beginning of this lesson we discussed there are several output columns the Fuzzy Grouping Transform provides. These columns include a Group Output Alias column that you now use in the Mappings tab. Set the OccupationLabel_clean to map to the OccupationLabel column in the destination. Once your Mappings tab looks like Figure 27-7, click OK.

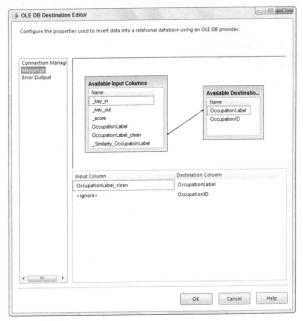

Figure 27-7

13. A successful run of this package should look like Figure 27-8.

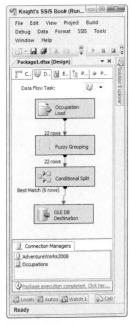

Figure 27-8

14. Figure 27-9 shows the results in the Occupation_FuzzyGrouping table you just populated. If you completed the last lesson, you might notice that you just created essentially the same table, except for the order, that was used as a reference table in Lesson 26.

	OccupationID	OccupationLabel
1	1	CUSTOMER SERVICE REPRESENTATIVE
2	2	ASSISTANT MANAGER
3	3	REGIONAL MANAGER
4	4	STORE MANAGER
5	5	SHIFT LEADER
6	6	DISTRICT MANAGER

Figure 27-9

 Please select Lesson 27 on the DVD to view the video that accompanies this lesson.

Section IV
Variables and Expressions

Making a Package Dynamic with Variables

Creating dynamic packages in SQL Server Integration Services (SSIS) enables you to have packages that can reconfigure themselves at runtime. Using variables is a significant part to making a package dynamic because with variables you are able to pass values directly into the properties of individual components.

A *variable* is essentially a placeholder for a value within a package that you can write to or read from as many times as you want. A process within the package can read the variable's value and use it or write to the variable and change the value directly.

Variables come in two forms: system variables and user-defined variables. *System variables* are predefined and include things like the package name and package start time, whereas *user-defined variables* are created solely by the developer.

To create a user-defined variable, simply right-click the design surface in Business Intelligence Development Studio (BIDS) and click Variables. This action opens the Variables window where you can create a new variable by clicking the icon in the top left. Once you create a new variable you need to populate the fields Name, Scope, Data Type, and Value.

All variables must be assigned to a specific access level in a package called *scope*. The scope can be set to an individual component so it is available only to that object, or it can be set to the package level so it can be used anywhere in the package. For example, in Figure 28-1 the variable has a scope set to the Lesson 28, or the package, level. Keep in mind that once you have set the scope of a variable it cannot be changed unless you delete the entire variable and start over.

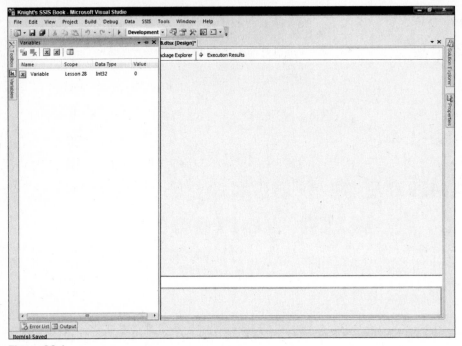

Figure 28-1

When you are configuring the variable data types, you might notice that they are named significantly different from Data Flow data types. In fact, you are going to find that only a subset of the data types typically available in the rest of the SSIS environment can be used for variables. The following table can be used to map the variable data types to standard data types found in the Data Flow:

Variable Data Type	SSIS Data Type	Description
Boolean	DT_BOOL	Value either True or False
Byte	DT_UI1	1-byte unsigned integer
Char	DT_UI2	Single character
DateTime	DT_DBTIMESTAMP	Standard datetime structure
DBNull	N/A	Declarative NULL value
Double	DT_R8	Double-precision, floating-point value
Int16	DT_I2	2-byte signed integer
Int32	DT_I4	4-byte signed integer
Int64	DT_I8	8-byte signed integer

Variable Data Type	SSIS Data Type	Description
Object	N/A	Object reference. Used to store data sets or large object structures
SByte	DT_I1	1-byte signed integer
Single	DT_R4	Single-precision, floating-point value
String	DT_WSTR	Unicode string value
UInt32	DT_UI4	4-byte unsigned integer
UInt64	DT_UI8	8-byte unsigned integer

To expand on a variable's potential, you can select a variable and press F4 to bring up the Properties window. From the Properties window you can set EvaluateAsExpression to True and enter an expression so the variable takes on a dynamic quality defined by the expression in the Expression property. To learn more about expressions and the SSIS expression language, read the next two lessons, Lessons 29 and 30, which are dedicated to expressions.

When you are referring to variables in expressions, you need to remember that variables are case-sensitive, meaning that however you initially created the variable name is how it must be referred to in the rest of the package. If you are referring to a variable in a task or transform, like you do in the following tutorial, you use question marks (?). For example, you have an Execute SQL Task that is given the duty of deleting rows from the DimEmployee table where the EmployeeNationalIDAlternateKey is equal to a value in a variable called @EmployeeID. To accomplish this you would write the following query in the Execute SQL Task:

```
DELETE FROM DimEmployee
    WHERE EmployeeNationalIDAlternateKey = ?
```

Next, on the Parameter Mappings tab you assign the @EmployeeID variable to the value of the question mark.

Try It

In this lesson, you create a flat file export of employees based on their level in the organization. The package you create should be easy to adjust based on what organization level you need. After this lesson, you will have an understanding of how to make a package dynamic using variables.

Lesson Requirements

Create a variable named OrgLevel to narrow down the number of employees returned based on the level in the organization. Create a flat file named OrganizationLevel.txt that contains all employees with an organization level of 2.

Hints

- ❏ Create a new variable that passes a value for the organization level to the OLE DB Source to return only employees with an organization level of 2

- ❏ Create a flat file that has the following rows:

    - ❏ NationalIDNumber

    - ❏ LoginID

    - ❏ OrganizationLevel

    - ❏ JobTitle

    - ❏ BirthDate

    - ❏ MaritalStatus

    - ❏ Gender

    - ❏ HireDate

Step-by-Step

1. Create a new package and name it Lesson28 or download the completed Lesson28.dtsx package from www.wrox.com.

2. Right-click the Control Flow design surface and click Variables to open the Variables window.

3. To create a new variable click the icon in the top left of the Variables window and name it Org-Level. Figure 28-2 shows the variable with a Data Type of Int32 and a value of 2.

Figure 28-2

4. Drag a Data Flow Task onto your designer and name it "DFT - Employee Export."

5. Switch to the new Data Flow Task by clicking on the Data Flow tab. Add an OLE DB Connection Manager that uses the AdventureWorks2008 database and then bring an OLE DB Source in your Data Flow that uses this connection manager.

6. Open the OLE DB Source Editor by double-clicking the OLE DB Source. In the OLE DB Source Editor change the data access mode to SQL Command and enter the following SQL statement:

```
SELECT NationalIDNumber
      ,LoginID
      ,OrganizationLevel
      ,JobTitle
      ,BirthDate
      ,MaritalStatus
      ,Gender
      ,HireDate
  FROM HumanResources.Employee
  WHERE OrganizationLevel=?
```

7. Next, click Parameters and set Parameter0 to use the variable created earlier: User::OrgLevel. Figure 28-3 shows the changes you have just made. Click OK twice to exit the OLE DB Source Editor.

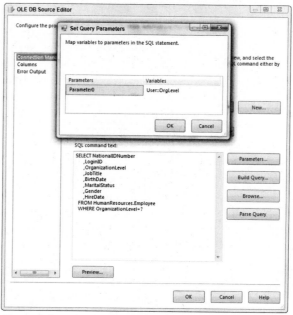

Figure 28-3

8. Create a new Flat File Connection Manager, name it "Organization Level," and point it to C:\ Projects\SSISPersonalTrainer\OrganizationLevel.txt. Also, check the "Column names in the first data row" option.

9. Bring a new Flat File Destination over, open the Flat File Destination Editor by double-clicking the Flat File Destination, and make the connection manager the newly created Organization Level with the proper mapping. Click OK.

10. The package is now complete using a variable in the WHERE clause of the SQL statement that retrieves data to load a flat file. You can now easily change what type of organization level is brought back by simply changing the variable making this package reusable. When the package is executed, your results will look like Figure 28-4.

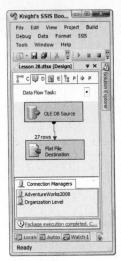

Figure 28-4

 Please select Lesson 28 on the DVD to view the video that accompanies this lesson.

Making a Connection Dynamic with Expressions

If you truly want to expand the possibilities of what you can accomplish with your packages, it is essential that you learn the SQL Server Integration Services (SSIS) expression language. One of the common uses for expressions in SSIS is to create a dynamic connection to allow packages to be altered by external or internal means.

> *In Lesson 17 you learned about the Derived Column Transform and many of the common functions used in expressions. This lesson focuses on using expressions in connection managers, so if you want a recap on the expression language itself, refer to Lesson 17.*

To configure a connection to take advantage of expressions, select the connection manager and press F4 to open the Properties window, as shown in Figure 29-1. Find the Expression property and click the ellipsis (. . .). This action opens the Property Expressions Editor where you can select which property inside the connection manager you want to add an expression to. Once you have selected the property from the drop-down box, click a second ellipsis in the Expression property to open the Expression Builder. Here you can begin building your expression for the given property you have selected.

Remember that each property can accept only one type of value, so often you have to cast the expression's value to the appropriate data type. Typically when dealing with connection properties you will find they require a string value using the cast function DT_WSTR(<<length>>).

A common example of using expressions in connection managers is if you have multiple flat files that you need to load using the same package. This setup would require a Foreach Loop Container, which are discussed in Lesson 33, to loop through a collection of flat files and an expression on the connection manager to change the connection string during each iteration of the loop to change the file name. To configure the Flat File Connection Manager to use expressions you would follow the steps mentioned earlier in this lesson.

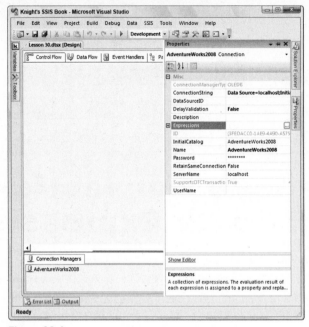

Figure 29-1

Try It

In this lesson, you create a flat file export that contains a count of employees in each department. The flat file that is created should have the current date as part of the file's name. After completing this lesson, you will understand how to use expressions in a connection manager.

Lesson Requirements

Create a package that uses the AdventureWorksDW2008 database and the DimEmployee table to load all the departments and a count of how many employees are in each to a flat file. The flat file should be named EmployeeCount_(*Current Date*).txt with the current date being populated by an expression after the underscore.

The date should be in the following *mmddyyyy* format: 02082010

You must have leading zeros when month or day is only one digit.

Hints

❑ With an OLE DB Source bring in a count of all the employees grouped by the departments they belong to from the DimEmployee table

❑ Place the results in a flat file that has an expression on the Flat File Connection Manager's ConnectionString property. The file name should have the current date as part of the name

Step-by-Step

1. Create a new package and name it Lesson29 or download the completed Lesson29.dtsx package from `www.wrox.com`.

2. Drag a Data Flow Task onto your designer and name it "DFT - Connection Expression."

3. Add an OLE DB Connection Manager that uses the AdventureWorks2008DW database and then bring an OLE DB Source in your Data Flow that uses this connection manager.

4. Open the OLE DB Source Editor by double-clicking the OLE DB Source. In the OLE DB Source Editor change the data access mode to SQL Command and enter the following SQL statement:

```
SELECT
    DepartmentName
    ,count(EmployeeNationalIDAlternateKey)EmployeeCount
FROM DimEmployee
GROUP BY DepartmentName
```

    Click OK twice to exit the OLE DB Source Editor.

5. Bring a new Flat File Destination over and connect the green arrow from the OLE DB Source to it. Open the Flat File Destination Editor and create a new Flat File Connection Manager.

6. The new connection manager should be comma delimited and named "Employee Count." Point the file to C:\Projects\SSISPersonalTrainer\EmployeeCount_.txt and check the "Column names in the first data row" option. Then click OK. Ensure the mapping is correct in the destination editor and then click OK again.

7. Click once on the connection manager named Employee Count and press F4 to bring up the Properties window. Click the ellipsis next to the Expression property to open the Property Expressions Editor, shown in Figure 29-2.

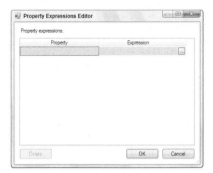

Figure 29-2

8. Click the Property drop-down box and select ConnectionString. Then click the ellipsis next to the Expression property. This action opens the Expression Builder.

9. Enter the following expression, shown in Figure 29-3, which gives the desired results for a file name:

```
"C:\\Projects\\SSISPersonalTrainer\\EmployeeCount_"+
RIGHT( "0"+(DT_WSTR, 2) Month(GETDATE() ), 2 ) +
RIGHT( "0"+(DT_WSTR, 2) Day(GETDATE() ), 2 ) +
(DT_WSTR, 4) Year(GETDATE() )+".txt"
```

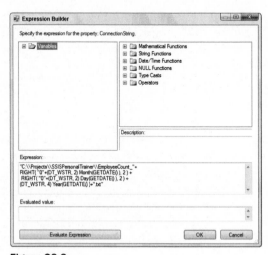

Figure 29-3

This expression is commonly used so take a look at some important functions that are used here:

❏ `Month(GETDATE() )` — Returns the current month

❏ `(DT_WSTR, 2)` — Converts the datetime to a string

❏ `RIGHT( "0"+(DT_WSTR, 2) Month(GETDATE() ), 2 )` — Adds a 0 to every month but displays only the last two digits. This is so months that already have two digits like December display only 12 instead of 012

❏ Also notice that there are two backslashes for each file directory but only one is displayed when the expression is run. A backslash is a special character in the SSIS expression language, so using \\ is how you make SSIS understand your intentions

Click OK in the Expression Builder and then OK again in the Property Expressions Editor.

10. The package is now complete using an expression to make the destination file name dynamic. Each day the package is run it creates a new file with a different name that contains the current date. When the package is executed, your results will look like Figure 29-4.

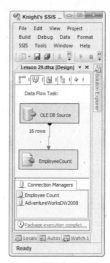

Figure 29-4

 Please select Lesson 29 on the DVD to view the video that accompanies this lesson.

Making a Task Dynamic with Expressions

When you consider the many places expressions can be applied, you begin to see how highly adaptable SQL Server Integration Services (SSIS) truly is. The previous lesson discussed the way expressions could be used to make connections dynamic. This lesson now turns to the use of expressions in tasks. Using expressions in tasks gives an SSIS developer the ability to alter individual properties within a task at runtime. A common example is using the Send Mail Task with an expression to populate the subject line to be unique based on the results of your package.

In Lesson 17 you learned about the Derived Column Transform and many of the common functions used in expressions. This lesson focuses on using expressions in tasks, so if you want a recap on the expression language itself, refer to Lesson 17.

You set up a task to use expressions exactly the same way you configure connections to use expressions. To configure a task to take advantage of expressions, select the desired task and press F4 to open the Properties window. Find the Expression property and click the ellipsis (...) next to it, shown in Figure 30-1. This action opens the Property Expressions Editor where you can select to which property inside the task you would like to add an expression. Once you have selected the property from the drop-down box, click a second ellipsis in the Expression property to open the Expression Builder. Here you can begin building your expression for the given property you have selected.

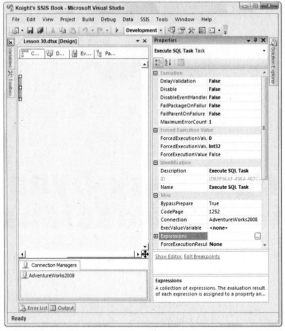

Figure 30-1

Remember that each property can accept only one type of value, so often you have to cast the expression's value to the appropriate data type. Before even writing an expression, take the time to think about what data type is going to be accepted in the property you have chosen. For example, if you have decided to make an Execute SQL Task using expressions on the SQLStatement property, then you know a string value must be returned from the expression.

To gain greater understandings of how useful expressions in tasks can be, go back to the first example we used at the beginning of this lesson when we mentioned the Send Mail Task. In that example, we mentioned with expressions you could have a dynamically changing subject line. So how would you accomplish a dynamic subject line in a Send Email Task?

The Send Mail Task was discussed in more detail in Lesson 11, so for this example, we assume you have everything set up except the desired subject. Say you need an email generated when the package begins so you know exactly what the start time was. Follow the steps stated earlier to open the Property Expressions Editor and select Subject from the Property drop-down box. Next, click the ellipsis in the Expression column and write the following expression in the Expression Builder that will populate the subject line:

```
"SSIS Package: "+@[System::PackageName] +" ran at " +
(DT_WSTR, 30)  @[System::StartTime]
```

This expression is broken down like this:

❏ `"SSIS Package: "` — Simply prints the text between the quotation marks including blank spaces

❏ `@[System::PackageName]` — System variable that displays the package name, in this case Lesson 30

❑   " ran at " — Simply prints the text between the quotation marks including blank spaces

❑   (DT_WSTR, 30) — Converts the contents of the @[System::StartTime] to a string

❑   @[System::StartTime] — System variable that display the start time of the package

Click OK twice to return to the Control Flow. When you run this package now, the resulting email subject line (depending on the date you run your package) will look something like this:

SSIS Package: Lesson 30 ran at 4/5/2009 4:59:27 PM

Try It

In this lesson, you create a package that deletes records from the Employee table based on an organization level that no longer exists in your company. After completing this lesson, you will understand how to use expressions in a task.

Lesson Requirements

Create a package that uses the AdventureWorks2008 database for a connection manager. Then create two variables that have a scope at the package level.

❑   The first variable should have a string data type and be called DeleteStatement with the following as a value:

```
Delete FROM HumanResources.Employee
Where NationalIDNumber =
```

❑   The second variable should have an int data type and be called ID with a value of 14

Combine the two variables in an expression that evaluates the property SQLStatementSource in an Execute SQL Task.

Hints

❑   The only task you need for this lesson is an Execute SQL Task

❑   You need two variables to create an expression that will complete the SQL statement

Step-by-Step

1.   Create a new package and name it Lesson30 or download the completed Lesson30.dtsx package from www.wrox.com.

2.   Add an OLE DB Connection Manager that uses the AdventureWorks2008 database. Then bring an Execute SQL Task in the Control Flow.

3. Next create a package-level variable named DeleteStatement with a string data type and the following for a value:

```
Delete FROM HumanResources.Employee
Where NationalIDNumber =
```

4. Create a second package-level variable named ID with an int data type and a value of 14. Figure 30-2 shows the variables you just created.

Creating variables is covered in more detail in Lesson 28.

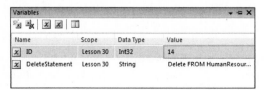

Figure 30-2

5. Click once on the Execute SQL Task and press F4 to bring up the Properties window. Click the ellipsis next to the Expression property to open the Property Expressions Editor.

6. Click the Property drop-down box and select SQLStatementSource. Then click the ellipsis next to the Expression property, shown in Figure 30-3.

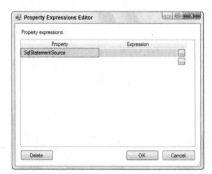

Figure 30-3

7. Enter the following expression, which gives the desired results for a SQL statement, in the Expression Builder shown in Figure 30-4:

```
@[User::DeleteStatement]+ (DT_WSTR, 10) @[User::ID]
```

With this expression you produce the following:

❑ `@[User ::DeleteStatement]` — Places the Delete statement you created in Step 3 in the expression

❑ `(DT_WSTR, 10)` — Converts the contents of the `@[User::ID]` variable to a string. This is necessary because the expression must have one data type

❑   @[User::ID] — Places the integer variable you created in Step 4 in the expression

Click OK in the Expression Builder and then OK again in the Property Expressions Editor

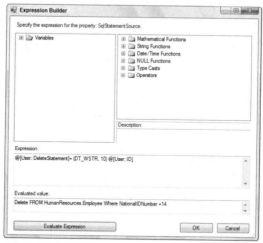

Figure 30-4

8. Double-click the Execute SQL Task to open it and set the Connection to AdventureWorks2008. Then click OK. You may still see a red *x* on the task indicating that it is not configured correctly. Remember expressions are evaluated at runtime so the task doesn't know you have entered a SQL statement in yet. Once the package runs, the SQL statement build with expressions will be inserted in the appropriate field.

9. The package is now complete using an expression to make the task dynamic. When the package is executed, your results should look like Figure 30-5.

Figure 30-5

If you open the task now, you find that the SQL statement you created with expressions has been entered in the SQLStatement property.

 Please select Lesson 30 on the DVD to view the video that accompanies this lesson.

Section V
Containers

Using Sequence Containers to Organize a Package

Sequence Containers provide a simple and easy method for organizing the flow of a package and can help you divide a package into more manageable pieces. When you first begin exploring the Sequence Container, you may think organization is the only benefit it provides. However, to the creative developer this container's uses go far beyond simple cleanliness. If you know how to use it, it can also grant you the following capabilities:

❑ Group tasks so that you can disable a part of the package that's temporarily not needed

❑ Narrow the scope of a variable to just the container

❑ Collapse and expand the container to hide the tasks within

❑ Manage the properties of multiple tasks in one step by setting the properties of the container

❑ Use one method to ensure that multiple tasks have to execute successfully before the next task executes

❑ Create a transaction across a series of data-related tasks, but not on the entire package

❑ Create event handlers on a single container so that you can send an email if anything inside one container fails and perhaps even page yourself if anything else fails (event handlers are discussed in more detail in Lesson 38)

To add a Sequence Container to a package, drag and drop the Sequence Container in the design pane just like you would any other task. To have a task as part of the container, just drag the task within the outlined box.

Once tasks have been placed inside the Sequence Container, they can be connected by precedence constraints only to other tasks within the same container. If you attempt to connect a task inside the container to one outside, you receive an error.

Try It

In this example, you explore how Sequence Containers can be used inside a package. After this lesson, you will have a better idea of the versatility that using Sequence Containers can give you when you are developing your own packages.

Lesson Requirements

Create a package with Sequence Containers and test different uses of the container. Just use Script Tasks to test inside the containers because Script Tasks do not require any configuration. You really are just learning more about Sequence Containers in this lesson.

Hints

❏   To do this example you need three Sequence Containers, with three Script Tasks inside each

Step-by-Step

1.   Create a new package and name it Lesson31 or download the completed Lesson31.dtsx package from www.wrox.com.

2.   Drag three Sequence Containers onto your designer and then place three Script Tasks inside each container. Connect the precedence constraints from each container to make your package look like Figure 31-1. Feel free to run this package as is because the Script Task requires no further configuration. The package will complete successfully without changing any data.

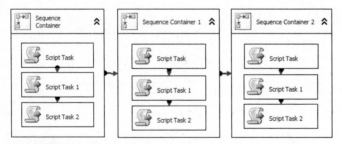

Figure 31-1

3.   The next several steps will help you better understand the benefits and limitations of this container. First, attempt to connect the precedence constraint from any Script Task inside Sequence Container 1 to any other object in the package. You will receive the error shown in Figure 31-2 because any object inside a Sequence Container cannot be connected to any component outside the container.

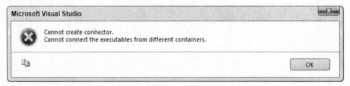

Figure 31-2

4. With individual tasks you have the ability to execute a single task while excluding the rest of the package. You can also do this with entire containers. Right-click on the first container and click Execute Container to execute just the tasks that are inside the container. Notice just the first container executes while the rest of the package remains inactive. Once you're ready to go to the next step, click the stop debugging button to continue.

5. Containers also give you the ability to scope variables exclusive to the contents of the container. Click once on Sequence Container 2 and open the Variables window. Create a variable called "Lesson 31" that has a scope set to "Sequence Container 2" (creating variables is discussed in Lesson 28).

6. Next, right-click and disable Sequence Container 1, the container in the middle, and then run the package. The results, in Figure 31-3, show how Sequence Containers give you the ability to disable entire sections of a package with the container. Though you can't see color in this figure, the outer two containers should be green, while the middle container is gray indicating it is disabled.

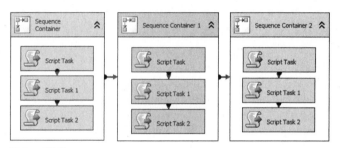

Figure 31-3

7. Last, you can collapse a container simply by clicking the two arrows pointing upward next to the container name. Figure 31-4 shows all three containers collapsed. This action does not change how the package runs but just hides the content. To expand the containers again click the arrows that are now pointed down.

Figure 31-4

This should give you a basic understanding of how Sequence Containers work. These same principles can be applied to containers that are discussed in the next lessons.

 Please select Lesson 31 on the DVD to view the video that accompanies this lesson.

Using For Loop Containers to Repeat Control Flow Tasks

Loops are a great tool that can be used in many programming languages. They provide a way to iterate over selected code repeatedly until it is conditionally told to stop. For example, in T-SQL a While loop is constructed so that a statement is repeated until a Boolean expression evaluates as false. The For Loop Container in SSIS works much the same way.

A common reason that you might use the For Loop Container is if you have a set of Control Flow tasks that need to be run until a condition has been met. For example, in the "Try It" section of this lesson a For Loop Container is used to check to see if a table has any rows of data. If the table has no records, then the loop continues to iterate until it finds that at least one row is present.

When you use a For Loop Container you first create a variable that the container can use to store an expression value of how many times the container has completed a run. The container runs three separate expressions at run time to formulate the loop. These three expressions require only one variable because the expressions change the same variable value each time they evaluate.

To configure the For Loop Container drag it on the design surface and double-click the top portion of the container to open the editor. Here you see the InitExpression, EvalExpression, and AssignExpression properties.

- ❑ The **InitExpression** sets the initial value of the variable, so if you want the package to perform the loop a set number of times you will likely start the variable at 1

- ❑ The **EvalExpression** is the expression that tells the loop when to stop. This must be an expression that always evaluates to true or false. As soon as it evaluates to false, the loop stops

- ❑ The **AssignExpression** is the expression that changes a condition each time that the loop repeats. Here you tell the loop to increment or decrement the number of runs the loop has completed

Try It

In this lesson, you explore how the For Loop Container uses expressions to determine how many times to run Control Flow items. The package you create continuously loops until data has been loaded in a table called ForLoop. After this lesson, you will understand how the For Loop Container is used to iterate through Control Flow tasks a set number of times.

Lesson Requirements

Create the table ForLoop in the AdventureWorks2008 database with the following query:

```
CREATE TABLE ForLoop
    (
    ID int NOT NULL IDENTITY (1, 1),
    Name varchar(50) NULL
    ) ON [PRIMARY]
```

The queries used in this lesson and the completed package are available for download on the book's website at www.wrox.com.

Create a package that runs an Execute SQL Task that checks to see if data has been loaded into the ForLoop table. Create a variable called Counter with an Int32 data type. Place the Execute SQL Task inside a For Loop Container that checks to see if new data has been loaded to the ForLoop table.

Hints

❑ After you start the package, generate an INSERT statement to insert several rows into it

❑ Once data has been loaded to the ForLoop table, the Execute SQL Task should change the Counter variable and, therefore, complete the package

Step-by-Step

1. Open SQL Server Management Studio and create the table ForLoop in the AdventureWorks2008 database with the following statement:

```
CREATE TABLE ForLoop
    (
    ID int NOT NULL IDENTITY (1, 1),
    Name varchar(50) NULL
    ) ON [PRIMARY]
```

2. After this table is created, open Business Intelligence Development Studio (BIDS) and create a new package named Lesson32, or download the completed Lesson32.dtsx package from www. wrox.com.

3. Create a New OLE DB Connection Manager that uses the AdventureWorks2008 database.

4. Next, open the Variables window by right-clicking on the design surface and select Variables. Click the Add Variable button to add a new variable named Counter with an Int32 data type, as shown in Figure 32-1.

Figure 32-1

5. Drag an Execute SQL Task into the Control Flow and open its editor by double-clicking the task.

6. On the General tab select AdventureWorks2008 as your connection, change the ResultSet to Single row, and type the following query into the SQLStatement property:

```
declare @RecordsInserted int

if exists(select Name
        from ForLoop )
set @RecordsInserted = 1
else

set @RecordsInserted = 0
select @RecordsInserted as RecordsInserted
```

This query checks to see if the ForLoop table has any records, and if it does, it returns the number 1. If there are no rows in the table, then it returns the number 0. Figure 32-2 shows the editor after these changes have been made.

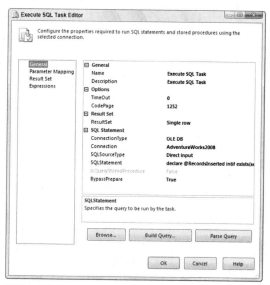

Figure 32-2

7. Select the Result Set tab and click Add. In the Result Name column change the default NewResultName to RecordsInserted and keep the Variable Name column the default of User::Counter. After you make these changes, the results of the Execute SQL Task will be loaded into the variable. After setting up this page, you are done with this editor so click OK.

8. Now drag a For Loop Container in the Control Flow and place the Execute SQL Task inside the new container.

9. Open the For Loop Editor and make the following changes:

❑ **InitExpression** — @Counter = 0

❑ **EvalExpression** — @Counter == 0

❑ **AssignExpression** — Leave blank

Remember that variables are case sensitive, so you must type the variable name exactly how you did when you created it.

Once these properties have been filled, click OK. Your screen should look like Figure 32-3.

Figure 32-3

10. The package is now complete and ready to run. After you execute this package you will see that because there is currently no data in the ForLoop table, the package will continue to run until new data is inserted into the table.

11. While the package is continuing to run open SQL Server Management Studio and run the following statement to load some records in the ForLoop table:

```
INSERT INTO ForLoop
          (Name)
Select Distinct
LastName
From Person.Person
```

This should cause the package to complete because the loop you created was waiting for new records to be inserted before it could complete. Figure 32-4 shows what the completed Lesson 32 package should look like after these rows have been inserted.

Figure 32-4

 Please select Lesson 32 on the DVD to view the video that accompanies this lesson.

Using the Foreach Loop Container to Loop Through a Collection of Objects

The Foreach Loop Container is a very powerful and very useful tool for repeating Control Flow items. It is often used when you have a collection of files that you want to apply the same changes to. If you provide the directory for a set of files, the Foreach Loop Container can apply the same Control Flow tasks to each file. You might ask yourself, how is this different from the For Loop Container? The easy answer is the For Loop iterates through the content of the container a number of times you define or you define with an expression, while the Foreach Loop Container iterates through its content as many times as it takes to effect the full collection.

The configuration of the Foreach Loop Container can differ depending on which enumerator you decide to use. An *enumerator* specifies the collection of objects that the container will loop through. All tasks inside the container will be repeated for each member of a specified enumerator. The Foreach Loop Editor can significantly change depending on what you set for this option:

- ❑ **Foreach File Enumerator** — Performs an action for each file in a directory with a given file extension

- ❑ **Foreach Item Enumerator** — Loops through a list of items that are set manually in the container

- ❑ **Foreach ADO Enumerator** — Loops through a list of tables or rows in a table from an ADO recordset

- ❑ **Foreach ADO.NET Schema Rowset Enumerator** — Loops through an ADO.NET schema

- ❑ **Foreach From Variable Enumerator** — Loops through a SQL Server Integration Services (SSIS) variable

- ❑ **Foreach Nodelist Enumerator** — Loops through a node list in an XML document

- ❑ **Foreach SMO Enumerator** — Enumerates a list of SQL Management Objects (SMO)

To configure the Foreach Loop Container, drag it on the design surface and double-click the top portion of the container to open the editor. Click the Collection tab to choose which type of enumerator you want to use, shown in Figure 33-1. For example, say you want to loop through a directory to load a group of flat files to a table, so you choose the Foreach File Enumerator. Then you must specify what folder directory the files are in and what kind of file extension they have. Assume the flat files are .txt files, so in the Files box *.txt is used to bring back only the text files in the directory. Last, because the flat files each have a different name you can use the Variable Mappings tab to dynamically change the Flat File Connection Manager's file name for each iteration of the loop. Don't worry if this explanation sounds complicated because the following "Try It" section gives you a step-by-step example of how to do this exact scenario.

Figure 33-1

Another commonly used enumerator is the Foreach ADO Enumerator. This enumerator is handy for looping through a set of records and executing every task inside the container for each record in that set. For example, you want to run each task in your package for every database on a server. With the Foreach ADO Enumerator you could loop through a table that lists all the database names on your server and dynamically change a connection manager's database name for each iteration of the loop.

Try It

In this lesson, you create a package that uses the most common type of enumerator, the Foreach File Enumerator, to loop through a collection of flat files and load them to a table. After this lesson, you will understand how to use the Foreach Loop Container to loop through a collection of files and load each to a table.

Lesson Requirements

Download the four flat files named File 1.txt, File 2.txt, File 3.txt, and File 4.txt from www.wrox.com to use as your source. Save these files to the C:\Projects\SSISPersonalTrainer\Lesson 33 directory.

Create a table named ForEachLoop in the AdventureWorks2008 database to load each flat file into.

Use a Foreach Loop Container to loop through and load each file in the C:\Projects\ SSISPersonalTrainer\Lesson 33 directory.

Hints

❑   Create a variable to store the location of the file that currently needs to be loaded. The loop will change the variable location after each run

❑   Use this variable as an expression for the connection manager that points to the flat file

Step-by-Step

1.   Create a new package and name it Lesson33 or download the completed Lesson33.dtsx package from www.wrox.com.

2.   Drag a Data Flow Task onto your designer and name it "DFT - Load Flat Files."

3.   Create a new Flat File Connection Manager, name it "File Extract," and point it to File 1.txt in the following directory: C:\Projects\SSISPersonalTrainer\Lesson 33\File 1.txt. Also, check the "Column names in the first data row" option; then click OK.

4.   In the Data Flow bring a new Flat File Source over and name it "File Extract." Open the Flat File Source Editor by double-clicking the Flat File Source and make the connection manager the newly created File Extract. Then click OK.

5.   Next, create another connection manager, this time an OLE DB Connection Manager, using the AdventureWorks2008 database.

6.   Bring an OLE DB Destination in the Data Flow and open the editor. Set the OLE DB Connection Manager to AdventureWorks2008 and create a new table with the following SQL statement by clicking New next to the table selection drop-down box:

```
CREATE TABLE [ForEachLoop] (
    [Name] varchar(50),
    [State] varchar(50)
)
```

Ensure the columns are mapped correctly; then click OK. Your Data Flow should now look like Figure 33-2.

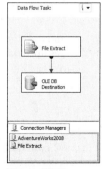

Figure 33-2

7. Your package is now set up to run just one file, but because you have four, you now go back to the Control Flow and drag over a Foreach Loop Container.

8. Place the Data Flow Task inside the Foreach Loop Container; then open the Foreach Loop Editor by double-clicking the top banner portion of the container. On the Collections tab select Foreach File Enumerator from the Enumerator property drop-down box. The Foreach File Enumerator is the default when you open the editor, but in order to get the needed configuration, you still need to select it again from the drop-down box.

9. Now, set the Folder property to the C:\Projects\SSISPersonalTrainer\Lesson 33 directory and the Files property to *.txt because you want to bring back all the text files in the directory. Everything else you can leave as the default. After you make these changes, your editor should look like Figure 33-3.

Figure 33-3

10. On the Variable Mappings tab create a new variable called "FlatFileLocation" by selecting <New Variable...> from the Variable drop-down box. Figure 33-4 shows the Add Variable dialog box.

Figure 33-4

11. This variable's value will change each time the container runs to the current file it is loading. In this specific case after File 1.txt is completed, the container will automatically change the variable's value to the next file name. After the variable is created, click OK. The Variable Mappings tab should look like Figure 33-5. Click OK again to return to the Data Flow.

Figure 33-5

12. The last step is to put an expression on the File Extract Connection Manager that uses the variable you just created inside the Foreach Loop Container. Select the File Extract Connection Manager called "File Extract" from your list of connection managers and press F4 to bring up the Properties window. Click the ellipsis next to the Expressions property to open the Property Expressions Editor. Select ConnectionString from the Property drop-down and then click the ellipsis in the Expression box.

13. In the top left of the Expression Builder expand the Variables and drag @[User::FlatFileLocation] down into the Expression box. If you try to click Evaluate Expression now, there will be no result. Remember that this expression will be populated at runtime, so you will see nothing here yet. Your screen should look like Figure 33-6. Click OK twice to return to the Data Flow.

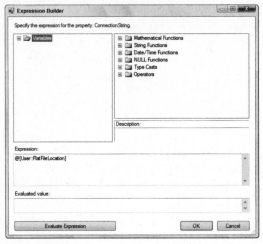

Figure 33-6

14. The package is now complete. A successful run will loop through and load all the files in the C:\Projects\SSISPersonalTrainer\Lesson 33 directory to the ForEachLoop table in the AdventureWorks2008 database. Figure 33-7 shows what a successful run should look like.

Figure 33-7

 Please select Lesson 33 on the DVD to view the video that accompanies this lesson.

Section VI
Configuration

Easing Deployment with Configuration Tables

Once you have a set of packages complete, the challenge is deploying those packages to a production environment without having to manually configure the packages for that environment. For example, your production server may not have the same directory to extract files from or the same user name to connect to a database. Configuration tables make the migrations seamless and the configuration automated to reduce the risk of errors. You can connect to a configuration table for each connection in a package, and each package that uses the connection can then reference the configuration table. When the packages are moved to production, you can change the configuration table's server name from development to production.

The SSIS Package Configuration option allows you to write any SSIS property for the package, connection, container, variable, or any task into a table. The value in the configuration table then can be used instead of the value in the package. This value is read at run time. The same configuration table can exist on the development and production server. When the package is moved to the production server, it then uses the production configuration table, which can point the package to the production server. This process makes deployment easier than your having to manually update all connections before deployment.

To create a configuration table for a package you right-click in the blank area of the package in the control flow and left-click Package Configurations, as shown in Figure 34-1. This action opens the Package Configurations Organizer. In this screen you can create, edit, and delete package configuration connections to the configuration table. First, you need to check the Enable Package Configurations check box, as shown in Figure 34-2.

Figure 34-1

Figure 34-2

To create the connection to the configuration table you click the Add button at the bottom of the Package Configurations Organizer. This button starts the Package Configuration Wizard. The first time you add a configuration table you see a welcome screen. You can check the option to not show this page again if you prefer. Select Next to move on.

On the next screen, you can then select SQL Server from the Configuration Type drop-down menu. With SQL Server as the type, your connection can be any SQL Server database. You can click the New button to the right of the Connection drop-down to create an OLE DB connection to a SQL Server instance. The SQL Server connection is not referring to connections in the package. This connection is strictly for the package's connection to the configuration table. The data in the table is where the connections in the connection manager look to for the configuration information.

After you have selected the SQL connection, you select the table to use. There is a default table named "SSIS_Configurations." If you want to create this table, click the New button next to the Configuration Table drop-down menu. This opens the SQL query that creates the database.

You also need to give the configuration a filter name. You need to make this name broad yet descriptive. Other packages are going to use the same configuration table, and you are going to see this filter listed when you set up configuration tables on other packages. Once you select the SQL Server and the table, the window should look like Figure 34-3.

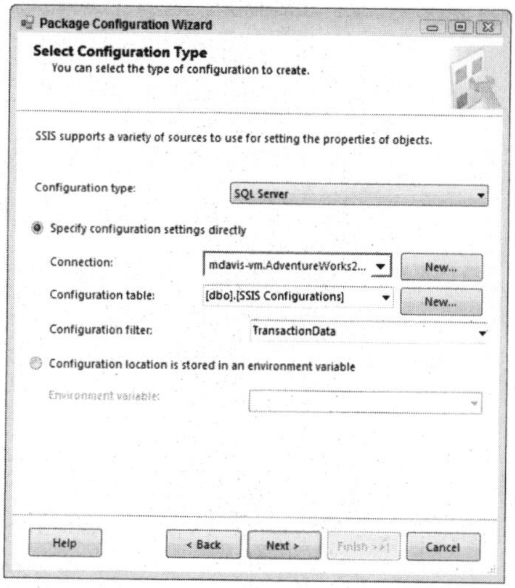

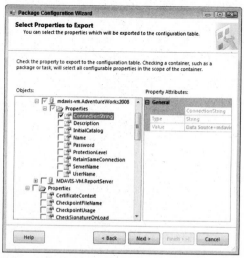

Figure 34-3

After you click Next, you see the list of objects in the package and the attributes for those objects. You can place a check next to the attribute you want to create in the configuration table. When you are using the configuration table for a connection, you can select the connection string attribute, as in Figure 34-4.

Figure 34-4

Now you can click Next and go to the final configuration window. Here you can name the configuration. This name is used for reference in the package only. You also see the configuration type, connection name, table, filter, and the target property (Figure 34-5).

Figure 34-5

Click Finish and you return to the Package Configurations Organizer. You can now see the new configuration table listed in this window, as shown in Figure 34-6. The Add, Edit, and Remove buttons at the bottom of this window allow you to alter or remove the existing configuration tables and add new ones.

Figure 34-6

Once you have a configuration table created, the package uses the data in the configuration table instead of the data in the package. The connection string in the package is not used when debugging the package now.

> *A common issue in troubleshooting occurs when a developer has a problem with a connection, and that developer continues making changes to the connection in the package, not realizing the configuration table is overruling the settings in the package. If you find yourself troubleshooting a connection, it is a good idea to disable package configurations first.*

Try It

In this lesson you are going to learn how to create a configuration table and use the data from the configuration table. After this lesson you should understand how configuration tables are used to pass information into a package.

Lesson Requirements

In this lesson you create a simple package with a Script Task that pops up a message with the configuration value instead of the value saved in the package. Then you create a configuration table and run the package to see the value in the configuration table.

The completed package for this lesson is available for download on the book's website at www.wrox.com.

Hints

❑   You need only a Script Task

❑   The value of the string is the value used in the configuration table

Step-by-Step

1.   Create a String variable named "strConfigTest" in a blank package.

2.   Set the value of the variable to "HardCoded."

3.   Drag a Script Task into the Control Flow and double-click on it.

4.   Select VB as the language for the Script Task.

5.   Select the variable you just created as a read-write variable in the ReadWriteVariable field.

6.   Click the Edit Script button and type the following code in the Script Task where it states "Add your Code here":

```
MsgBox(Dts.Variables("strConfigTest").Value)
```

7.   Close the Script Task Editor and click OK in the Script Task.

8.   Right-click in the Control Flow and select Package Configurations.

9.   Click Next in the wizard welcome screen (if it appears).

10. Set the Configuration Type as SQL Server.

11. Set the SQL Connection to AdventureWorks2008.

12. Select the SSIS Configurations table (click New and create it if does not exist).

13. Set the Configuration Filter to strConfigTestVariable.

14. Place a check in the Value attribute of the strConfigTest variable, as in Figure 34-7.

15. Click Next.

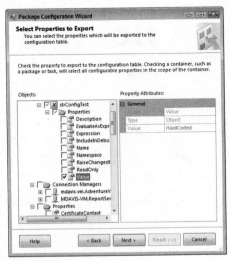

Figure 34-7

16. Name the configuration "Config Variable"; click Finish.

17. Click Close in the Package Configurations Organizer.

18. Run the package and a popup appears with the text "HardCoded."

19. Open SQL Server Management Studio.

20. Navigate to the SSIS_Configurations table on the AdventureWorks2008 database. Right-click the table and select Edit Top 200.

21. Change the Configured Value from "HardCoded" to "Config Data."

22. Run the package again, and you should see a popup box with the text "Config Data."

 Please select Lesson 34 on the DVD to view the video that accompanies this lesson.

Easing Deployment with Configuration Files

Once you have a set of packages complete, the challenge is deploying those packages to a production environment without having to manually configure the packages for that environment. For example, your production server may not have the same directory to extract files from or the same user name to connect to a database. Configuration files make the migrations seamless and make the configuration process automated to reduce the risk of errors. You can create a configuration file for each connection in the packages, and each package that uses the connection can then reference the configuration file. When the packages are moved to production, you can then change the configuration file's server name from development to production.

The SSIS Package Configuration option allows you to write any SSIS property for a package, connection, container, variable, or task into an XML file or a table. The value in the configuration file is then used instead of the value in the package. This value is read at runtime. The same configuration file can exist on the development and production servers. So, when the package is moved to the production server, it can use the production configuration file, which can point the package to the production server. This makes deployment easier than your having to manually update all connections before deployment.

To create a configuration file for a package, you right-click in the blank area of the package in the Control Flow and left-click Package Configurations, as shown in Figure 35-1. This action opens the Package Configurations Organizer. In this screen you can create, edit, and delete package configuration files. First, you need to check the Enable Package Configurations check box, as shown in Figure 35-2.

Figure 35-1

Figure 35-2

To create the configuration file you click the Add button at the bottom of the Package Configurations Organizer. This button starts the Package Configuration Wizard. The first time you add a configuration file you see a welcome screen. You can check the option to not show this page again if you prefer. Select Next, and on the next screen you can select the configuration file type and the location of the configuration file.

You select XML Configuration File as the type and the location can be anywhere on the file system. You can click Browse to find a location or already existing configuration file. When you are creating a configuration file for a connection, it is a best practice to name the configuration file something descriptive about the connection, like the server or database name. Once you select the type and configuration file location, the window should look like Figure 35-3.

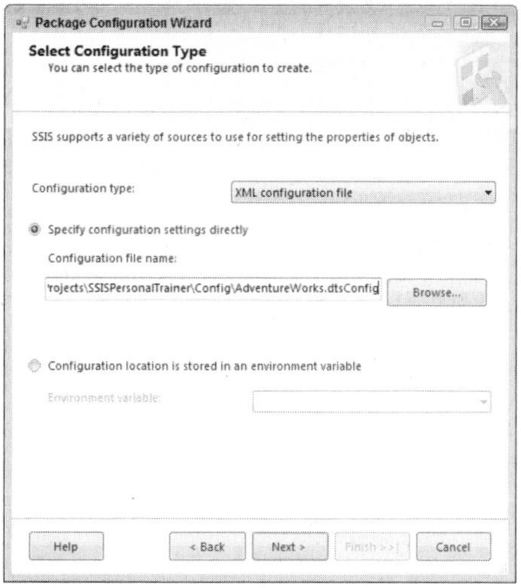

Figure 35-3

After you click Next, you see the list of objects in the package and the attributes for those objects. You can place a check next to the attribute you want to create in the configuration file. For example, when using the configuration file for a connection, you can select the connection string attribute, as in Figure 35-4.

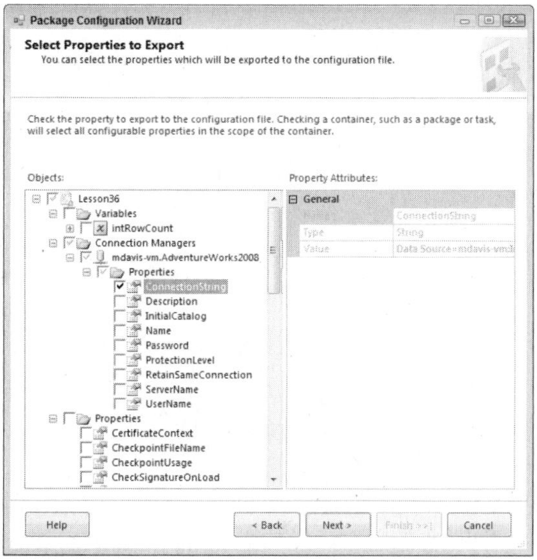

Figure 35-4

Now you can click Next, and you see the final configuration window. Here you can name the configuration. This name is used for reference in the package only. You also see the configuration type, file name, and properties along with the statement that a new configuration file will be created, as shown in Figure 35-5.

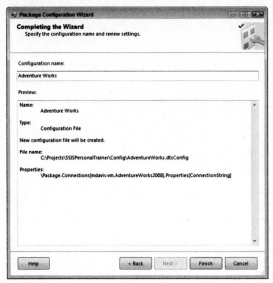

Figure 35-5

Click Finish and you return to the Package Configurations Organizer. You now see the new configuration file listed in this window, as in Figure 35-6. Add, Edit, and Remove buttons at the bottom of this window allow you to alter or remove the existing configuration files and add new ones.

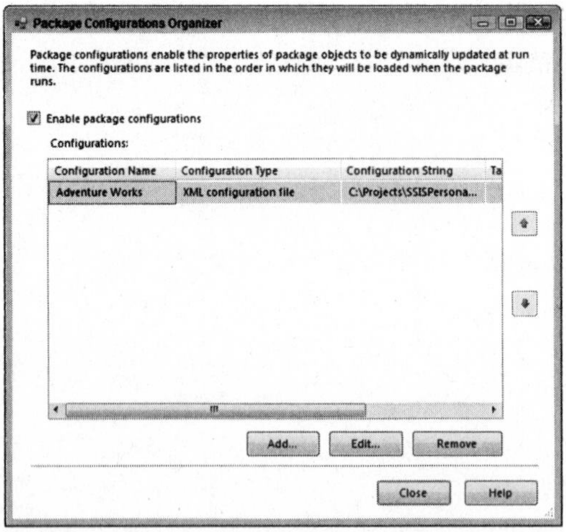

Figure 35-6

Once you have a configuration file created, the package uses the data in the configuration file instead of the data in the package. The connection string in the package will not be used when debugging the package now.

A common issue in troubleshooting occurs when a developer has a problem with a connection, and that developer continues making changes to the connection in the package, not realizing the configuration file is overruling the settings in the package. If you find yourself troubleshooting a connection, it is a good idea to disable package configurations first.

Try It

In this lesson you are going to learn how to create a configuration file and show the data from the configuration file. After this lesson you should understand how configuration files are used to pass information into a package.

Lesson Requirements

In this example, you first create a simple package with a Script Task that will pop up a message with the configuration value instead of the value saved in the package. Then you create a configuration file and run the package to see the value in the configuration file.

The completed package for this lesson is available for download on the book's website at www.wrox.com.

Hints

- ❑ You need only a Script Task
- ❑ The value of the string is the value used in the configuration file

Step-by-Step

1. Create a String variable named strConfigTest in a blank package.
2. Set the value of the variable to "HardCoded."
3. Drag a Script Task into the Control Flow and double-click it.
4. Select VB as the language for the Script Task.
5. Select the variable you just created as a read-write variable.
6. Click Edit Script and type the following code in the Script Task where it says "Add your code here":

```
MsgBox(Dts.Variables("strConfigTest").Value)
```

7. Close the Script Task Editor and click OK in the Script Task.
8. Right-click in the Control Flow and select Package Configurations.
9. Click Next in the wizard welcome screen (if it appears).
10. Leave the configuration type as XML Configuration File.
11. Set the Configuration File Name to C:\projects\SSISPersonalTrainer\Config\ConfigTest. dtsConfig.
12. Place a check in the Value attribute of the strConfigTest variable, as in Figure 35-7.

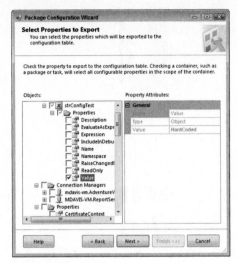

Figure 35-7

13. Click Next.

14. Name the configuration "Config Variable" and click Finish.

15. Click Close in the Package Configurations Organizer.

16. Run the package and a popup appears with the text "HardCoded."

17. Navigate to the configuration file and open with a text editor.

18. Change the value from "HardCoded" to "Config Data."

19. Run the package again, and you should see a popup box with the text "Config Data."

Please select Lesson 35 on the DVD to view the video that accompanies this lesson.

Configuring Child Packages

After creating many packages in your environment you may realize that you have the same tasks performing the exact same functions in multiple packages. This kind of repetition can be simplified with a child package. A *child package* is a package called from another package. The package calling the child package is called a *parent package*. The parent package calls the child package by using the Execute Package Task in the Control Flow.

The Execute Package Task can be placed anywhere in the Control Flow of a parent package just like any of the tasks in the Toolbox. You can use expressions and precedence constraints to decide if the Execute Package Task runs in the parent package, allowing you to control when and if the child package executes. The child package does not have to be the last task in the parent package.

If the Execute Package Task is not the last task in the parent package, then after the child package completes, the parent package resumes at the point after the Execute Package Task. If the child package runs successfully, the parent package continues as if the tasks completed successfully just like any other task in the Control Flow. If the child package fails, the Execute Package Task reports failure. If the precedence constraint coming from a failed Execute Package Task is set to success, the next task in the Control Flow of the parent package is not executed.

When a child package fails to run, the parent package does not report the error from the child package. The message from the parent package only states "Task (*Name of the Execute Package Task*) Failed." This message is not very descriptive and does not tell you what step failed in the child package. To troubleshoot a child package, you have to open the child package and find the exact error message from the child package. Troubleshooting a package is covered in more detail in Lesson 39.

Configuring an Execute Package Task

Drag in an Execute Package Task to the Control Flow and double-click to open its editor. The first screen of the Execute Package Task Editor shows the General node with some basic properties of the task. Under the General node you see the name and description of the Execute Package Task.

These do not affect the Execute Package Task. They are used for ease of reference when viewing the tasks in the Control Flow. The name shows on the tasks in the Control Flow, and the description is usually a longer line of text describing the purpose of the Execute Package Task. It is a best practice to always change the values of these fields to values that make it easy for anyone to see and understand the function of the task.

The next node on the left pane is the Package node. These are the properties used to tell the parent package where the child package is located. The first property is the Location property. The Location can be set to SQL Server or File System. If you have deployed your child package to a SQL Server, you need to select SQL Server. If you are running your packages from a folder on the file system, you need to select File System.

If you select SQL Server as the Location, your next two options are Connection and Package Name. The connection will be an OLE DB Connection to a SQL Server–like connection. Once you have the connection set in the connection manager, you can see it in the Connection drop-down in this menu. You can also click the <New connection…> option in the drop-down menu and open the OLE DB Connection Manager Editor. This editor creates the OLE DB connection to the SQL Server in the connection manager of the package.

After you select the connection in the Execute Package Task, the package name shows all of the packages in the SQL Server selected. Clicking the ellipsis next to the Package Name property opens the Select Package window showing the Packages folder of the SQL Server. The Maintenance Plans folder and any other folders on the server show in this window, as shown in Figure 36-1.

Figure 36-1

As mentioned earlier in the lesson, when you are using a package saved in a folder on the file system you need to select File System from the Location drop-down menu. When this option is selected, the Package property changes to PackageNameReadOnly and becomes grayed out. The Package property is not needed in this situation because the name of the package will be in the file location selected in the Connection property.

The Connection drop-down now lets you select a file on the file system. If you do not have the connection created in the connection manager, you can select the <New connection…> option and create the file connection. Once the file connection exists in the connection manager, you can select it in the Connection drop-down menu.

The next property of the Execute Package Task is Password. This is the password of the child package. If the child package does not have a password, you can leave this field unchanged. Although the password property shows asterisks in the field as a default, as shown in Figure 36-2, this does not mean a password is entered into the task. Clicking the ellipsis next to the Password property opens the Password Property Editor.

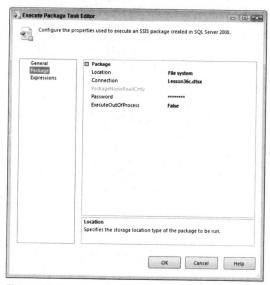

Figure 36-2

In the Password Property Editor you need to enter the password twice and click OK to save the password (Figure 36-3). Saving the password does not make any changes to the asterisks in the password property. If you are unsure if a password is set and want to remove a password, leave both password fields blank in the Password Property Editor and click OK.

Figure 36-3

The next property is ExecuteOutofProcess. When this property is set to True, the child package runs in a separate process from the parent package. Running a child package in a separate process uses more memory, but it provides more flexibility. Running the child package in a separate process allows the parent package to continue when the child package fails, which is useful when you have other tasks in the parent package that you want to complete regardless of the success of the child package.

When you need the parent and child packages to fail together as one unit, you need to leave the ExecuteOutofProcess property set to False. Leave this property set to False also when you do not want to incur the additional overhead of another process.

Configuring a Child Package

In most situations involving a parent package and child package, you are going to need to pass information from the parent package to the child package. The Package Configuration options in the child package allow you to do this. To open the Package Configuration Organizer, right-click in the blank area in the Control Flow, and left-click Package Configurations. Place a check next to Enable Package Configurations to turn on configuration options for the package. Clicking Add at the bottom of the Package Configuration Organizer starts the Package Configuration Wizard. In the drop-down menu of Configuration Types one of the options is Parent Package Variable.

Once Parent Package Variable is selected, the option for Parent Variable is shown. The name of the variable from the parent package must be typed in the text box. Keep in mind that the variable name is case sensitive. On the next screen you see the list of the objects available in the child package and the attributes for those objects. Select the attribute where the parent package's variable value is to be saved in the child package by clicking the attribute.

The next screen gives the option of Configuration Name. This is the name saved in the child package and is used for reference in the Configuration Organizer only. The Configuration Name can be anything but should be descriptive of the reason for the configuration.

Once the Package Configuration for the parent package variable is created, as seen in Figure 36-4, the value of the variable in the parent package will be passed to the child package, and it will be the value of the variable at the time the Execute Package Task is executed in the parent package.

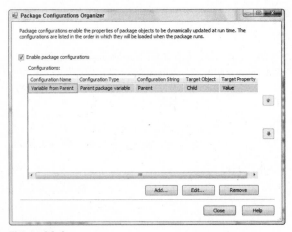

Figure 36-4

Try It

In this lesson you create a parent package and a child package and then you pass a variable value to the child package. After you complete this lesson you should understand the relationship between a parent and child package and how to pass information between them.

Lesson Requirements

Create a parent package with an Execute Package Task and a string variable named "Parent" with a value of "From Parent." Then create a child package with a string variable named "Child" with a value of "From Child." Create a Parent Package Configuration on the child package to pass the value of the "Parent" variable to the "Child" variable. The child package will have a Script Task to show a popup with the value of the "Child" variable. Run the child package and see the value of the variable, and then run the parent package and see the new value of the variable.

The completed parent and child packages for this lesson are available for download from www.wrox.com. The parent package is Lesson36p.dtsx, and the child package is Lesson36c.dtsx.

Hints

- ❏ You need two packages
- ❏ The value of the variable should be different in the packages
- ❏ The Script Task code is `msgbox(DTS.Variables("Child").Value)`

Step-by-Step

1. Create two packages, one to be a parent and one to be a child.
2. In the parent package right-click in the blank Control Flow and click Variables.
3. Click Add Variable and name the variable "Parent."
4. Set the Variable Type to String.
5. Set the Value of the variable to "From Parent."
6. Drag out an Execute Package Task to the Control Flow.
7. Double-click the Execute Package Task and set the Name to "Call Child" and the Description to "This calls a Child Package."
8. Click the Package node in the left pane of the Execute Package Task Editor.
9. Set the Location to File System.
10. Set the Connection to the child package you just created using the <New connection…> option in the drop-down menu.
11. Click OK in the Execute Package Task Editor.
12. Open the child package and create a string variable named "Child" with a value of "From Child."
13. Drag a Script Task into the Control Flow of the child package.
14. Double-click the Script Task to open the Script Task Editor.
15. Set the Script Language to Visual Basic.
16. Click the ellipsis next to ReadOnlyVariables and select the Child variable.

17. Click the Edit Script button and enter the following script: `MsgBox(DTS.Variables("Child").Value)`

18. Close the Script Editor and click OK in the Script Task Editor.

19. Right-click the blank area of the Control Flow and select Package Configurations.

20. Place a check next to Enable Package Configurations and click Add.

21. Click Next on the wizard start up screen if it appears.

22. Select Parent Package Variable from the Configuration Type menu.

23. Type "Parent" in the Parent Variable text box and click Next.

24. Select the Value of the Child variable in the left pane (Figure 36-5). Then click Next.

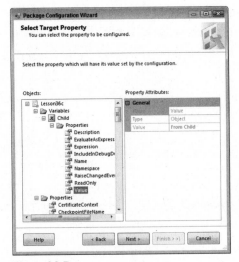

Figure 36-5

25. Set the Configuration name to "Variable from Parent."

26. Click Finish and then click Close.

27. Click the green debug arrow on the toolbar. The value in the popup should be "From Child."

28. Close the popup and stop debugging the child package.

29. Open the parent package.

30. Click the green debug arrow on the toolbar. The value in the popup should be "From Parent."

 Please select Lesson 36 on the DVD to view the video that accompanies this lesson.

Section VII

Troubleshooting and Logging

Logging Package Data

Most businesses want to keep track of the packages running on their servers. The logging options in SSIS allow you to record package information at runtime. This lesson shows you how to use those built-in logging options.

> *Although the logging options built into SSIS are limited, you have other ways to log information. One example is creating Execute SQL Tasks in the event handlers and passing in the system variables. However, creating and maintaining this type of logging can be time-consuming. There is also software available that creates a robust auditing framework on your packages, such as BI xPress from Pragmatic Works, Inc.*

To set up logging with the built-in SSIS logging option, right-click in the Control Flow of a package and select Logging. This action opens the Configure SSIS Logs window, as shown in Figure 37-1. To log information from the package you need to place a check next to the package name in the left pane.

The drop-down menu of provider types has the available logging locations where you can save the information from the package. The options are as follows:

- ❑ **Windows Event Log** — The Windows Event Log option logs the data to the Windows Event Log

- ❑ **Text File** — The Text File option saves the information into a plain text file with the data comma separated

- ❑ **XML File** — The XML File option saves the data in an XML File parsed into XML nodes

- ❑ **SQL Server** — The SQL Server option logs the data to a table in your SQL Server. The table logged to on the server is named "sysssislog." If it does not exist, this table is created automatically by SSIS when the package runs

- ❑ **SQL Server Profiler** — The SQL Server Profiler option logs the data to a file as SQL that can be captured in SQL Server Profiler

Regardless of the provider type you select, options are available as to what data you want to log and when this data is logged. You can see these options under the Details tab of the Configure SSIS Logs window, as shown in Figure 37-2.

Figure 37-1

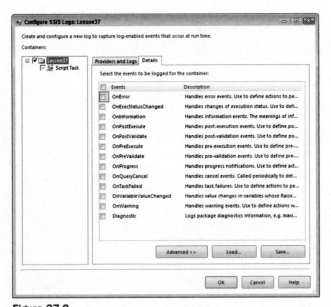

Figure 37-2

Under the Details tab you select the event you want to cause logging. If the event occurs during the run of the package, it logs data to the selected provider. The most commonly used events are onError, onWarning, onPreExecute, and onPostExecute.

If you select onError, if an error occurs during the execution of the package, data is stored in the selected log provider. If an error never occurs during the package execution, then obviously no data is logged for this event. The same holds true for onWarning and warnings occurring during the package execution.

The onPreExecute event logs all the data before the package begins execution. This gives you a chance to see what the data values were before the packages performed any tasks. The onPostExecute event option logs all of the data after the package has completed execution.

The data that is saved by the SSIS logging options is shown in the Advanced window, as shown in Figure 37-3, which you bring up in the Details tab by clicking the Advanced button at the bottom of the screen. In the advanced screen you can select what data you want to log and on what event. You can select or unselect each item on each event. So if you want to log the computer name, but only on the onPreExecute, you can place a check under the Computer column next to the onPreExecute event only and make sure it is unchecked for the other events. This is the limit of the customization allowed to the built-in SSIS logging.

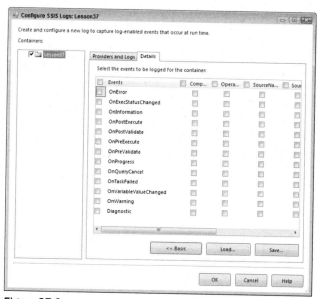

Figure 37-3

To create a log provider, select a provider type from the Provider Type drop-down menu on the Providers and Logs tab in the Configure SSIS Logs window, and then click the Add button. The log provider then appears in the "Select the logs to use for the container" pane below the drop-down menu. Place a check under the Name column to turn on the log provider. If you want to disable a log, but not remove it from this log menu, you need only remove the check in the Name column next to that log provider.

After you have created the log provider and checked the name column to activate it, click the Configuration drop-down menu. If a connection type exists in the connection manager that is used by the selected provider, it shows in this window. If the connection does not exist, you can create it by clicking the <New connection...> option.

Next click the Details tab to choose the events you want to log. If you want to log all events, click the check box next to the Events title at the top of the events list to select all. If you want just individual events, place a check next to the event you want to cause logging.

After you have selected the events click the Advanced button and uncheck any data you do not want to log on the events you prefer so you don't have that data saved. You can also save the configuration you have selected to an XML file with the Save button that appears at the bottom of the Details tab. Later you can use this XML file in another package to select the same check boxes in this logging configuration screen automatically by clicking the Load button that also appears at the bottom of the Details tab.

Try It

In this lesson you are going to create a package with a Script Task that causes an error and logs the package information on the error, before it runs, and after it completes. After this lesson, you will have an understanding of how to use SSIS logging to audit the running of your packages.

Lesson Requirements

Create a package with a Script Task. Edit the Script Task to open a message box popup with a variable that does not exist. Log the package onError, onPreExecute, and onPostExecute.

The completed package for this lesson is available for download on the book's website at www.wrox.com.

Hints

❑   You need to turn on three event logs

❑   Do not alter the advanced logging options

Step-by-Step

1. Create a new package.

2. Drag a Script Task into the Control Flow.

3. Open the Script Task and set the language to Visual Basic.

4. Click Edit Script and enter the following:

```
msgbox(DTS.Variables("Test").Value)
```

Do not create the "Test" variable.

5. Close the Script Editor and click OK in the Script Task.

6. Right-click the Control Flow and select Logging.

7. Place a check next to the package name in the left pane.

8. Select the SSIS log provider for text files in the Provider Type drop-down menu and click Add.

9. Place a check in the Name column of the Log Provider.

10. Click the Configuration drop-down menu and select <New connection...>.

11. Create a connection to a text file named "LogTest.txt" on your local drive and select create file as the usage type. Then click OK.

12. Click on the Details tab.

13. Place a check next to onError, onPreExecute, and onPostExecute.

14. Click OK.

15. Run the package by clicking the green debug arrow on the toolbar.

16. After the Script Task turns red open the LogTest.txt file on your desktop.

17. You should see the error "The Element cannot be found in a Collection." This is the error indicating the variable name in the Script Task is invalid.

18. You should also see the pre- and post-execute lines in the text file.

 Please select Lesson 37 on the DVD to view the video that accompanies this lesson.

Using Event Handlers

While the main tasks of SSIS packages exist in either the Control Flow or the Data Flow, the Event Handlers tab, the subject of this lesson, is another tab that is very useful when you are creating a package. *Event handlers* are what enable you to call tasks when events like errors or warnings occur during the execution of a package, which can be helpful in logging errors or sending notifications. The Event Handlers tab is used to call a task when an event has occurred in the package. The tasks in the event handler run only if the proper event is called in the package. Therefore, it is possible to have tasks in the event handlers of a package that don't run during the execution of the package because the proper event is not called.

Several events can occur in a package to cause an event to fire and call an event handler:

- ❏ OnError
- ❏ OnExecStatusChanged
- ❏ OnInformation
- ❏ OnPostExecute
- ❏ OnPostValidate
- ❏ OnPreExecute
- ❏ OnPreValidate
- ❏ OnProgress
- ❏ OnQueryCancel
- ❏ OnTaskFailed
- ❏ OnVariableValueChanged
- ❏ OnWarning

The most commonly used events are OnError, OnWarning, OnPreExecute, and OnPostExecute. The OnError event fires when the executable selected has an error occur during its execution. The OnWarning event fires when the executable selected has a warning occur during its execution. The OnPreExecute event fires just before the selected executable starts executing. The OnPostExecute event fires just after the selected executable finishes executing.

Creating Event Handlers

When you open the Event Handlers tab for the first time, it looks similar to Figure 38-1. Notice there is a blue link in the middle. When clicked, this link creates an event handler on the package. At the top of the Event Handlers tab are two drop-down menus. The left drop-down menu contains a list of all the executables in the package. This is a list of all the tasks in the package. If no tasks have been created in the package, the only executable listed is the package.

Figure 38-1

When you are creating an event handler, it is important to select the proper executable from the drop-down menu to ensure the tasks in the event handler execute when intended.

The second drop-down menu, on the top right of the Event Handlers tab, contains a list of all the events that can be chosen for the selected executable.

In Figure 38-2 there is a Script Task in the Control Flow of the package and a Data Flow with a source and destination. Notice the source and destination do not show in the drop-down menu of executables. Rather, the entire Data Flow is the executable. Placing an OnPostExecute Event Handler on the Data Flow means the task in the event handler will fire after the entire Data Flow finishes executing. Placing an OnError Event Handler on the Script Task means the tasks in the event handler will fire only if an error occurs on the Script Task. So, for example, if no error occurs or if an error occurs in the Data Flow (as opposed to in the Script Task), the OnError event on the Script Task will not fire.

Figure 38-2

When you first open the Event Handlers tab and click the blue link in the middle of the tab, it creates an OnError event for the package. This causes the tasks in the event handler to execute if any errors occur during any tasks in the package. Sometimes you may want the tasks in the event handlers to fire only for a certain task in the package. To do this, first select the task in the left drop-down menu and then click the blue link in the event handler. This action creates an event handler for the specific tasks and executes only when the proper event occurs on the tasks selected.

Common Uses for Event Handlers

Two of the most common uses for the event handlers are notification and logging. When you want to be notified via email that an error has occurred, the event handlers are the right place to execute this task. Simply place a Send Mail Task in the OnError Event Handler for the package. When you want to be notified via email that a package has completed, again the event handlers are the right place to execute this task. Just place a Send Mail Task in the OnPostExecute Event Handler for the package.

These Send Mail Tasks can contain information about the package. You can include any system variables in the message to tell you what occurred in the package and when.

Another useful purpose of the event handlers is logging. You can create your own custom logging framework if you are not satisfied with the built-in logging of SSIS. By creating Execute SQL Tasks in the event handlers you can write information from the package to a database. These Execute SQL Tasks execute only when the proper event occurs, allowing you to log errors when they occur with the OnError Event Handler and warnings with the OnWarning Event Handler.

After several event handlers have been created and these event handlers are on different executables, you might find it hard to keep track of which executable has an event handler and which does not. The Executable drop-down menu shows all of the event handlers on the package and each executable. There is also an Event Handler folder under the package and each executable. Clicking the plus next to this folder opens the folder and shows the event handlers in each of them.

Under the event handler is an Executables folder showing each task in the event handler. In Figure 38-3 you can see the package has three event handlers each with an Execute SQL Task. The Data Flow and Script Task have OnError Event Handlers with Send Mail Tasks in them. This information can also be seen in the Package Explorer tab.

Figure 38-3

When you click the plus next to any task in an event handler, you see there is another Event Handler folder. The task in the event handler can have an event handler of its own. So, you can have a Send Mail Task in the OnPostExecute Event Handler of a package and then have an Execute SQL Task in the OnError Event Handler of the Send Mail Task. If the Send Mail Task has an error, the error can then be logged with the Execute SQL Task.

Try It

In this lesson you are going to create a package with an Execute SQL Task with an OnError Event Handler. The event handler is going to cause a popup message from a Script Task to show the error. After this lesson you will understand how to create and use event handlers on a package.

Lesson Requirements

Create a package with an Execute SQL Task. Run it with no error, and run it with an error. The OnError Event Handler should fire when there is an error.

The completed package for this lesson is available for download on the book's website at www.wrox.com.

Hints

❑ Create an Execute SQL Task in the Control Flow

❑ Create an OnError Event Handler

❑ Create a Script Task in the event handler

Step-by-Step

1. Create a new package.

2. Drag in an Execute SQL Task.

3. Set the Connection to AdventureWorks2008.

4. Set the SQL statement to "Select 1." When you are ready to cause an error, change the SQL to "Select a."

5. Click the Event Handlers tab.

6. Select the package in the Executables menu.

7. Select the OnError Event Handler in the Event Handler menu.

8. Click the blue link to create the OnError Event Handler.

9. Drag a Script Task into the event handler.

10. Double-click the Script Task.

11. Set the Script Language to VB.

12. Click the ReadOnlyVariables ellipses.

13. Place a check next to System::ErrorDescription.

14. Click the Edit Script button.

15. In the Main class type in `MsgBox(Dts.Variables("ErrorDescription").Value)`

16. Close the Script Editor.

17. Click OK in the Script Task Editor.

18. Click the Control Flow tab.

19. Click the green debug arrow on the toolbar to run the package.

20. The Execute SQL Task should turn green, and no error should occur.

21. Click the stop debug button on the toolbar.

22. Change the query in the Execute SQL Task to "Select a."

23. Click the green debug arrow on the toolbar to run the package.

24. A popup message will appear matching Figure 38-4.

25. Click OK in the message box and stop the debugging.

Figure 38-4

 Please select Lesson 38 on the DVD to view the video that accompanies this lesson.

Troubleshooting Errors

After creating a package with all of the tasks needed, you almost always face some necessary amount of troubleshooting. For example, a package running in your production database might suddenly stop working due to some change to the environment. You need the ability to analyze the errors from the package to determine what is going wrong and how to fix it. That's the focus of this lesson.

For example, validation errors are easy to stop in a package because the task with the error has a small red circle with a red x on it. This icon indicates the task is not passing the validation phase of the package. In this case the package pops up a message showing the validation error. These errors look like Figure 39-1. The error seems long but the key message is in the fourth line. It states "Invalid object name" and then gives the object name "MailingErrorQueue." This is an object being referred to by the package that does not exist and is therefore causing this error.

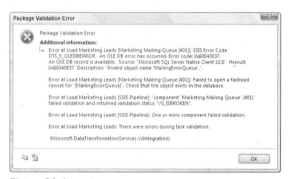

Figure 39-1

In cases like the one just mentioned, the error may not be caused by a problem with the package but rather the environment. The object that is not found might need to be created, or the connection manager might be set up incorrectly. In this case a table is missing.

Working in the Progress Tab

When you are debugging a package, errors show in the Progress tab. During troubleshooting you spend a lot of time in the Progress tab, so it is important to get familiar with the messages and icons located there. Figure 39-2 shows a typical Progress tab with an error.

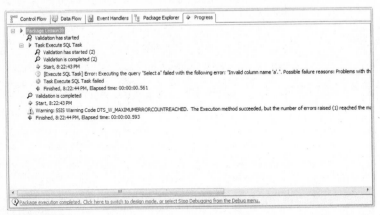

Figure 39-2

You need to become familiar with several icons in the Progress tab for troubleshooting purposes. They indicate key places in the flow of the package. Figure 39-3 has a list of the icons in the Progress tab and their abbreviated meanings.

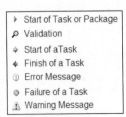

Figure 39-3

The first item listed in the Progress tab is the name of the package. There is a small blue triangle next to the package name. These blue arrows appear next to the package and the tasks in the package. This makes it easier to distinguish where the messages about a task start and stop.

There is also a negative symbol next to the package name and task names. Clicking this negative symbol collapses the executable next to it. If you are troubleshooting a package and you know the errors appear only in a certain task, you can collapse the other tasks to make it easier to read through the errors on the task in question.

A small magnifying glass appears next to lines to indicate validation has started and finished. *Validation* is the process of checking for the sources and destinations in the particular task.

A green arrow pointing to the right indicates the start of the task listed above the arrow. The start time of the task is listed next to the green arrow. A red arrow pointing to the left indicates the stopping point of a task. The total time the task ran is listed next to the red arrow.

Three icons indicate an error or warning has occurred in the package:

❑   The red exclamation point in a circle indicates an error has occurred, and the full error message is usually listed next to this icon. The icon can show several times in the Progress tab and have several different messages. The first error is usually the one that contains the meaningful information. In some cases you may even see a message referring you to the preceding error.

      If the error message next to the red exclamation point is too long to read or if you need a copy of the error, you can right-click the error, click the "Copy Message Text" option that appears, and then paste it in an email or in a text editor.

❑   The next icon seen after the red exclamation point is the red circle with an x in the center. The message next to this icon is usually not very useful. It does not give details of what caused the failure; it just states the task failed. This icon is easy to spot and makes it easy to find the error messages in the Progress tab. This is especially true when the package has a lot of tasks and the Progress tab has many screens to look through.

❑   The last icon you should be familiar with is the yellow triangle with the black exclamation point in the center. This icon indicates a warning has occurred on the package. Warnings can occur on a package without stopping the package. It is normal to run a package and to have warnings occur during runtime, but to still have all of the tasks in the package complete successfully.

      Warnings may not cause a package to fail, but it is important to read them and decide if changes should be made to the package to prevent possible package failures in the future. One of the more common warning messages seen in Data Flows is "Truncation may occur . . ." This Message does not stop a package from executing. This message indicates that a source column is set to a length that is greater than the destination column. Unless the data in the source column is actually longer than the destination, truncation will not occur, and the package will execute successfully. But that might not always be the case, and the warning is pointing out that the potential exists for a problem to occur later.

Troubleshooting Steps

Thousands of errors can occur in a package, and the methods to correct these errors are almost always specific to the package. Too many possibilities exist to list every error message and how to fix them. However, the steps to correcting errors are the same:

1.   Check the Progress tab and read all error messages.

2.   Determine which tasks needs adjusting, if any; keep in mind the error could be caused by something outside of the package.

3.   Stop debugging.

4.   Adjust the task that caused the error.

5.   Debug.

6.   Repeat if more errors occur.

One of the pitfalls of troubleshooting a package is assuming the error has not changed. Once you have gone through the steps of troubleshooting and the package still fails, it is always important to return to the Progress tab and check the error message again. The error message can change; you may have fixed the first error and are now getting a new error. As you can imagine, it is even more difficult to fix a package when you are troubleshooting the wrong error.

Try It

In this lesson you open the package named Lesson39.dtsx (which you can download at www.wrox.com) and troubleshoot the errors to get it working. After completing this lesson, you will have a better understanding of how to troubleshoot errors in SSIS.

Lesson Requirements

Open the package named Lesson39.dtsx. Run the package in debug mode. Look at the errors and make the necessary corrections to the package for it to run with no errors. The package should cause a popup box to appear with the words Adjustable Race.

Hints

❏   The Execute SQL Task has Syntax errors

❏   The Execute SQL Task has Result Set errors

❏   The Script Task is missing variable parameters

❏   The Script Task has a typo in the code

Step-by-Step

You can troubleshoot the package correctly and fix the errors in a different order than what is listed in this step-by-step walkthrough.

1.   Click the green debug arrow on the toolbar.

2.   An error occurs stating the variable may have been changed.

3.   Rename the variable to "strName."

4.   Debug the package again.

5.   Check the Progress tab to see the invalid column name reference.

6.   Change the column names in the Execute SQL Task to "Name" instead of "Names."

7.   Debug the package again.

8.   Click the Progress tab and read the error "The element cannot be found in a collection."

This error is not very descriptive; it indicates the task is referring to an object that does not exist. In this case it is the variable.

9.   Open the Script Task Editor and select the "strName" variable in the ReadOnlyVariables property.

10. Debug the package again.

11. Notice the same error in the Progress tab.

12. Open the Script Task and change the message box code to `MsgBox(Dts.Variables("strName").Value)`.

13. Debug the package again.

14. A message box should appear matching Figure 39-4.

Figure 39-4

 Please select Lesson 39 on the DVD to view the video that accompanies this lesson.

Using Data Viewers

The Data Flow Task moves data from sources to destinations with some transforms in between. When you are running a Data Flow in development, it might seem difficult to determine if the data is being transformed correctly. The columns might not be passed through the Data Flow at all.

You could open the destination to check on the status of the data, but this approach might not always be the best solution. Imagine a Data Flow with dozens of transforms moving thousands of rows to a destination. Opening the destination shows the columns are not showing the data you expected. Which transform is causing the problem? It may be hard to determine by just examining the data in the destination. This situation is where Data Viewers make tracking data changes much easier. *Data Viewers* are a development tool used to glance at the data during the Data Flow execution phase of a package. They cause a small popup window to show the data at certain points in a Data Flow.

Data Viewers should be removed before moving a package to production to be scheduled to run. If the Data Viewer remains on a package, the package will not stop at the point the Data Viewer is called, and the Data Viewer will load in memory and use unnecessary buffers.

To create a Data Viewer on a Data Flow, double-click the green or red line that connects the tasks in the Data Flow. This opens the Data Flow Path Editor, as shown in Figure 40-1. In the General node you find the common properties of the Data Flow Path. The Metadata node shows the metadata for each column in the Data Flow at that point.

Figure 40-1

The last node is the Data Viewers node. Under the Data Viewers node are three buttons: Add, Delete, and Configure. If no Data Viewers exist, the Delete and Configure buttons are disabled.

To add a Data Viewer to the Data Flow click the Add button. This action opens the Configure Data Viewer window. You have four types of Data Viewers to choose from in this menu:

- ❑ Grid
- ❑ Histogram
- ❑ Scatter Plot (x, y)
- ❑ Column Chart

No matter which Data Viewer you select, they all stop the Data Flow at about 10,000 rows unless the default buffer size property of the Data Flow has been changed. You click the small green arrow in the top left of each Data Viewer to pass in approximately the next 10,000 rows. This presentation allows you to view chunks of data and is an efficient way to view lots of data as it passes through the Data Flow.

The Grid option shows the values in each column, as shown in Figure 40-2. It shows the data in a table structure similar to Excel. You can change the size of the columns and highlight one row or multiple rows. A Copy Data button allows you to copy all of the data from the Grid View to the clipboard to be used in a text editor. A Detach button at the top of the Grid View detaches the Data Viewer from the debugging process. It allows the package to continue running without populating the rest of the data in the Data Viewer. When you click the Detach button, the last set of rows remains in the Data Viewer.

Figure 40-2

The Histogram Data Viewer shows the data in a chart. When you are creating a Histogram chart, it is important to click the Histogram tab at the top of the Configure Data Viewer window and select the column you want to view in the chart. The chart will show the column selected on the bottom axis and the number count on the side axis. Each range is auto-generated by the Data Viewer to show all the data. The bottom of the chart shows the Data Viewer is attached, the total rows, buffers, and the number of rows currently displayed, as shown in Figure 40-3. These numbers can change each time the green continue arrow is clicked.

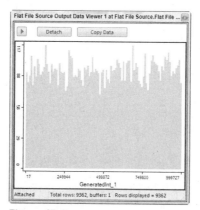

Figure 40-3

The Scatter Plot Data Viewer shows the data in a different type of chart. This Data Viewer is not just a count of the values; it is a plot of two values against each other, as shown in Figure 40-4. When selecting the Scatter Plot Data Viewer, you need to select the X and Y axis in the Scatter Plot (x, y) tab. The column names are listed in both fields. This allows you to see trends in your data. If you want to determine if the price and weight of a product have a correlation, the scatter plot shows this in a chart that makes the trend easy to spot.

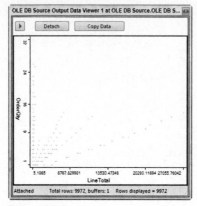

Figure 40-4

The Column Chart Data Viewer shows the data in a chart with columns. The column data is along the bottom axis and the count is along the side axis, as shown in Figure 40-5. Just as was the case in the scatter plot, these values are automatically calculated by SQL Server Integration Services (SSIS) to show all of the data. When configuring the Column Chart Data Viewer, click the Column Chart tab in the Configure Data Viewer window and select the column to display in the Data Viewer.

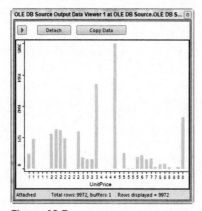

Figure 40-5

When you are done using the Data Viewers in the Data Flow of a package, double-click the Data Flow connectors that contain Data Viewers. These are indicated by the small table with glasses shown next to the Data Flow lines, as shown in Figure 40-6. In the Data Flow Path Editor, click the Data Viewers node and click the Delete button at the bottom.

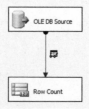

Figure 40-6

Try It

In this lesson you create a package with a Data Flow and create a Data Viewer on the Data Flow. After this lesson, you will understand how to use Data Viewers to assist you in developing Data Flows in SSIS. You will know how to view data between each task in a Data Flow. You can download the completed lesson at www.wrox.com.

Lesson Requirements

Create a package with a Data Flow and create a Data Viewer after the source to see the data in the Data Viewer window.

Hints

❑ Connect to an OLE DB Source

❑ The source can connect to a Row Count Task

❑ You need a row count variable

Step-by-Step

1. Create a new package.

2. Drag in a Data Flow Task.

3. Double-click the Data Flow.

4. Drag in an OLE DB Source to the Data Flow.

5. Connect the OLE DB Source to the AdventureWorks2008 database.

6. Select the SalesOrderDetail table in the OLE DB Source.

7. Drag in a Row Count Transform.

8. Connect the OLE DB Source to the Row Count Transform with the green Data Flow line from the bottom of the OLE DB Source.

9. Right-click in the Data Flow and select Variables.

10. Create a variable named "intRowCount."

11. Close the Variable window.

12. Double-click the Row Count Transform.

13. Select the intRowCount variable in the Row Count Transform.

14. Close the Row Count Transform.

15. Double-click the green Data Flow.

16. Click the Data Viewers node.

17. Click the Add button.

18. Select Grid in the Type menu.

19. Click OK in both open windows.

20. Click the green debug button on the toolbar.

21. You should see a Grid Data Viewer appear showing data.

22. Click the green continue arrow in the Data Viewer until all rows have passed through.

23. Close the Data Viewer.

24. Stop debugging the package.

 Please select Lesson 40 on the DVD to view the video that accompanies this lesson.

Using Breakpoints

When you are developing a package, many times you will need to troubleshoot issues in the package. It is helpful to know the status of data, variables, and tasks at certain points in the execution of the package. Breakpoints allow you to stop a package during execution and view the status of these items. Breakpoints also allow you to see value of variables immediately before and after a task.

To create a breakpoint on a task, right-click the task and select Edit Breakpoints. This action opens the Set Breakpoints window as shown in Figure 41-1. The left-hand column of this window is a set of check boxes that enable the breakpoint listed. Figure 41-1 shows the Set Breakpoints window for a For Loop Container. Notice the last breakpoint option is "Break at the beginning of every iteration of the loop." This option is available only on the For Loop and Foreach Loop.

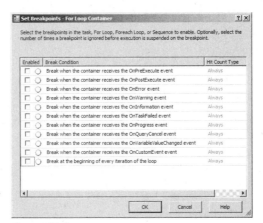

Figure 41-1

Each option in the Set Breakpoints window will stop the package execution at a different point during in the task:

❑ **OnPreExecute**—Just before the task executes

❑ **OnPostExecute**—Directly after the task completes

❑ **OnError**—When an error occurs in the task

❑ **OnWarning**—When a warning occurs in the task

❑ **OnInformation**—When the task provides information

❑ **OnTaskFailed**—When the task fails

❑ **OnProgress**—To update progress on task execution

❑ **OnQueryCancel**—When the task can cancel execution

❑ **OnVariableValueChanged**—When the value of a variable changes (the RaiseChangedEvent property of the variable must be set to true)

❑ **OnCustomEvent**—When the custom task-defined events occur

❑ **Loop Iteration**—At the beginning of each loop cycle

The most commonly used events in breakpoints are OnPreExecute, OnPostExecute, OnError, OnWarning, and Loop Iteration. By using OnPreExecute and OnPostExecute on a task you can see the value of a variable before and after a task, which allows you to determine if the task changed the value of the variable to the expected value. The OnError and OnWarning events allow you to stop a package with a breakpoint if something goes wrong. Imagine having a package that contains two Data Flows: the first loads the data into a flat file and the second loads the data into a table. If the first Data Flow encounters a warning, you do not want the second Data Flow to load the data. An OnWarning Breakpoint on the first Data Flow can stop the package from executing the second Data Flow.

The Loop Iteration Breakpoint stops the package at the beginning of either a Foreach Loop or a For Loop. If a loop is executed ten times, the breakpoint will fire ten times. If a loop never occurs in a package, the breakpoint will never fire. If you have a Foreach Loop set to loop through each file in a folder and the breakpoint never fires, check the folder to ensure the files exist.

While a package is stopped at the breakpoint, you can click the green arrow on the toolbar to continue to the next breakpoint or through the rest of the package if there are no other breakpoints. You can also click the square blue stop button on the toolbar to stop the execution of the package at the breakpoint. Keep in mind that the package is stopped at that point and the tasks before the breakpoint have executed. This may require some manual resetting before you can test the package again.

The other properties in the Set Breakpoints window are Hit Count and Hit Count Type. These properties set the maximum number of times that a Breakpoint condition occurs before the Breakpoint stops the package. There are four Hit Count Types:

❑ **Always**—The breakpoint stops the package when the breakpoint fires every time

❑ **Hit Count Equals**—The breakpoint stops the package when the breakpoint fires the number of times listed in Hit Count

❑ **Hit Count Greater than or Equal to**—The breakpoint stops the package when the breakpoint reaches the number listed in Hit Count and every time afterwards

❑ **Hit Count Multiple**—The breakpoint stops the package when the breakpoint reaches the number listed in Hit Count and every multiple of the Hit Count number; a Hit Count of 2 stops the package on every other breakpoint event

Once you have decided which breakpoint to set, and close the Set Breakpoints window by clicking OK, you see a red dot on the task, as in Figure 41-2 (though note that the figure in the book doesn't show color). The red dot indicates a breakpoint exists on a task. In truth, there may be several breakpoints on a task with the red dot. You can also tell when a package is stopped at a breakpoint during debugging here. A small yellow arrow appears in the middle of the red dot on the task.

Figure 41-2

When a breakpoint has stopped a package from running, you can use the Watch window during debugging to see the values of the variables in the package at that time. To open a Watch window, click Debug on the toolbar and then under Windows click Watch and Watch 1. This opens a Watch window at the bottom of Visual Studio by default. Type in the name of the variables you need to monitor to see the values of the variables. In Figure 41-3 you can see the value of some variables in the Watch window during a breakpoint and the variable types.

Figure 41-3

Using breakpoints and the Watch window to debug a package makes it very easy to determine what the tasks in your package are doing. You can quickly determine where the error is occurring and not occurring. In some cases a package might be running with no error messages but might still not be performing correctly. These types of errors would be hard to track down without breakpoints. Errors or no errors, breakpoints allow you to stop a package and examine the results up to that point. You should use breakpoints often during the development of any package.

Try It

In this lesson you create a package with a For Loop to count from 1 to 10. Then you verify the value of the variable in the loop. After this lesson, you will understand how to use breakpoints to aid in the development and debugging of an SSIS package.

Lesson Requirements

Create a package with a For Loop to count from 1 to 10. Use breakpoints and a Watch window to see if the loop is actually incrementing the variable value.

You can download the completed lesson at www.wrox.com.

Hints

- ❏ Use an integer variable
- ❏ Use a For Loop
- ❏ Increment the integer variable by one each loop

Step-by-Step

1. Create a blank package.
2. Create an Integer variable named "intCounter."
3. Set the Value of intCounter to 1.
4. Drag in a For Loop to the Control Flow, and double-click to open the editor.
5. Set the InitExpression of the For Loop to "@intCounter = 1."
6. Set the EvalExpression to "@intCounter < = 10."
7. Set the AssignExpression to "@intCounter = @intCounter + 1." Now the For Loop should match Figure 41-4.

Figure 41-4

8. Close the For Loop Editor by clicking OK.
9. Right-click the For Loop and select Edit Breakpoints.
10. Place a check next to Break at the beginning of every iteration of the loop and click OK.
11. Click the green debug arrow on the toolbar.
12. When the package stops at the breakpoint open a Watch window by clicking Debug on the toolbar. Then under Windows, click Watch and Watch 1.
13. Type in the name of the variable intCounter (it is case-sensitive).
14. The value of intCounter should be 1.
15. The red dot on the For Loop should have a yellow arrow on it, as seen in Figure 41-5, though again you can't see the colors in the book.

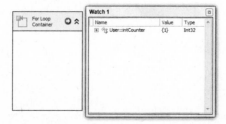

Figure 41-5

16. Click the green debug arrow on the toolbar to continue the package.

17. The value of intCounter in the Watch window should change to 2.

18. Continue clicking the debug arrow until the value reaches 10 and the package completes. The For Loop should turn green.

19. Click the blue square stop debugging button on the toolbar.

 Please select Lesson 41 on the DVD to view the video that accompanies this lesson.

Section VIII
Deployment and Administration

Deploying Packages

So you've created a set of packages, and you're now ready to get those packages to production. This lesson focuses on the deployment of packages from your development environment to each subsequent environment like Q&A or production. You can use several mechanisms to deploy your packages:

- ❑ By using the deployment utility
- ❑ From within BIDS or Management Studio
- ❑ From a command line using `dtutil` or `xcopy`

Each mechanism has its pros and cons that really depend on if you're storing your packages in the msdb database in your SQL Server instance or in the file system. This lesson touches on each of these deployment approaches and these two storage methods.

Deploying Packages Using a Deployment Utility

In SSIS, you can create a deployment utility that helps a user install your project of packages and any dependencies. This deployment utility is like creating a program like InstallShield and is perfect for times when you want to pass a set of packages to a customer or a production DBA that may not know how to install SSIS packages manually. When you create a deployment utility, all the files that are necessary to install the project are copied into a centralized directory and an .SSISDeploymentManifest file, which opens the Package Installation Wizard, is created for the installer to run.

To create a deployment utility, simply right-click the SSIS project in the Business Intelligence Development Studio (BIDS) and select Properties. In the Property Pages dialog box, go to the Deployment Utility page and change the CreateDeploymentUtility property to True, as shown in Figure 42-1. This property is set to False by default. The AllowConfigurationChanges property is a key setting as well and when set to True prompts the installer to ask if he or she wants to change any settings that may be exposed via a configuration file at installation time. The DeploymentOutputPath property shows you where the deployment utility is outputted to underneath the project folder. Click OK to save that property.

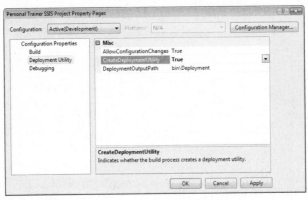

Figure 42-1

Back in the BIDS main screen, under the Build menu, select Build <Project Name>, where <Project Name> represents your project's name. This opens each package and builds the package. If any errors exist in the package, you see them at this point. As BIDS builds the project, each package and the project's .SSISDeploymentManifest file is validated then outputted into the \bin\deployment directory under your project's folder.

> *After building the deployment utility, change the CreateDeploymentUtility to False again. Otherwise, each time you click the Play button to execute the package, each package is validated and executed, which can take an enormous amount of time for a large project.*

Now that you have created a deployment .SSISDeploymentManifest file, you're ready to send the contents of the <project location>\bin\deployment folder to the installation person. The installation person then needs to copy the contents of the folder to the server he or she wishes to deploy to and double-click the .SSISDeploymentManifest file. This action runs the Package Installation Wizard. The installer can also run it remotely, but it is preferable to run it on the same server as the target deployment server to simplify the installation.

After skipping over the introduction screen, you are asked where you want to deploy the packages. You can choose either a File System Deployment or a SQL Server Deployment. A File System Deployment just copies the files to a directory on the server. A SQL Server Deployment stores the packages in the msdb database on the target server. You can also have the wizard validate each package after you install the package. This validation ensures the package, including the data sources, that was delivered to you is valid on your machine.

So, which do you choose—a File System Deployment or a SQL Server Deployment? One of the more common questions that we hear in the forums and in our classes is about the pros and cons of where to put your SSIS packages. The following table shows you a quick guideline of where you'd want to put your packages because the answer really varies based on your needs.

Functionality	Best in File System	Best in msdb
Security		X
Backup and recovery	X	
Deployment	X	
Troubleshooting	X	
Execution speed	X	X

If security concerns you greatly, you may want to consider placing your packages in the msdb database. To secure your packages on the file system, you could have multiple layers of security by using the Windows Active Directory security on the folder on the file system where the packages are located. You could also then place a password on the packages to keep users who may have administrator rights to your machine from executing the package. However, all these measures do add extra complexity to your package deployments in some cases. On the other hand, if you store your packages in the msdb database, you can assign package roles to each package to designate who can see or execute the package. The packages can also be encrypted in the msdb database, which strengthens your security even more.

Backup and recovery is simpler but recovery becomes complex when you store your packages in the msdb database. If you store your packages in the msdb database, you must wrap the msdb database into your regular maintenance plan to back up all the packages. As packages are added, they are wrapped into the maintenance plan. The problem with this is that you cannot restore a single package using this mechanism. You have to restore all the packages to a point in time, and that also restores the jobs and history. The other option is a file system backup, which would just use your favorite backup software to backup the folders and files. However, you must rely on your Backup Operator to do this for you, which makes some uneasy. You could at that point restore individual packages to a point in time. In reality, you may just go ahead and redeploy the packages from SourceSafe if you couldn't retrieve a backup file.

File system deployments are much simpler but less sophisticated than msdb deployments. To deploy packages onto the file system, you must only copy them into the directory for the package store. You can create subdirectories under the parent directory to subdivide it easily. You can also copy a single package over easily as well in case you need to make a package change. To import packages into the package store using the msdb database, you must use Management Studio (or a command-line tool called dtutil.exe) and import them package by package. To do a bulk migration, you can use the deployment utility discussed earlier.

Troubleshooting runs along the same lines as deployment in the file system versus msdb question. If something were to go bump in the night and you wanted to see if the packages in production were the same release as the packages you thought you had deployed, on the file system you only need to copy the files down to your machine and perform a comparison using SourceSafe or another similar tool. However, if the files are stored in the msdb database, you have to right-click each package in Management Studio and select Export.

The good news is no matter what storage option you choose, the performance is the same. As you can see, each storage option has many pros and cons and neither overwhelmingly wins. The main reason that we choose to use the file system generally is for simplicity of deployment.

So when you are faced with the deployment storage choice in the Package Installation Wizard, if you select SQL Server Deployment, the next screen prompts you for which SQL Server 2008 instance you want to deploy the packages. (If you select a File System Deployment, the next screen prompts you for the file path you want the packages to be deployed to.) The last option in the SQL Server Deployment screen is to specify whether you want to rely on the SQL Server for protecting the package by encrypting the package. This is the preferred option and changes the ProtectionLevel package property to ServerStorage as it installs each package.

Even though you have selected a SQL Server Deployment, there may still be files that must be deployed like configuration files and readme files. The next screen prompts you for where you'd like to put these files. Generally, they go under a folder named after the project under the C:\Program Files\Microsoft SQL Server\100\DTS\Packages folder.

After you click Next, the packages are installed in the package store on the server. After the packages are installed, if the developer selected True to the AllowConfigurationChanges in BIDS (shown in Figure 42-1), you receive an additional screen giving you, as an installer, a chance to edit the values in the configuration file at deployment time.

Other Methods of Deploying Packages

As mentioned at the start of the lesson, you do have other methods for deploying packages at your disposal. One way to deploy your packages is from within SQL Server Management Studio, which you can do by first connecting to the SSIS service. Once you are connected, right-click the folder you want to have the packages moved to and select Import Package.

Another way you can deploy the package is with a command-line utility called `dtutil`. This utility is not for the faint of heart but allows you to build a batch file to install your packages quickly if you're a vendor or want to make things easy for your client. To run the command, use the `/FILE` switch to specify where the source package is located and then the `/DestServer` to choose which server to target as shown in the following command line:

```
dtutil /FILE c:\sourcepkg.dtsx /DestServer <servername> /COPY SQL;destpkgname
```

Finally, there is one additional way to migrate and that is from BIDS itself. You can send a single package to production by going to File ⇨ Save Copy of XX.dtsx As. This action saves a single package to either the file system or the msdb database.

Some third-party vendors like Pragmatic Works (`http://www.pragmaticworks.com`) have developed solutions to simplify this migration as well if these options seem complex.

Try It

In this lesson, you learn how to deploy the project of packages you've been using throughout this book to QA or production. You've learned several ways to deploy a single package or set of packages, and although you can choose from many methods to solve the requirements of this lesson, the step-by-step instructions here are going to refer to the Package Installation Wizard. After this lesson, you'll have a better understanding of the options in the Package Installation Wizard and how to deploy packages easily to the msdb database.

Lesson Requirements

You have now completed development of a set of packages and are ready to move those packages to production. The requirements of this lesson are simple: deploy the project of packages that you've been using throughout this book to your SQL Server msdb database.

Hints

❑ Right-click the project in BIDS and select Properties to create a deployment manifest to deploy the packages

❑ This action creates an .SSISDeploymentManifest file that you can then run to launch the installer

Step-by-Step

1. Open the project that you've been using throughout this book.

2. Right-click the project and select Properties. This will launch the SSIS Project Property Pages (shown in Figure 42-1). Go to the Deployment Utility page and set the CreateDeploymentUtility to True.

3. Select Build ➪ *<Project Name>* to build the project.

4. Go to the location of your project file and then go under the \Bin\Deployment folder and run the *<ProjectName>*.SSISDeploymentManifest. (You can find the location of the project file by selecting the project and looking in the Properties window.) This opens the Package Installation Wizard.

5. In the Deploy SSIS Packages screen (shown in Figure 42-2) in the Package Installation Wizard, select SQL Server Deployment, and click Next.

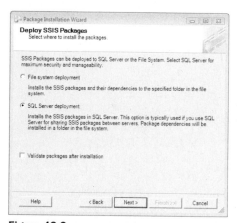

Figure 42-2

6. Type the location of your SQL Server and set the Package Path to \. In addition, check "Rely on server storage for encryption" and click Next.

7. Click Next a few times to complete the wizard and confirm the packages are there in Management Studio after completion by connecting the SSIS Server.

 Please select Lesson 42 on the DVD to view the video that accompanies this lesson.

Configuring the SSIS Service

When you deploy your packages, they are stored into what is called the SSIS Package Store. The Package Store in some cases actually physically stores the package, such as the msdb database option. If you're using file system storage, the Package Store just keeps a pointer to the top-level directory and enumerates through the packages stored underneath that directory. In order to connect to the Package Store, the SSIS service must be running. This service is called SQL Server Integration Services, or MSDTSServer100. There is only one instance of the service per machine or per set of clustered machines.

Though you can run and stop packages programmatically without the service, the service makes running packages more manageable. For example, if you have the service run the package, it tracks that the package is executing and people with the proper permission can interrogate the service and find out which packages are running. Those people that are in the Windows Administrators group can stop all running packages. Otherwise, you can stop only packages that you have started.

The service can also aid in importing and exporting packages into the Package Store. This lesson covers other uses for the service, but one last great use for the service worth mentioning at the start is how it can enable you to create a centralized ETL server to handle the execution of your packages throughout your enterprise.

The MSDTSServer100 service is configured through an XML file that is located by default in the following path: C:\Program Files\Microsoft SQL Server\100\DTS\Binn\ MsDtsSrvr.ini.xml. This path will vary if you're in a cluster. If you cannot find the path, go to the

HKEY_LOCAL_MACHINE\SOFTWARE\Microsoft\Microsoft SQL Server\100\SSIS\ServiceConfigFile registry key in the Registry. By default, the XML file should look like the following:

```
<?xml version="1.0" encoding="utf-8" ?>
  <DtsServiceConfiguration xmlns:xsd="http://www.w3.org/2001/XMLSchema"
xmlns:xsi="http://www.w3.org/2001/XMLSchema-instance">
  <StopExecutingPackagesOnShutdown>true</StopExecutingPackagesOnShutdown>
  <TopLevelFolders>
  <Folder xsi:type="SqlServerFolder">
  <Name>MSDB</Name>
  <ServerName>.</ServerName>
  </Folder>
  <Folder xsi:type="FileSystemFolder">
  <Name>File System</Name>
  <StorePath>..\Packages</StorePath>
  </Folder>
  </TopLevelFolders>
  </DtsServiceConfiguration>
```

There isn't a lot to really configure in this file, but it does have some interesting uses. The first configuration line tells the packages how to react if the service is stopped. By default, packages that the service is running will stop if the service stops or fails over. You could also configure the packages to continue to run until they complete after the service is stopped by changing the StopExecutingPackagesOnShutDown property to false as shown here:

```
<StopExecutingPackagesOnShutdown>false</StopExecutingPackagesOnShutdown>
```

The next configuration sections are the most important. They specify which paths and servers the MSDTSServer100 service reads from. Whenever the service starts, it reads this file to determine where the packages are stored. In the default file, you have a single entry for a SQL Server that looks like the following SqlServerFolder example:

```
<Folder xsi:type="SqlServerFolder">
<Name>MSDB</Name>
<ServerName>.</ServerName>
</Folder>
```

The <Name> line represents how the name will appear in Management Studio for this set of packages. The <ServerName> line represents where the connection points to. There is a problem, however: If your SQL Server is on a named instance, this file still points to the default non-named instance (.). So, if you do have a named instance, simply replace the period with your instance name.

The next section shows you where your file system packages are stored. The <StorePath> property shows the folder where all packages are enumerated from. The default path is C:\program files\ microsoft sql server\100\dts\Packages, which is represented as ..\Packages in the default code that follows. This part of the statement goes one directory below the SSIS service file and then into the Packages folder.

```
<Folder xsi:type="FileSystemFolder">
<Name>File System</Name>
<StorePath>..\Packages</StorePath>
</Folder>
```

Everything in the Packages folder and subfolders is enumerated. You can create subdirectories under this folder, and they immediately show up in Management Studio without your having to modify the service's configuration file.

Each time you make a change to the MsDtsSrvr.ini.xml file, you must stop and start the MSDTSServer100 service.

Try It

In this lesson, you are going to learn how to configure the SSIS service to create a new grouping of packages in a new folder that is going to be monitored.

Lesson Requirements

Configure the SSIS service so that the Package Store contains three folders: File System, MSDB, and File System New, which points to a directory with a few packages in it or your project like C:\Projects\ Personal Trainer (if the directory exists).

Hints

❑ To achieve the goal of this lesson, modify the C:\Program Files\Microsoft SQL Server\100\ DTS\Binn\MsDtsSrvr.ini.xml file

Step-by-Step

1. Prepare for this lesson by creating a new directory if it doesn't exist yet called C:\Projects\Personal Trainer. Open the C:\Program Files\Microsoft SQL Server\100\DTS\Binn\MsDtsSrvr.ini. xml file to edit (in Notepad or your favorite XML editor).

2. Copy and paste the FileSystemFolder node and replace it with the cloned version as follows:

```
<Folder xsi:type="FileSystemFolder">
<Name>File System New</Name>
<StorePath>C:\projects\Personal Trainer</StorePath>
</Folder>
```

3. Save the file and then stop and start the SSIS service (SQL Server Integration Services or MSDTSServer100) in the Services applet. You must have access to perform these actions.

4. Open Management Studio and connect to Integration Services to confirm the results. If you see the new File System New folder, then you have successfully completed this lesson.

 Please select Lesson 43 on the DVD to view the video that accompanies this lesson.

Securing SSIS Packages

Once you deploy your packages, you are going to want to prevent those who aren't authorized from executing the packages. That's the focus of this lesson. The way you lock down your packages depends on where your packages are installed: the msdb database or the file system.

However, before you can dive into the topic of securing the package execution, you must first understand a few things about connecting to the SSIS service. The only login option for connecting to the SSIS service is to use your Active Directory account. Once you connect, you see only packages that you are allowed to see. This protection is accomplished based on package roles. Package roles are available only on packages stored in the msdb database. Packages stored on the file system must be protected with a password and with Windows security.

Package roles can be accessed in Management Studio by right-clicking a package that you want to protect and selecting Package Roles. The Package Roles dialog box shown in Figure 44-1 allows you to choose the msdb role to be in the writer role and reader role.

❏ The **writer role** can perform administration-type functions such as overwrite a package with a new version, delete a package, manage security, and stop the package from running.

❏ The **reader role** can execute and view the package. The reader role can also export the package from Management Studio.

Figure 44-1

Package roles use database roles from the msdb database. By default, people who are in the db_ dtsadmin and db_dtsoperator database roles or the creator of the package can be a reader. The writer role is held by members of the db_dtsadmin database role or the creator of the package by default. When you select the drop-down box in the Package Roles dialog box, you can change the package role from the default one to another customized role from the msdb database.

You may want to customize a group of people as the only ones who can execute the accounting set of packages. As a quick example, consider how to secure a package to a role called Accounting for the writer and reader package role. First, open Management Studio and connect to your development or local database engine instance. Then, expand System Databases ➪ msdb ➪ Security, right-click Roles, and select New Role. This opens the Database Role - New dialog box (shown in Figure 44-2). Of course, you need the appropriate security to create a new database role.

Name the role "Accounting" and make your own login a member of the role by clicking the Add button. Additionally, make your own user or dbo an owner of the role. You may have to add your login as a user to the msdb database prior to adding the role if it's not there already.

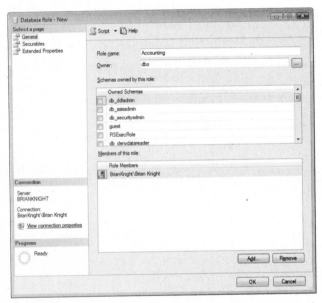

Figure 44-2

You're now ready to tie this role to a package. In Management Studio, connect to Integration Services. Right-click any package stored in the msdb database and select Package Role to secure the package. For the writer and reader roles, select the newly created Accounting role and click OK. Now, members of the Accounting role will be able to perform actions to the package such as execute the package. If you're a member of the sysadmin role for the server, you will be able to perform all functions in SSIS, such as execute and update any package and bypass the package role.

If your packages are stored on the file system, you must set a package password on the package to truly secure it. You can also enforce security by protecting the directory with Windows Active Directory security on the file or folder where your packages are stored. To set a package password in BIDS, you can set the ProtectionLevel property to EncryptSensitiveWithPassword and type a password for the PackagePassword property. You can also set a package password using a utility called DTutil.exe, which is covered in Lesson 42.

To connect to a package store, the SSIS service must be started on the given server. Additionally, you must have TCP/IP port 135 open between your machine and the server. This is a common port used for DCOM, and many network administrators will not have this open by default. You also need to have the SQL Server database engine port open (generally TCP/IP port 1433) to connect to the package store in the msdb database.

Try It

You have just deployed a set of packages, and you now want to lock them down to where no one but the HR group can execute the package. In this lesson, you are going to make sure that only members of the HR group can execute a package of your choosing. After this lesson, you'll have an understanding of how to secure your packages to allow only a given user rights to execute a package.

Lesson Requirements

To successfully complete this lesson, you want to protect one of your packages from executing by anyone but employees in the HR group. First, you need to create an HR role and make yourself a member of the role. Then create a package role to prevent anyone but the HR group from running the package.

Hints

❏ Connect to the database instance and create an HR database role in the msdb system database

❏ Connect to the database instance and set a given package to where the HR role is in the reader role

Step-by-Step

1. Open Management Studio and connect to the database engine for the SQL Server that has your packages installed.

2. Drill to Databases ⇨ System Databases ⇨ msdb ⇨ Security ⇨ Roles.

3. Right-click Roles and select Add Database Role.

4. Type HR for the role name and make yourself a member of the role by clicking Add. The final screen should resemble Figure 44-3. Click OK to save the role.

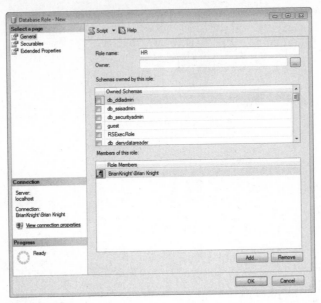

Figure 44-3

5. In the Object Browser in Management Studio, click Connect ⇨ Integration Services to connect to the service.

6. Go to the stored packages in the msdb database and right-click any package to secure and select Package Roles.

7. For the reader role, select HR from the drop-down box, as shown in Figure 44-4. Your package can now be run only by the HR group.

Figure 44-4

 Please select Lesson 44 on the DVD to view the video that accompanies this lesson.

Running SSIS Packages

Now that your packages are deployed, you're ready to run them. In this lesson, you see how to execute a package from a variety of places like Management Studio and from the command line. You also see some of the key differences between 32- and 64-bit machines and some of the items that may not work on a 64-bit machine.

Before we begin, one important caveat is that even though your package is deployed onto a server, the package uses the resources and runs from whichever machine executes it. For example, say you deploy a package to your production server and then you connect through Management Studio and execute the package from your work laptop. In this case, the package will use your laptop's resources, not the production server's resources, to run the package and will likely overwhelm your laptop.

One way to run a package is through Management Studio. Simply open Management Studio for SQL Server 2008 and connect to the Integration Services service.

> *In case you're skipping around, Lessons 42 and 43 discuss how to connect and configure the SSIS service.*

Once connected, you can right-click any package that's stored on the msdb database or in the file system and click Run Package to execute the package.

After you click Run Package, the Execute Package Utility opens. You can also access this utility by double-clicking any package in Windows Explorer or by just running DTExecUI. The tool wraps a command-line package executor called DTExec.exe.

> *The Execute Package Utility tool executes packages only in 32-bit mode, so if your package requires 64-bit support, you'll need to run the package from a command line with the instructions mentioned later in this lesson.*

When you first open the Execute Package Utility (shown in Figure 45-1), you see that the package is automatically selected for you in the General page. If you enter the tool by just typing the command DTExecUI, it does not have the package name already filled out. In this lesson, we cover the important pages in the tool and just touch on the pages that you'll rarely use.

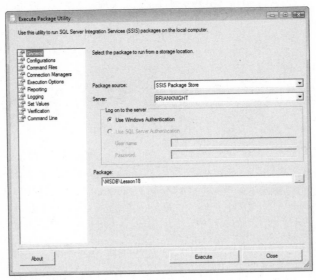

Figure 45-1

The next page in the Execute Package Utility is the Configurations page. In this page, you can select additional configuration files that you want to use for this execution of the package. If you do not select an additional configuration file, any configuration files that are already on the server will be used. Even though you may have configuration files already defined in the package, the existing ones will not show in the list here. This is a place where you can only add additional configuration files.

The Command Files page passes additional custom command-line switches into the DTExec.exe application.

The Connection Managers page shows the power of connection managers. This page allows you to change the connection manager settings at runtime to a different setting than what the developer had originally intended by simply checking the connection you would like to change and making your changes. For example, perhaps you'd like to move the AdventureWorks connection for a package to a production server instead of a QA server (shown in Figure 45-2). Another typical example is when you don't have the same drive structure in production as they had in development and you need to move the connection manager to a different directory.

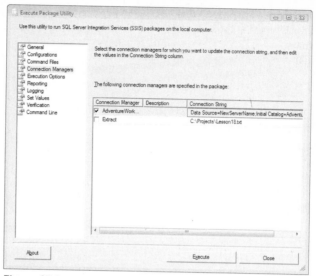

Figure 45-2

The Execution Options page is where you configure the package's execution runtime environment like the number of tasks that will run in parallel.

The Reporting page controls what type of detail will be shown in the console. The default option is Verbose, which may be too detailed for you. You may decide that you'd rather show only Errors and Warnings, which would perform slightly better than the Verbose message. You can also control which columns will show in the console.

The Logging page is where you can specify additional logging providers.

Another powerful page is the Set Values page (shown in Figure 45-3). This page allows you to override nearly any property you want by typing the property path for the property. The most common use for this is to set the value of a variable. To do this, you would use a property path that looked like \Package.Variables[VariableName].Value and then type the value for the variable in the next column. This page is also a way to work around some properties that can't be set through expressions. With those properties, you generally can access them through the property path.

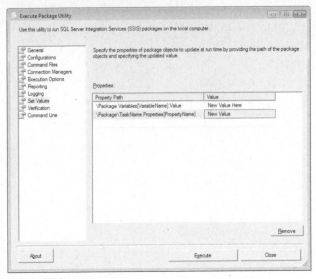

Figure 45-3

In the Verification page, you can ensure that the package will only run if it's the correct build of the package.

The Command Line page (shown in Figure 45-4) is one of the most important pages in the interface. This page shows you the exact DTExec.exe command that will be executing. You can also edit the command here as well. After the command is edited how you like it, you can copy and paste it in a command prompt after the command DTExec.exe.

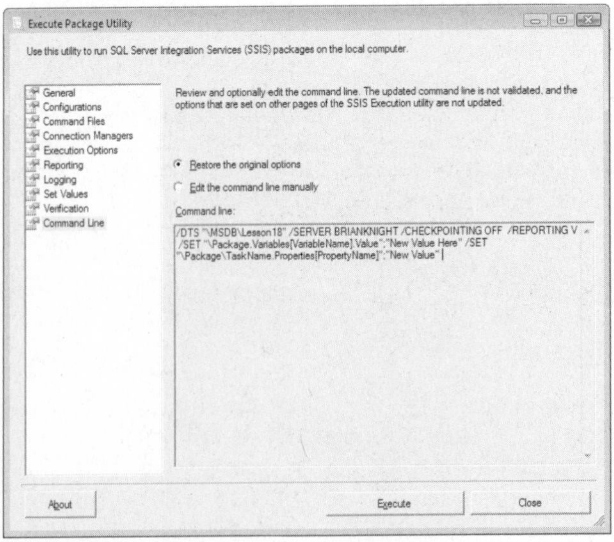

Figure 45-4

Keep in mind that on a 64-bit machine, there are two Program Files directories: C:\Program Files (x86) for 32-bit applications and C:\Program Files for 64-bit applications. A copy of DTExec.exe resides in each of these folders under Microsoft SQL Server\100\Dts\Binn. If you must execute a package in 32-bit mode, you can copy and paste the command from the Command Line page to a command prompt and append this command after the word DTExec.exe (once you're in the appropriate directory). For example, if you're on a 64-bit machine, packages that use Excel at the time of this writing will not work. You'll need to run those packages in 32-bit mode.

You can also execute the package by clicking the Execute button at any time from any page. After you click the Execute button, you see the Package Execution Progress window, which shows you any warnings, errors, and informational messages, as shown in Figure 45-5. You'll only see a fraction of the message in some cases, but you can hover over the message to see the full message.

Figure 45-5

Try It

In this lesson, you learn how to execute a previously created package and change some basic properties prior to execution. You have realized that the original developer of the package left old directory information in the package, and you now need to point the connection manager to a different directory to see the file without modifying the package. After this lesson, you will understand how to run a package in Management Studio and change the properties to point to a new directory.

Lesson Requirements

To simulate this problem, you are going to execute the package that was created in Lesson 18, which creates a flat file. Instead of writing the file to C:\Projects, point the package to C:\Temp if you have the directory or some arbitrary directory of your choosing. Do this connection manager modification without opening the package in BIDS. If you did not complete Lesson 18, you can download Lesson18. dtsx from the Wrox website for this book at www.wrox.com.

Hints

❑ Run the package in Management Studio by right-clicking on the package and selecting Run Package. Go to the Connection Managers page to change the connection

Step-by-Step

1. Open Management Studio and connect to your SSIS service.

2. Find Lesson18 if it has been deployed. If it has not been deployed, you can double-click the package in Windows Explorer.

3. Go to the Connection Managers page of the Execute Package Utility and check the Extract Connection Manager. Once you have checked that, change the path to a path of your choosing.

4. Run the package by clicking Execute and confirm that the file was placed in the new directory.

 Please select Lesson 45 on the DVD to view the video that accompanies this lesson.

Scheduling Packages

Once your packages are deployed, you can schedule them as a job to run automatically through SQL Server Agent. SQL Server Agent runs jobs under its own Windows account, which can pose some security issues when it comes to accessing components in your package. For example, you may have a package that uses Windows Authentication to access a database. When the package is run through SQL Server Agent, Agent will pass its credentials to the database, which may not be adequate. To fix those issues, you can also run packages under a separate Windows account called a proxy account.

To schedule a package through SQL Server Agent, open Management Studio and expand SQL Server Agent ⇨ Jobs. Right-click Jobs and select New Job. Name the job something that you'll recognize at a later time and then go to the Steps page. A *step* is the smallest unit of work in a job, and it can have a number of different types. For SSIS, the type of job is SQL Server Integration Services Package so that is the type you select for your step. Next, point to the package you'd like the step to execute as shown in Figure 46-1. The other tabs that you see look identical to what was discussed in Lesson 45 in the Package Execution Utility (DTExecUI).

The only difference between the job scheduling page and DTExecUI is that when you schedule a job, you additionally have an option in the job system to run the package in 32-bit mode. To do this, check the "Use 32 bit runtime" property in the Execution Options tab. This option will be required for packages that use Excel files or Access databases, to name just a couple scenarios.

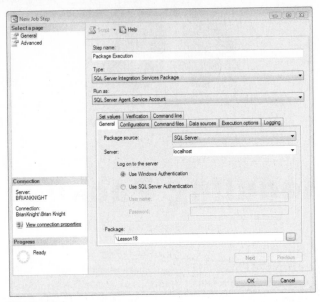

Figure 46-1

After configuration of the step, click OK and then go to the Schedule page. Click New to create a new schedule and then set the schedule of how often you want the package to execute and click OK. You can also manually execute the job by right-clicking it and selecting Start Job at Step. To look at the job history, right-click the job and select View History.

Using Proxy Accounts

A classic problem in SSIS is that a package may work in the design environment but not work once scheduled. Typically, this is because you have connections that use Windows Authentication. At design time, the package uses your credentials, and when you schedule the package, it uses the SQL Server Agent service account by default. This account may not have access to a file share or database server that is necessary to successfully run the package. Proxy accounts in SQL Server 2008 allow you to circumvent this problem.

With a *proxy account*, you can assign a job to use an account other than the SQL Server Agent account with the Run As drop-down box, as shown in Figure 46-1. Creating a proxy account is a two-step process:

1.   First, you must create a credential that will allow a user to use an Active Directory account that is not his own.

2.   Then, you specify how that account may be used.

To first create a credential, open Management Studio, right-click Credentials under the Security tree, and select New Credential. This action opens the New Credential window (shown in Figure 46-2). For this example, you create a credential called Admin Access. The credential allows users to temporarily gain administrator access. For the Identity property, type the name of an administrator account or an account with higher rights. Lastly, type the password for the Windows account, and click OK.

> As you can imagine, because you're typing a password here, be careful of your company's password expiry policies. Credential accounts should be treated as service accounts.

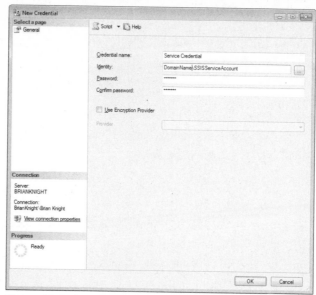

Figure 46-2

The next step is to specify how the credential can be used. Under the SQL Server Agent tree, right-click Proxies and select New Proxy, which opens the New Proxy Account dialog box. Type a name for the Proxy Name property, and the credential name you created earlier as the Credential Name. Check SQL Server Integration Services Package for the subsystem type allowed to use this proxy.

Optionally, you can go to the Principals page in the New Proxy Account dialog box to state which roles or accounts can use your proxy from SSIS. You can explicitly grant server roles, specific logins, or members of given msdb roles rights to your proxy. Click Add to grant rights to the proxy one at a time.

You can now click OK to save the proxy. Now if you create a new SSIS job step as was shown earlier, you can use the new proxy by selecting the proxy name from the Run As drop-down box. Any connections that use Windows Authentication then use the proxy account instead of the standard account. This allows you to connect with the account of your choosing for packages using Windows Authentication and prevent failure.

Try It

In this lesson, you are in the position of having already created a package and are now ready to schedule it to run nightly. To do this, you're going to schedule a SQL Server Agent job to run nightly to execute your package. After you have completed this lesson, you will know how to schedule your packages.

Lesson Requirements

Find a package that you've already deployed to your database (and is safe to run) and schedule the package to run nightly. If you're looking for a sample package, you can use Lesson18.dtsx, which is a package that we use in the following "Step-by-Step" and is available on the Wrox website (www.wrox .com) with the Lesson 18 materials.

Hints

❑ Create a new job in Management Studio under SQL Server Agent. The type of the job is SQL Server Integration Services

Step-by-Step

1. Open Management Studio and connect to your SQL Server instance.

2. Right-click SQL Server Agent (after making sure it is started) and select New ⇨ Job.

3. In the General page, name the job "Test Job."

4. In the Steps page, click New and name the step "Package Execution."

5. Select SQL Server Integration Services from the Type drop-down box.

6. Change the properties in the General page in the New Job Step dialog box to point to Lesson18, as shown in Figure 46-1.

7. Click OK to return to the Steps page and go to the Schedules page.

8. Select New to create a new schedule and schedule the package to run daily by changing the Frequency drop-down box to Daily, as shown in Figure 46-3.

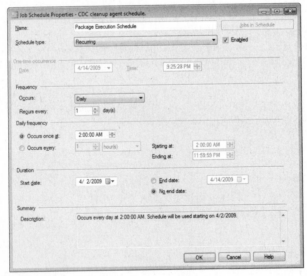

Figure 46-3

9. Click OK several times to save the job. Right-click on the job and select Start Job at Step to begin the job execution. If a failure occurs, you can right-click on the job and select View History to see the failure.

 Please select Lesson 46 on the DVD to view the video that accompanies this lesson.

Section IX
Data Warehousing

Loading a Dimension Table

If you have a data warehouse, you've probably been thumbing through this book looking for a way to load your dimension tables. Luckily, what used to take thousands of lines of code is now done with a simple wizard in SSIS. This Slowly Changing Dimension Wizard is a Data Flow object that takes all the complexity out of creating a load process for your dimension table. (Note: This lesson does not cover a step-by-step example on how to build a data warehouse from a design perspective because that is a book in itself.)

Before we discuss the Slowly Changing Dimension Wizard, you must understand a bit of terminology. The wizard can handle three types of dimensions: Type 0, Type 1, and Type 2. Each of these types is defined on a column-by-column basis.

- ❑ A **Type 0 (Fixed Attribute) dimension** column will not allow you to make updates to it, such as a Social Security number

- ❑ A **Type 1 (Changing Attribute) dimension** handles updates but does not track the history of such a change

- ❑ A **Type 2 (Historical Dimension) dimension** tracks changes of a column. For example, if the price of a product changes and it's a Type 2 column, the original row is expired, and a new row with the updated data is created

The last term you need to be familiar with because you see it in the wizard is *inferred members* (also called *late arriving facts*). These happen when you load a fact table and the dimension data doesn't exist yet, such as loading a sale record into the fact table when the product data is not up to date. In that case, a dimension stub record is created. When the dimension record finally comes from the source, the transform updates the dimension as if it were a Type 1 dimension, even if it's classified as a Type 2.

To use the Slowly Changing Dimension (SCD) Wizard, connect the Slowly Changing Dimension Transform to a source or transform after dragging the SCD Transform onto the Data Flow tab. After connecting it to a source or another transform, double-click the transform to open the Slowly

Changing Dimension Wizard. The first screen (Figure 47-1) specifies which destination you want to load. First select the destination connection manager, then the table, and then map the source input column to the target dimension column. Lastly, select one key to be your business key (the primary key from the source system is sometimes called the alternate key).

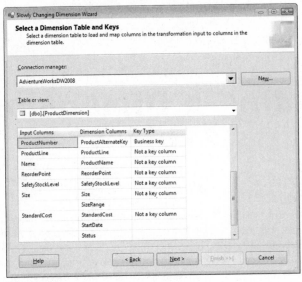

Figure 47-1

In the next screen (shown in Figure 47-2) you select what type of dimension (Type 0, 1, or 2) each column is going to be. A Type 0 maps to a Fixed Attribute, a Type 1 is a Changing Attribute, and a Type 2 is an Historical Attribute.

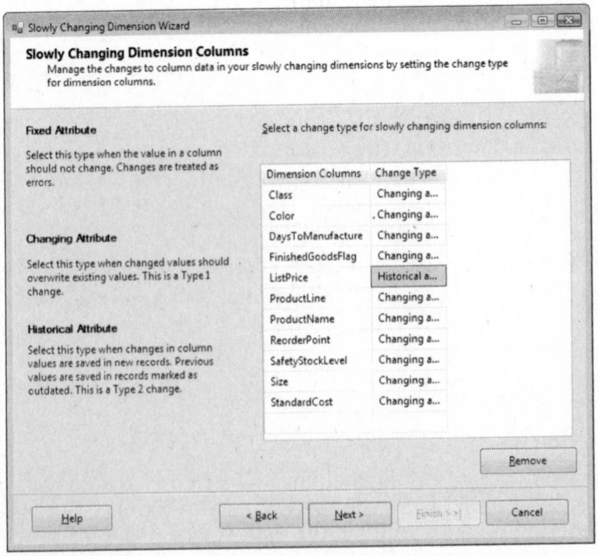

Figure 47-2

If any of those columns are set to a Historical Attribute, then in a few screens (shown in Figure 47-3) you are asked how you want to expire the row and create a new row. The top section allows you to have a column where you just set an value to "Expired" or "Active" or whatever value you want. The bottom section sets a start date and an end date column to a date system or user variable. Don't worry—all of this can be customized later.

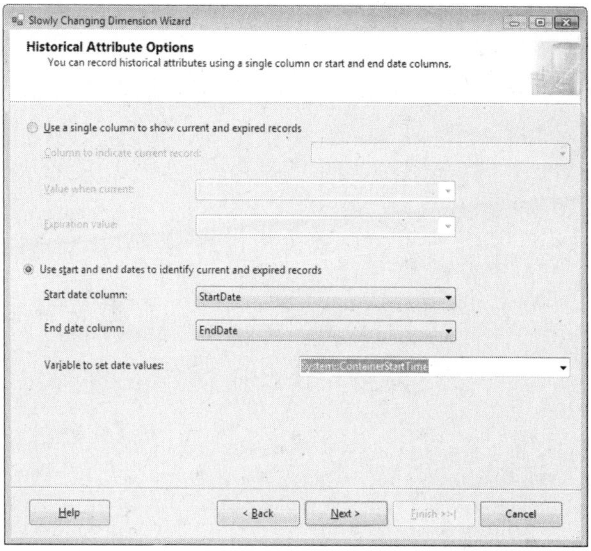

Figure 47-3

After you complete the wizard, the template code is created, and your dimension is ready to load. As the Data Flow Task runs, every row is checked to see if the row is a duplicate, new row, or a Type 1 or Type 2 update. Inferred members are also supported. All the code that you see can be customized, but keep in mind that if you change any code and rerun the wizard, the customization will be dropped and the template code will be re-created.

Try It

In this lesson, you learn how to use the Slowly Changing Dimension Wizard to load a new product dimension. You then make some changes to the source data and see the changes flow into the dimension table. After this lesson, you will understand how to load a dimension table using the Slowly Changing Dimension Wizard.

Lesson Requirements

To load the ProductDimension dimension table (Lesson47CreateTable.sql creation script available at www.wrox.com), you use the Slowly Changing Dimension Wizard. Your source table is in the AdventureWorks2008 database and is called Production.Product, and the ListPrice column is a Type 2 dimension column. To successfully implement this example, you need to ensure that as you pull data out of the Production.Product table, you replace NULL data in the Color column with the word "Unknown." After you run the package, run Lesson47Changes.sql to make changes to the source table and watch those changes propagate to the destination dimension table.

The completed package for this lesson is also available for download on the book's website at www. wrox.com.

Hints

- ❏ Use the OLE DB Source to pull data out of the Production.Product table

- ❏ You can use the Derived Column Transform to change the Color column to "Unknown" if it is NULL

- ❏ Use the Slowly Changing Dimension Wizard to load the dimension

Step-by-Step

1. Create a new package called Lesson47.dtsx.

2. Create a connection manager to the AdventureWorks2008 and AdventureWorksDW2008 databases.

3. Create a Data Flow Task, and in the Data Flow tab, drag an OLE DB Source over. Point the OLE DB Source to the Production.Product table in the AdventureWorks2008 database.

4. Connect a Derived Column Transform and configure it to replace the Color column with the following expression:

```
ISNULL(Color) ? "Unknown" : Color
```

5. Drag over the Slowly Changing Dimension Transform from the toolbox and connect the transform to the Derived Column Transform. Open the wizard and go to the Mappings page (shown in Figure 47-1). The Connection Manager property should be set to AdventureWorksDW2008, and the table should be ProductDimension (this table is created by Lesson47Create.sql). Map all the columns by name, but the Name column from the source left side should map to Product-Name in the dimension. The ProductNumber will map to the ProductAlternateKey. Additionally, the ProductAlternateKey should be set to the Business Key. Keep in mind that some of the columns from the source won't be used.

6. The next screen is the Slowly Changing Dimension screen where you define each column to its dimension type. Set each column to a Changing Attribute except for the ListPrice, which should be a Historical Attribute, as shown back in Figure 47-2.

7. Click Next twice to go to the Historical Attribute screen (shown back in Figure 47-3). Select the "Use start and end dates to identify current and expired records" option. Set the Start Date Column to StartDate and the End Date Column to EndDate. Set the "Variable to set date values" to System::ContainerStartTime.

8. For the remainder of the screens, you can keep the default options. The "Fail the transformation if changes are detected in a fixed attribute" checkbox tells the transform how to handle Type 0 changes, which we don't have. Click Next a few times until the wizard is complete. Run the package, and the results should look like Figure 47-4.

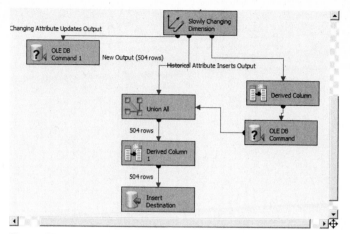

Figure 47-4

9. Run Lesson47Changes.sql to make changes to the underlying data. This will make one Type 1 change and one Type 2 change to the underlying Production.Product table. There is also a SELECT script in the SQL script so you can view the Type 2 change as it flows.

 Please select Lesson 47 on the DVD to view the video that accompanies this lesson.

Loading a Fact Table

A fact table is generally much easier to load than a dimension table. Typically, you only insert into the table and don't update. Additionally, the components you use for a fact table load are much simpler than the Slowly Changing Dimension Transform you used in the previous lesson.

In a fact table load, the source data coming in contains the natural keys (also known as alternate or business keys) for each of the dimension attributes in the fact table. The first thing you do is perform a lookup against the dimension table to pass in the natural key (also known as the alternate key) and retrieve the surrogate key (the dimension table's primary key).

Additionally, you may have to apply a formula to the data prior to it being loaded into the destination. For example, your fact table may have a Profit column but your source data only has a Cost and SellPrice column. In that case in the Data Flow Task you would create a Derived Column Transform that applies a formula in the expression, creating the new Profit column.

The last type of example you see often is where you have to roll the granularity of the data up to a higher grain. For example, say you have a source file that includes columns for CustomerID, Date, ProductID, and SalesAmount but your fact table only includes ProductID, Date, and SalesAmount. In this case, you will want to roll the data up by using an Aggregate Transform. You would do a Group By ProductID and set the operation on Date to Max and SalesAmount to Sum.

Try It

Now that you know the components that are involved in a fact table load, in this lesson you load one. After you complete this lesson, you'll have a better understanding of how SSIS **can** help you load a fact table in your own data warehouse. To load this warehouse fact table, you'll need to retrieve the surrogate keys from the business key.

Lesson Requirements

Load a fact table called FactFinanceLesson (Lesson48CreateTable.sql creates the table) in the AdventureWorksDW2008 database. The source data is a flat file called Lesson48Data.csv. You can download both Lesson48CreateTable.sql and Lesson48Data.csv as well as a completed package of this lesson (Lesson48.dtsx) off the book's website at www.wrox.com.

Hints

❑   Keep in mind that a fact table is a series of surrogate key lookups. Your lookup will have a series of five Lookup Transforms, where you pass in the alternate key and return the surrogate key

❑   Use a Lookup Transform against the DimOrganization, DimScenario, DimDate, DimAccount, and DimDepartmentGroup dimension tables

Step-by-Step

1.   Run the Lesson48CreateTable.sql script to create the necessary table.

2.   Create a new package in BIDS called "Lesson48.dtsx."

3.   Create a connection manager to AdventureWorksDW2008.

Creating connection managers is discussed in Lesson 6.

4.   Create an additional connection to the Lesson48Data.csv file that you download from www.wrox.com. In the General page, select the "Column names in the first data row" check box. In the Advanced page, set the FullDateAlternateKey column's data type to a "database date." Set the OrganizationName, DepartmentGroupName, and ScenarioName columns to "Unicode string." Lastly, set AccountCodeAlternateKey and ParentAccountCodeAlternateKey to "four-byte signed integer." The Amount column can be left alone. Click OK to exit.

5.   Create a Data Flow Task and in the task drag a Flat File Source onto the design pane and link it to the Flat File Connection Manager you just created.

Working with Data Flow Tasks and using sources are covered in Lessons 13 and 14, respectively.

6.   Drag a new Lookup Transform onto the Data Flow design pane and link it to the Flat File Source. Name the Lookup Transform "Organization." In the transform select DimOrganization as your reference table in the AdventureWorksDW2008 database in the Connection page. In the Columns page, connect OrganizationName from the source to OrganizationName on the Dim-Organization table. Check OrganizationKey, as shown in Figure 48-1.

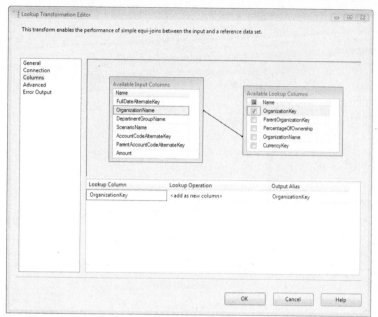

Figure 48-1

Lookup Transforms are covered in detail in Lesson 20.

7. Now, repeat the same steps for the DimScenario, DimDate, DimAccount, and DimDepartment-Group tables. For the DimScenario table, match ScenarioName columns and retrieve the Scenario-Key. For the DimDate table, match FullDateAlternateKey and retrieve DateKey. For DimDe-partmentGroup, match DepartmentGroupName and retrieve DepartmentGroupKey. Finally, for DimAccount, pass in AccountCodeAlternateKey and ParentAccountCodeAlternateKey and return AccountKey. Connect each of the Lookup Transforms together in any order.

8. Connect the final Lookup Transform into a newly created OLE DB Destination. Configure the destination to load the FactFinanceLesson table.

Loading information into destinations is discussed in Lesson 15.

9. Run the package and the final result should look like Figure 48-2.

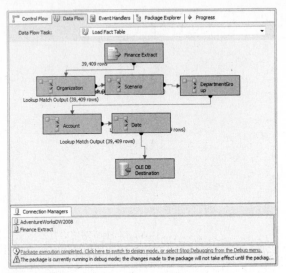

Figure 48-2

 Please select Lesson 48 on the DVD to view the video that accompanies this lesson.

Section X

Wrap Up and Review

Bringing It All Together

In the past 48 lessons, you've see most of the common SQL Server Integration Services (SSIS) components, but now it's time to think a little out of the box, or maybe just make the box bigger and try a complete solution. In this solution, you create a package that performs a load of a few dozen files into a table and audits the fact that you did this. You also build steps in the package to prevent you from loading the same file twice.

In this lesson, we're assuming that you've gone through the rest of the book to learn the components in a more detailed fashion than will be covered in this lesson. Some of the low-level details in this lesson have intentionally been left out for that reason, but you can see those steps in this lesson's companion video.

To work the solution in this lesson, you need to download a few files from the book's website at www.wrox.com. The files that accompany this lesson are as follows:

❑ **Lesson49Create.sql** — This is the file that creates the schema you'll be using throughout this lesson

❑ **Lesson49Data.zip** — This contains the data that you'll be using to load

❑ **Lesson49DataNextDay.zip** — This contains the data to simulate the next day's data

❑ **Lesson49.dtsx** — This is a completed version of the package for this lesson

Lesson Requirements

The AdventureWorks, Inc., sales department wishes to communicate with voters who signed a certain petition. They also want to ensure that you never load the same file twice, wasting the salesperson's time. Your requirements are as follows:

❑ Unzip Lesson49Data.zip into a new folder called C:\InputFiles

❑ Load all the files from the C:\InputFiles directory into the PetitionData table in the AdventureWorks database

❏ Log each time you load a file (file name), the amount of rows loaded from the file, and when it was loaded (today's date in your case) into the AdventureWorks database in the [VoterLoadAudit] table

❏ As you load the data, ensure the zip codes are the standard 5-digit length

❏ Archive the file to a new directory called C:\InputFiles\Archive

❏ You should be able to re-run the package multiple times and never load the same files twice **even if the duplicate file is in the same directory**

❏ Whether or not you've already loaded the file, you want to archive the file to an archive folder after loading it or detecting it as a duplicate file

The files have text qualifiers (double quotes) around the columns. You need to handle this in the connection manager.

❏ After your package successfully runs the first time, unzip Lesson49DataNextDay.zip into the C:\InputFiles directory to test the duplicate file requirement and re-run your package

Hints

To accomplish these goals:

❏ You need a Foreach Loop Container to loop over the files in the directory

❏ Set an expression on your Flat File Connection Manager to set the connection string property to be equal to the variable that holds the file name

❏ Load the flat file into the table by using a Data Flow Task and audit the row count with a Row Count Transform

❏ Once loaded, audit the fact that the load occurred by using an Execute SQL Task

❏ Lastly, place an Execute SQL Task as the first task to ensure that the same file can't be loaded twice. The query in the Execute SQL Task should look something like the following: `SELECT COUNT(*) from VoterLoadAudit where FileName = ?`. Set the necessary property to capture the single row returned from the query into a variable. Then connect the Execute SQL Task to the Data Flow Task and set the precedence constraint to evaluate the expression, to prevent the double-loading of a file

Step-by-Step

At this point, the step-by-step instructions aren't going to be quite as detailed as before because it's assumed that you know some of the simpler steps. If you still need more granular information, watch the video for this lesson on the accompanying DVD for very incremental steps. If you have any questions regarding specific tasks or transforms, please review the lessons focusing on them earlier in the book.

1. Run Lesson49Create.sql, which creates the necessary tables for this lesson.

2. Unzip Lesson49Data.zip into the C:\InputFiles directory. Also create a C:\InputData\Archive directory.

3. Create a new package called "Lesson49.dtsx."

4. In the Control Flow tab, create two new variables called FileCount and RowCount that are both Int32 and default to 0. Make sure they are scoped to the package name.

5. Create a connection manager to point to the AdventureWorks2008 database.

6. Create another connection manager, this time a Flat File Connection Manager, to point to any file in the C:\InputFiles directory. The file is comma delimited and has a text qualifier of a double-quote.

7. Create a new Data Flow Task, and in the Data Flow tab, drag over a Flat File Source. Configure the Flat File Source to point to the Flat File Connection Manager you just created.

8. Add a Derived Column Transform and connect it to the Flat File Source. In the transform, add the following code to use only the first five characters for the Zip column:

```
SUBSTRING([ZIP],1,5)
```

Set the Derived Column drop-down box to "Replace Zip" column.

9. Drag a Row Count Transform over and connect it to the Derived Column Transform. Set the VariableName property to "User::RowCount."

10. Drag an OLE DB Destination onto the design pane and connect the Row Count Transform to it. Point the destination to the PetitionData table and set the mappings based on column names.

11. Run the package once to make sure the Data Flow works.

12. In the Control Flow tab, drag a Foreach Loop Container. Drag the Data Flow Task into the container.

13. Double-click the Foreach Loop Container to open the Foreach Loop Editor. Go to the Collection page. Set the Enumerator option to the "Foreach File Enumerator." Set the Folder to "C:\InputFiles" and the Files option to "*.dat", as shown in Figure 49-1. In the Variable Mappings page, select <New variable> from the Variable drop-down box and type the new string variable of FileName.

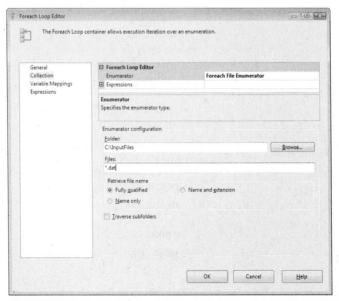

Figure 49-1

14. Drag an Execute SQL Task into the Foreach Loop Container and connect it after the Data Flow Task. Set the Connection property to AdventureWorks2008 and set the SQLStatement to the following statement:

```
INSERT INTO VoterLoadAudit
    (LoadFile, LoadFileDate, NumberRowsLoaded)
    VALUES (?, GETDATE(), ?)
```

15. In the Parameter Mapping page, add two parameters, as shown in Figure 49-2. The first variable should be set to FileName and the second one to RowCount. The FileName variable needs the Data Type property set to Varchar and the Parameter Name of 0. The RowCount variable should be set to Long for the Data Type and the Parameter Name of 1.

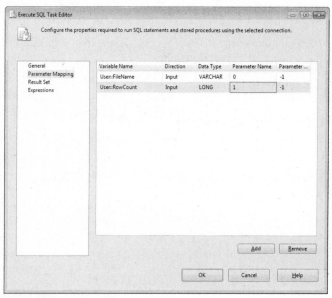

Figure 49-2

16. Drag another Execute SQL Task into the Foreach Loop Container and connect it before the Data Flow Task. Inside the task configuration, set the connection to point to the AdventureWorks2008 Connection Manager and the ResultSet property to Single Row. Finally, set the query to the following:

```
SELECT COUNT(*) From VoterLoadAudit
WHERE LoadFile = ?
```

17. In the Parameter Mapping page add a new parameter that maps to the FileName variable that's a Varchar and a Parameter Name of 0. In the Result Set page, add a new result to be captured by setting the Result Name property to 0 and the Variable Name to FileCount.

18. Drag a File System Task onto the design pane and connect it to the last Execute SQL Task that inserts into the auditing table. To configure the task, set the DestinationConnection property to a new connection manager that uses an Existing Folder property in the drop-down box of C:\InputFiles\Archive. Set the OverwriteDestination property to True. Last, set the SourceConnection property to the Flat File Connection Manager.

19. Connect the precedence constraints as shown in Figure 49-3. The first Execute SQL Task should connect to the auditing Execute SQL Task and the Data Flow Task.

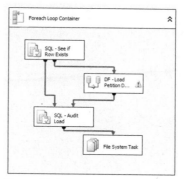

Figure 49-3

20. Double-click the precedence constraint between the first Execute SQL Task and the Data Flow Task. To make sure the Data Flow Task will execute only if the file hasn't loaded yet, set the Evaluation Operator to "Expression and Constraint" and the @FileCount == 0. Repeat the same step for the other precedence constraint coming out of the Execute SQL Task but this time set the Expression property to @FileCount > 0.

21. Next, you must make the Flat File Connection Manager file name dynamic by selecting the connection and then clicking the ellipsis button in the Properties pane next to the Expression property. Select the ConnectionString property from the Property drop-down box and type "@FileName variable" for the Expression property.

22. Finally, double-click the precedence constraint coming out of the Data Flow Task and change the Multiple Constraints property to a Logical Or. When you click OK, it will make both precedence constraints connecting into the second Execute SQL Task dotted.

23. Run the package and the final results should look like Figure 49-4. If it runs successfully, unzip the Lesson49DataNextDay.zip file into the C:\InputFiles folder and run it again. This time, some of the files will process and others will skip the processing.

Section X: Wrap Up and Review

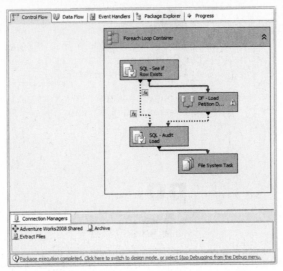

Figure 49-4

 Please select Lesson 49 on the DVD to view the video that accompanies this lesson.

SSIS Component Crib Notes

In this appendix you find a list of the most commonly used tasks and transforms in SSIS with a description of when to use them. Reference these tables when you have a package to build in SSIS and you are not sure which SSIS component to use to perform the needed actions.

When to Use Control Flow Tasks

Tasks	When to Use
For Loop Container	Use this container when you need to perform a task or set of tasks a certain number of times. This container will loop until a condition is false. The initial value of a number is set, and the value can be changed at each iteration of the loop. This task can be used to perform a loop until a condition is true, like a file existing.
Foreach Loop	Use this container when you need to perform a task or set of tasks for a list of objects. The object can be files, an ADO object, or an XML list. This container can look at each object and save the value in a variable to be used in each iteration of the loop. This is commonly used to loop through a set of files and load them each in a Data Flow.
Sequence Container	Use this container when you need to group tasks together. The tasks in the container will all finish before the container sends a message down the precedence constraint to the next task.
Bulk Insert Task	Use this task to load data from a flat file into a table. This is a very fast way to load data. The task loads all the data or none. No transforms can be performed on the data with this task.

Continued

(continued)

Tasks	When to Use
Data Flow Task	Use this task when you need to pass data from a source to a destination. The source and destination can be a flat file, an OLE DB Connection, or any other connections supported in the connection manager.
Execute Package Task	Use this task when you need to call another package from within a package. The package performing the call is the parent package. The called package is the child package. Information can be passed from the parent package to the child package with configurations.
Execute Process Task	Use this task to call an executable. The executable can be a batch file or an application. This task can call applications to perform functions on the files in SSIS, such as compressing a file. This task is commonly used to call third-party programs like compression or FTP tools.
Execute SQL Task	Use this task to perform any T-SQL operation. The SQL can be saved directly in the task, in a file, or in a variable. This task is commonly used to call stored procedures.
File System Task	Use this task to manipulate files. This task can move, rename, copy, and delete files and directories. You can also change the attributes of a file. A common use is archiving files after loading them.
FTP Task	Use this task to send or receive a file via the FTP protocol. You must have a valid FTP connection to perform this task. This task is commonly used to receive files from an FTP host for loading in a database.
Message Queue Task	Use this task to send or receive messages to a message queue. You must have a valid MSMQ connection to perform this task.
Script Task	Use this task to perform complex tasks that are not available in SSIS. This task allows you to leverage the .NET Framework to perform just about any task. Checking for the existence of a file is common use of this task.
Send Mail Task	Use this task to send email via SMTP. You must have a valid SMTP server connection to use this task. You can use this task to send notification of the package information to recipients. You can also send files via the attachments on the email.
Web Service Task	Use this task to call a web service. You need a valid web service URL to perform this task.
XML Task	Use this task to perform XML functions. This task can perform common XML tasks such as Diff, used to compare two XML files and find the differences.

When to Use Data Flow Transforms

Transforms	When to Use
Aggregate	Use this transform to perform grouping and summing of data. This is similar to the "Group By" function in T-SQL.
Audit	Use this transform to add a column to a Data Flow with package information. You can add items like the package name and user name as a new column in the Data Flow.
Conditional Split	Use this transform to divide data into different paths based on a Boolean expression. You can use all the paths from the split or ignore some outputs.
Copy Column	Use this transform to create a new column in the Data Flow that is an exact copy of another column.
Data Conversion	Use this transform to convert data from one data type to another. For example, you can change unicode to non-unicode or change a string to an integer.
Derived Column	Use this transform to create or replace a column in the Data Flow with a column created by an expression. You can combine columns or use functions like getdate to create new data.
Export Column	Use this transform to send a column in a Data Flow to a file. The data types can be DT_TEXT, DT_NTEXT, and DT_IMAGE.
Fuzzy Grouping	Use this transform to group data together based on a percentage match. In this transform the data does not have to be an exact match to be grouped together. You can control the percentage of matching needed to group the data.
Fuzzy Lookup	Use this transform to find matching data in a table. The data does not have to match exactly. You can control the percentage of matching needed to group the data.
Import Column	Use this transform to import data from files into rows in a data set.
Lookup	Use this transform to compare data in a Data Flow to a table. This will find exact matches in the date and give you a match and no-match output from the transform.
Merge	Use this transform to combine two sets of data similar to a Union All. This transform requires both inputs to be sorted.
Merge Join	Use this transform to combine two sets of data similar to a left outer join. This transform requires both inputs to be sorted.

Continued

(continued)

Transforms	When to Use
Multicast	Use this transform to clone the data set and send it to different locations. This transform does not alter the data.
OLE DB Command	Use this transform to send T-SQL commands to a database. This can be used to insert data into a table using the T-SQL Insert command.
Percentage Sampling	Use this transform to select a percentage of the rows in a Data Flow. The rows are randomly selected. You can set a seed to select the same rows on every execution of the transform. The unselected rows will follow a different path in the Data Flow.
Pivot	Use this transform to convert normalized data to denormalized data. This transform changes the rows into columns.
Row Count	Use this transform to write the row count in a Data Flow to a variable.
Row Sampling	Use this transform to select a number of rows in the Data Flow. The number of rows is set in the transform. The unselected rows will follow a different path in the Data Flow.
Script Component	Use this transform to perform complex transforms that are not available in SSIS. This transform allows you to leverage the .NET Framework to perform just about any transform.
Slowly Changing Dimension	Use this transform to create a dimension load for a data warehouse. This is a wizard that will walk you through all the decision making in setting up a dimensional load.
Sort	Use the transform to order the data by a column or more than one column. This is similar to an "order by" command in T-SQL.
Term Extraction	Use this transform to find words in a Data Flow and create an output with the words listed and a score.
Term Lookup	Use this transform to compare to data in a Data Flow and determine if a word exists in the data.
Union All	Use this transform to combine two sets of data on top of each other. This is similar to the "Union" command in T-SQL.
Unpivot	Use this transform to convert denormalized data to normalized data. This transform changes the columns into rows.

Problem and Solution Crib Notes

This appendix is a result of the culmination of many student questions over years of teaching SSIS classes. After a week of training students would typically say, "Great, but can you boil it down to a few pages of crib notes for me?" This table shows you common problems you're going to want to solve in SSIS and a quick solution on how to solve it. These solutions are just crib notes and most of the details can be found throughout the book or in *Professional Microsoft SQL Server 2008 Integration Services* (Wrox, 2008).

Problem	Quick Solution
Loop over a list of files and load each one	**Tasks Required:** Foreach Loop, Data Flow Task **Solution:** Configure the Foreach Loop to loop over any particular directory of files. The loop should be configured to output to a given variable. Map the given variable to a connection manager by using expressions. More of this can be found in Lesson 33.
Conditionally executing tasks	**Solution:** Double-click the precedence constraint and set the Evaluation property to Expression and Constraint. Type the condition that you want to evaluate in the Expression box.
Pass in variables when scheduling or running a package	**Solution:** Use the /SET command in the DTExec command line or change the Property tab in the Package Execution Utility to have the property path like \Package.Variables[User::VariableName] .Properties[Value]. More on this can be seen in Lesson 45.

Continued

(continued)

Problem	Quick Solution
Move and rename the file at the same time	**Tasks Required:** File System Task **Solution:** Set the File System Task to rename the file and point to the directory you'd like to move it to. This enables you to rename and move the file in the same step. More on this can be found in Lesson 8.
Loop over an array of data in a table and perform a set of tasks for each row	**Tasks Required:** Execute SQL Task, Foreach Loop **Solution:** Use an Execute SQL Task to load the array and send the data into an object variable. Loop over the variable in a Foreach Loop by using an ADO Enumerator. More of this can be found in Lesson 33.
Perform an incremental load of data	**Tasks Required:** Two Execute SQL Tasks, Data Flow Task **Solution:** Have the first Execute SQL Task retrieve a date from a control table of when the target table was last loaded and place that into a variable. In the Data Flow Task, create a date range on your query using the variable. Then, update the control table using a second Execute SQL Task to specify when the table was last updated.
Perform a conditional update and insert	**Components Required:** Data Flow Task, Conditional Split, Lookup Transform or Merge Join, OLE DB Command Transform **Solution:** Use the Lookup Transform or Merge Join to determine if the row exists on the destination and ignore a failed match. If the row yields blank on the key, then you know the row should be inserted into target (by a Conditional Split). Otherwise, the row is a duplicate or an update. Determine if the row is an update by comparing the source value to the target value in the Conditional Split. The update can be done by an OLE DB Command Transform or by loading the data into a staging table. More of this can be found in Lesson 47.

Problem	Expression

Create a file name with today's date	**Expression on the Flat File or File Connection Manager:**
	
	`"C:\\Projects\\MyExtract" + (DT_WSTR, 30)`
	`(DT_DBDATE)GETDATE() + ".csv"`
	
	Results in:
	
	`C:\Projects\MyExtract2009-03-20.csv`

Use a two-digit date. For example, retrieve a month in two-digit form (03 for March instead of 3)	`RIGHT("0"+(DT_WSTR,`
	`4)MONTH(Getdate()),2)`
	
	Results in:
	
	03 (if the month is March)

Multiple condition if statement. In this example, the statement determines that if the ColumnName column is blank or null, it will be set to unknown. To make a Logical AND condition, use && instead of the || operator	`ISNULL(ColumnName) ||`
	`TRIM(ColumnName)== "" ? "Unknown" :`
	`ColumnName`

Return the first five characters from a zip code	**Derived Column Transform in the Data Flow:** `SUBSTRING(ZipCodePlus4,1,5)`
Remove a given character from a string (example shows how to remove dashes from a Social Security number)	**Derived Column Transform in the Data Flow:** `REPLACE(SocialSecurityNumber, "-","")`
Uppercase data	**Derived Column Transform in the Data Flow:** `UPPER(ColumnName)`

Replace NULL with another value	**Derived Column Transform in the Data Flow:**
	
	`ISNULL(ColumnName) ? "New Value":`
	`ColumnName`

Replace blanks with NULL values	**Derived Column Transform in the Data Flow:**
	
	`TRIM(ColumnName) == "" ?`
	`(DT_STR,4,1252)NULL(DT_STR,4,1252) :`
	`ColumnName`

Continued

(continued)

Problem	Expression
Remove any non-numeric data from a column	**Script Transform in the Data Flow Task with the code as follows:** ```Imports System.Text.RegularExpressions

Public Overrides Sub
Input0_ProcessInputRow(ByVal Row As
Input0Buffer)
  If Row.ColumnName_IsNull = False Or
Row.ColumnName = "" Then
    Dim pattern As String =
String.Empty
    Dim r As Regex = Nothing
    pattern = "[^0-9]"
    r = New Regex(pattern,
RegexOptions.Compiled)
  Row.ColumnName =
Regex.Replace(Row.ColumnName, pattern,
"")
    End If
End Sub``` |
| Convert text to proper case (first letter in each word uppercase) | **Script Transform with the line of partial code as follows (note that this code should go on one line):**

```Row.OutputName = StrConv(Row.
InputName, VbStrConv.ProperCase)``` |

What's on the DVD?

This appendix provides you with information on the contents of the DVD that accompanies this book. For the latest and greatest information, please refer to the ReadMe file located at the root of the DVD. Here is what you will find in this appendix:

❑ System Requirements

❑ Using the DVD

❑ What's on the DVD

❑ Troubleshooting

System Requirements

Make sure that your computer meets the minimum system requirements listed in this section. If your computer doesn't match up to most of these requirements, you may have a problem using the contents of the DVD.

❑ PC running Windows XP, Windows Vista, Windows 7, or later

❑ An Internet connection

❑ At least 512MB of RAM

❑ A DVD-ROM drive

Using the DVD

To access the content from the DVD, follow these steps.

1. Insert the DVD into your computer's DVD-ROM drive. The license agreement appears

   The interface won't launch if you have autorun disabled. In that case, click Start ⇨ Run (For Windows Vista, Start ⇨ All Programs ⇨ Accessories ⇨ Run). In the dialog box that appears, type D:\Start.exe. (Replace D with the proper letter if your DVD drive uses a different letter. If you don't know the letter, see how your CD drive is listed under My Computer.) Click OK.

2. Read through the license agreement, and then click the Accept button if you want to use the DVD.

The DVD interface appears. Simply select the lesson number for the video you want to view.

What's on the DVD

This DVD is the most exciting part of this book. With this DVD you can listen to three geeks who love SSIS work through the lessons you've worked with throughout the book. Because we believe strongly in the value of video training, this DVD contains hours of instructional video. At the end of each lesson in the book, you will find a reference to an instructional video on the DVD that accompanies that lesson. In that video, one of us will walk you through the content and examples contained in that lesson. All you need to do is play the DVD and select the lesson you want to watch.

Troubleshooting

If you have difficulty installing or using any of the materials on the companion DVD, try the following solutions:

❑ **Reboot if necessary**. As with many troubleshooting situations, it may make sense to reboot your machine to reset any faults in your environment

❑ **Turn off any anti-virus software that you may have running.** Installers sometimes mimic virus activity and can make your computer incorrectly believe that it is being infected by a virus. (Be sure to turn the anti-virus software back on later.)

❑ **Close all running programs.** The more programs you're running, the less memory is available to other programs. Installers also typically update files and programs; if you keep other programs running, installation may not work properly

❑ **Reference the ReadMe:** Please refer to the ReadMe file located at the root of the CD-ROM for the latest product information at the time of publication

Customer Care

If you have trouble with the CD-ROM, please call the Wiley Product Technical Support phone number at (800) 762-2974. Outside the United States, call 1(317) 572-3994. You can also contact Wiley Product Technical Support at http://support.wiley.com. John Wiley & Sons will provide technical support only for installation and other general quality control items. For technical support on the applications themselves, consult the program's vendor or author.

To place additional orders or to request information about other Wiley products, please call (877) 762-2974.

Index